THE SEDUCTION
OF MADNESS

THE SEDUCTION of MADNESS

REVOLUTIONARY INSIGHTS INTO THE WORLD OF PSYCHOSIS AND A COMPASSIONATE APPROACH TO RECOVERY AT HOME

Edward M. Podvoll, M.D.

HarperCollins*Publishers*

FIRST EDITION

Designed by Ruth Kolbert

Library of Congress Cataloging-in-Publication Data
Podvoll, Edward M., 1936–
   The seduction of madness : revolutionary insights into the world of psychosis and a compassionate approach to recovery at home / Edward M. Podvoll.—1st ed.
        p.   cm.
   Includes bibliographical references.
   Includes index.
   ISBN 0-06-016029-2
   1. Psychoses—Treatment.   2. Psychoses—Patients—Home care.   3. Family—Psychological aspects.   I. Title.
   [DNLM: 1. Family.   2. Psychotic Disorders.   WM 200 P742s]
RC512.P63   1990
616.89—dc20
DNLM/DLC
for Library of Congress   89-45702
                                                                     CIP

90 91 92 93 94 CC/RRD 10 9 8 7 6 5 4 3 2 1

Contents

Acknowledgments

The structure of *The Seduction of Madness* follows closely to that of the course on psychosis and recovery that I and my colleagues have taught for the past thirteen years at the Naropa Institute in Boulder, Colorado. This book is written with the intent of giving the reader something of the experience of those who take the course: a sense of a personal relationship with insanity, and also the inspiration, knowledge, and courage to be of service.

Over the several years it has taken to write the book I have received a great amount of personal support, encouragement, editorial commentary, and financial aid from many friends, students, patients, colleagues, and private funders. I am extremely grateful to all of them for helping me through this labor of writing.

Mr. Jeffrey Fortuna has been my constant companion throughout the course of writing the book, as well as my friend and collaborator in all the treatment work described herein. His dedication to propagating this method of treatment has been a vital force in bringing the book to completion.

Mrs. Rachel Anderson and Mr. Reed Bye have done intensive editorial work on several chapters, and did their best to teach me how to write. I am especially grateful to Mr. John Michel of HarperCollins for his careful attention to the meaning of this book, for his final editing of every line of text, and for seeing this book into production.

This book offers and explores an alternative approach to the treatment of mental illness that involves home recovery without drug dependency. The course of treatment discussed in this book should not be followed without the advice and close supervision of a qualified psychiatric practitioner. In particular, mentally ill patients who are under medication are advised to consult with their doctor before discontinuing such medication or any other aspect of prescribed treatment. The author and publisher expressly disclaim responsibility for any adverse effects resulting from the information contained herein.

Introduction

More than 70 percent of the people who enter intensive care for mental illness return home to their families, and almost always need further care. This means that over 10 million people are living in households with someone who is in one stage or another of attempting to recover.[1] Those in this position find themselves alone, with few professional services available, and with very little advice. Certainly, they have not been given the accumulated wisdom about how to care for themselves and their family during and following a psychological catastrophe. This situation has led to increasing frustration and suffering by patients and their families, who have long relied solely on systems of professional psychiatric service. But there is just no "system," mental health or otherwise, that can deal with the scope of this problem. It is a situation of increasing urgency. In this day and age, when the world is proliferating with armies of dispossessed and homeless people, it is important to learn about the nature of "recovery" and, if need be, how one's own home can become a household for recovery.

The desperate condition of the world of mental health care is already common knowledge. This is especially true in the care and treatment of people in extreme states of mind, psychosis and the so-called chronic mentally ill. This care is confounded by opposing views, personal outrage, resentment, and staggering social challenges. The suffering of the millions of people in extreme mental states has understandably led their families and their doctors to become dependent on the ever-proliferating medication designs intended to effect a "biological cure."

An almost exclusive focus of interest on the biological and chemical origins of mental derangement has developed over the past ten years. Government and private funding have become devoted to the so-called medical model, leaving other areas of clinical study in danger of atrophy. This arises out of a fascination with high-technology research in brain mechanics and a total trust that someday it will solve the problem of mental illness and discover the chemistry of mental health. Once again,[2] the solution is just around the laboratory corner.

It is now popularly believed that an authoritative scientific judgment on this enigmatic illness will soon appear, making any great effort at individual or social treatment futile and impractical. Hardly even considered anymore is the simple notion that psychosis might be one of the unfortunate permutations and conditions of being human; rather than the comforting notion that psychosis is only a rare disease, psychosis may be the natural consequence of the way anyone has lived. Perhaps the medicalization of insanity has created for all of us a false sense of security. The fact is that people have lost control of their minds and they become psychotic at any age, from infancy to the moments before death. Believing that psychosis begins and ends with idiosyncrasies of the brain nullifies it as a human tragedy, and contributes to the steadily deteriorating conditions of care that today face almost all of the chronic mentally ill.

Current care has reached such a level of confusion and competition that the overuse of multiple medications is commonplace, and along with that has come the health-consuming battle against their enfeebling side effects: bodily dysfunctions, lethargy, distance from others, clouded concentration, loss of interest, and what is called "the boredom." Electroconvulsive therapy has become fashionable to the degree that some major teaching hospitals are delivering it as the primary treatment for severe neurotic depressions. It is now used on over thirty thousand patients a year.[3] And there is a renewed interest in the use of psychosurgery based almost exclusively on the argument of cost-effectiveness.

The outrageous predictions of Ivan Illich in *Medical Nemesis: The Expropriation of Health*[4] have already come true. That is, with such wholesale and gullible acceptance of the "medical model," people have abandoned all the traditional wisdom of caring for themselves or other ill persons. The healing professionals as well have become ignorant of the skills to be learned and practiced in order to care for their own mental health properly. What has been called the "industrialization of mental health"[5] is almost complete: Timeless healing wisdom and simple common sense are now called "anachronistic"—outmoded and no longer useful in the modern era. But the "modern era" of treatment is already a grim sociological case history. All modern treatment facilities are bound by three powerful conditions that restrain and govern the therapy of people who need intensive care: cost-effectiveness, insurance regulations, and the fear of malpractice allegations. These three conditions guarantee a continuation of the unquestioned yet very false belief in the virtues of treating many people in one place, with its resulting "asylum mentality." These conditions have always justified a wide variety of therapeutic aggressions ("furor therapeuticus," as the elder clinicians used to call it). Most modern treatment situations, without realizing it, promote a fear of the intimate relationships that are so precious and vital to the recovery from madness.

Almost as distressing as the ill effects of modern mental treatment is that the training for people working with patients who are in extreme mental states has been grossly neglected. Those in charge of training also seem to be waiting for a biological key to be discovered. While they wait, there is a continual stream of indictments from many who have been treated in our hospitals and asylums—of inattention, neglect, and violation. The study of mind and its functions has virtually ceased within medical, psychiatric, and most psychological curricula. Training in the psychotherapy of highly disturbed people, or in the disciplines of interpersonal healing in general, is becoming increasingly rare in academic realms—already, nearly all the chairmen of psychiatry departments are biochemists or geneticists. *From where will the training come that allows one to overcome the fear and helplessness one experiences in confronting a mind that has become psychotic?*

Consumer groups made up of former mental patients disagree with each other about treatment procedures. But even they tend to be united in their opposition to those who endorse all the popular medical theories of incurable brain dysfunction. Wherever you look, in fact, there is disagreement, frustration, and rivalry about psychiatric treatment, and many people feel that the current situation is approaching hopelessness.

But at the same time, it is not the whole story—there is evidence for another point of view. There is a wisdom within the history of caring for insane people that is not well known, yet contains the freshness and simplicity needed to meet the current crisis.

It is from this wisdom that *The Seduction of Madness* draws its inspiration and offers a different perspective on the nature of psychosis and its treatment. In spite of the bewildering and discouraging biases that determine current treatment, something inspiring and hopeful can still be pointed to by refocusing attention on the inner or personal reality of insanity and the fundamental mental functions that propagate it. One needs to learn directly from intimate relationships with people in psychosis about the abysmal struggle taking place within psychotic turmoil itself. It would be a misunderstanding to see this refocusing as associated with what is popularly called "antipsychiatry." But it does stem from a long psychiatric tradition that is definitely not in vogue. Perhaps it has never been in vogue. It is a tradition that has always taken many risks in the pursuit of alternative treatments for mental illness.

Motivation toward an alternative, more natural, and homelike treatment is a long and venerable tradition within psychiatry itself. At one point in his career, in the late 1800s, the great Swiss psychiatrist Eugen Bleuler (the founder of the concept of "schizophrenia") lived with his psychotic patients for twelve years: He farmed, cooked, ate, chopped wood, and shared his life with them in an experimental healing community that he founded at the old monastery at Rhineau. At around the same time, William James took a young man from the state asylum to live and recuperate within his own family. Bruno Bettelheim did the same with two autistic children.

It is in such settings that one can hear the truth and learn from people who are in psychosis: about the bewitchment and seduction of psychotic mind, and about the effort and discipline required for recovery. But the world of mental health appears to have totally ignored or forgotten what our patients have told us, and continue to tell us, about psychosis and other extreme states of mind. That is, *whatever* the trigger to that state might be, the experience must still be related to at its subtle stirrings, during the midst of psychological anarchy, and during the fragile process of awakening. One must work directly and precisely with ongoing and seemingly bizarre mental and physical events. Failure to do so drives one deeper into madness.

However, recovery, not reform, is the fundamental issue of this book. First and foremost it is written from the point of view that authentic recovery from psychosis is possible.

Moments of natural recovery, "islands of clarity" as I have come to call them, happen all the time within the experience of psychosis; not only can these be recognized and acknowledged, they need to be protected. Ultimately this book is about perceiving and nurturing islands of clarity, for in this way full recovery from psychosis has been accomplished and will continue to occur without aggressive or physically intrusive methods of treatment. Yet the possibility of anyone fully recovering from psychosis is generally doubted and disputed, and there is still a reluctance to develop noninvasive methods—as if to say there is no continuity between psychosis and sanity, that we can ignore our own minds and the frightening potential for insanity in all of us.

Some years ago I wrote to Professor Manfred Bleuler, a dean of international psychiatry who for twenty-seven years assumed his father's seat as director of the Burghölzli Hospital in Zürich (renowned for Carl Jung), and shared with him some of my own concerns and dilemmas in treating people in psychosis. I was as troubled as I am now at our culture's failure to assist these people. He answered like an opening hand.

In response to descriptions of the treatment work I was doing, he wrote:

> May I mention some particular points in regard to which I found your presentation particularly excellent: the importance of the 'history of sanity' is rarely mentioned in the psychotherapeutic literature. As far as I know you are the first who describes it in such a convincing way. It plays also a great role in my psychiatric work. The need to become free from the prejudice that a person who has become insane will always be so, is extremely urgent and you are formulating it very well. I have been much attacked within the last years as I have seen and described the recovery of many

schizophrenics who had been severely sick for long periods. The critic of my teaching and my experience consists in the following opinion: 'A schizophrenic patient can never recover—if you imagine to have seen recoveries of schizophrenic patients the reason is: you have made a wrong diagnosis.' In my opinion this criticism is unrealistic and is harmful to our patients. I am glad to know that you fight with me against this criticism.[6]

It is in this spirit that I hope to present the view of recovery, and to give patients and those around them who are able to give care the means to recognize the actual sequence of events in becoming insane and likewise the sequence of events that occur during natural recovery. For example, it is terribly important to become aware of the spiritual dimension of the psychotic ordeal and how closely related it is to actual bodily experiences. Such insights into how psychotic suffering is created may bring treasured moments of clarity and relaxation. In short, this book is meant to provide to those who have suffered in psychosis and may do so again, to their families, psychiatrists, or others who work with them, a practical knowledge of the ways and means of handling and protecting themselves and of improving their conditions in the different stages of illness and recovery.

Over the past thirty years I have witnessed many people recover from the most severe psychotic states, sometimes for months or years, sometimes for life. And, occasionally the level of recovery surpassed the best of health achieved before a mental illness occurred. In each case, I have observed "what it takes" to recover: the individual strengths, the qualities of character, and the personal intelligence of the patients. I have been in close therapeutic relationships with these people for sometimes many years and have examined the nature of the intimate relationships that either obstruct or nurture their recovery. Also, while working in more than a dozen hospitals and therapeutic communities I have come to recognize those aspects of an environmental setting and culture that inspire the attitudes and disciplines necessary for recovery, and those that do not.

More recently, I had occasion to create and direct for six years a specialized treatment community (the Windhorse project, the basis for the second part of this book) in which all the above clinical experiences came to fruition. Caring for people in this way deepened my understanding of the nature of psychosis and how recovery is possible. I believe that what I have learned from this experience can be communicated by telling the stories of patients' lives—before, during, and after psychosis.

These descriptions are from published accounts and from my own clinical encounters. Each case was carefully chosen for the insight it offers and because these insights have been repeatedly verified by my clinical experience. These cases resonate with what I also have heard and understood about hundreds of people who have been presented to me in clinical supervision. I have discussed these accounts with many present and former patients, at one time or another. Those who went on to read the autobiographical works on which these cases are based have confirmed the profundity of them and found much wisdom as well as practical advice. Aspects of themselves are always recognizable.

Although there are many different styles of becoming insane, each of these cases has a certain universality about it. These are not necessarily exotic cases or cases of elite people but they are about exceptional individuals who have the capability and talent to express and communicate the ordinary psychotic drama. Each means to speak *for* all people who have been in psychosis and each demonstrates the clarity and intelligence available even to one in acute confusion. This may come as a surprise to anyone who thinks that psychosis is only abject confusion. Yet each case tells of the subjective reality of psychosis, narratives that are arduous, painful, and possibly even dangerous to tell; such narratives have been known to agitate one's mind, and provoke angry criticism. Many of these people have recovered to one degree or another and each case points to and clarifies basic principles of recovery. All of them give or indicate urgently needed advice and recommendations for one's self-treatment in psychosis and, just as importantly, what is needed from others. These recommendations have been transformed into a treatment design, the subject of the final chapters, that offers valuable advice and instructions to anyone involved in creating a healing environment.

While many cases appear throughout the book, there are four large portraits that reveal ordinarily hidden dimensions of the psychotic experience, including the working of a subtle intelligence that is ultimately what makes recovery possible. The insights of these four stories are so critical to the issues involved in creating a therapeutic home that they stand on their own as the first part of the book. As if turning a microscope to successively higher powers, they follow the evolution of psychosis from an impelling sequence of events down to momentary flickers of consciousness. The first chapter describes the full panorama of the psychotic experience, from beginning to end, of one person's heroic recovery while totally alone and against all odds. The second chapter presents a portrait of the face of our human extremes—the wild energy and power of mania and depression. The third comes from the personal logbooks of a man becoming insane while alone at sea. He takes one into the depths of psychotic self-transformation and down to the switch-point where mania becomes megalomania. The fourth portrait is of a French poet who looked directly into psychotic mind in order to understand the most basic, elemental workings and constituent parts of consciousness.

The second part of the book follows a reverse sequence of events: The view expands outward from a flickering awareness of the intelligence of the recovering mind ("islands of clarity") to the totality of a healing environment, with recommendations for treatment and social policy. The first chapter, a case history of recovery, reveals just how greatly one's recovery from psychosis depends on the sanity of the surrounding environment. The next chapter describes how a specialized "therapeutic team" can create and protect a sane and compassionate healing environment. The final chapter explains how to apply the information about madness and recovery presented in this book to one's own life, including how to create a "therapeutic household" and a plan for a small hospital.

Several different lines of medical thinking have been brought to bear on the ageless problems of psychosis throughout this book. As well as the view I bring from psychiatry and psychoanalysis, there is also the view of mind and its actions that I bring from years of practice and study of Buddhist psychology, particularly of Vajrayana Buddhism. Also, the views of Native American healing traditions, the science of Yoga, and other shamanic traditions will find some expression here. This combination of psychological insights and practices has made it possible to track the moment-to-moment events of mind in psychosis; revealing a "micropsychology" of psychosis and a deeper understanding of its innermost experiences. This union of healing disciplines also helps illuminate the nature of human sanity and points to the universal experiences that facilitate the recovery of sanity.

PART ONE

PARABLES of MADNESS

Perceval's Courage

*I open my mouth for the dumb . . . I entreat you to place
yourself in the position of those whose suffering I describe,
before you attempt to discuss what course is to be pursued
toward them. Feel for them; try to defend them. Be their
friends—argue not hostilely.*

—JOHN THOMAS PERCEVAL

HERESY

Walking in the rain on the fogbound beach of Port Glasgow, he
knew he was converted. He got what he had come for, but he
never expected it would be so *sensible*. From the top of his head,
running downward through his whole body, he felt a "spirit" or
a "humor" infusing him, washing him with a benign influence.
Its effect caused the most "cheerful, mild, and grateful peace
and quiet" that he had ever experienced.

How could he have doubted this gift? He did, and then he
didn't; he went back and forth in an intense agony of indecision.
But he wanted it to happen. He had come to this coastal town

in northern Scotland in dreary September weather to explore extraordinary psychic occurrences that were widely rumored to have been happening here. It was a scandal to the church, known as the Row Heresy. At Port Glasgow, and just across the ferry in Row, a small congregation of evangelical Christians were "speaking in tongues." After leaving the university at Oxford, it had taken Perceval three months of traveling to get here. Now, among them, in their inspired presence, he wanted this divine gift of the Holy Spirit that the others seemed to have. When it came to him, it came in great surges, it undermined his nervous system and disordered his mind, and for the next forty years he would struggle with the experience of insanity.

John Thomas Perceval (1803–1876) was a Victorian English nobleman, and even though he was the son of a beloved prime minister of England he was confined to an insane asylum against his will at the age of twenty-nine. He largely recovered from psychosis during the first year of hospitalization but was not released until two years later, at which point he began to devote his life to telling the hard-won truths of his experience: that recovery *is* possible, and *how* it is possible. It was with this confidence that Perceval saw through the mechanisms of insanity, and cracked the code of his bondage to psychosis.

Interest in, even fascination with, the mind of psychosis never seems to end. Its origin and intriguing peculiarities have been discussed and written about by madmen and healers since the beginning of time. Philosophers, psychologists, scholars, and saints of all kinds continue to speculate about it. Yet, the experience of psychosis maintains an ageless impenetrability. Always, there are hints and suggestions that in knowing the mind of psychosis one will come to understand some of the mind's most fundamental and powerful energies. But psychosis is an endlessly interesting dark corner of the mind, which, when once illuminated, might change one's vision of the whole room. This was the experience of John Perceval, and of every other character of this book.

The outward story of Perceval's psychosis is quite familiar and surprisingly up-to-date. He was a college student who gradually turned all his attention to his spiritual development because it added a richness and meaning to his otherwise dull and constricted life. He became an enthusiast and follower of a religious sect that practiced exercises in "transcendence," or enlightenment. In a short time, he became covetous of spiritual experiences. He was insistent on trying to intensify the altered states of consciousness that different mind-altering practices brought about in him. Eventually, he came to endure oscillations between the ecstatic and terrifying experiences of living in heaven and hell.

He was immediately hospitalized by his family and treated for almost three years under court order at two prestigious hospitals. His condition worsened for some months, and he alternately lived in a state of complete compliance to, or else in defiance against, "command hallucinations." During the last year of his hospitalization, he became single-minded in obtaining his release from the hospital, and he vehemently opposed all attempts made to treat him. Finally, he gained his release "against medical advice," only after threatening just about everyone connected with his treatment with negligence and malpractice prosecution.

Similar stories can be found among the medical records of countless young people who have lost control of their minds. In this way, the story of John Perceval becoming insane is a parable of madness.

But, the *inner* story of John Perceval is unlike most others. Single-handedly he accomplished a dangerous path through recovery from psychosis, and in his great energy of determination to document his return to sanity he kept a daily journal. Then he published it against the bitter objections of his family and the medical authorities. After 150 years of obscurity, Perceval's writings were unearthed by Gregory Bateson, and they are as fresh and urgently relevant to our times as when they were first written.[1]

In Perceval's time, psychosis was believed to be incurable, or beyond anything but minimal repair; in any case, one was lost to the world. Perceval's indomitable hope was that the destructive beliefs about psychosis could be undone by a true, in-depth understanding of psychotic mind. Yet learning from Perceval's experience brings one to the border of heresy; one has no choice but to become involved with what he called the "magical" and "miraculous" dimensions of psychosis.

This degree of inquisitiveness into psychosis is not the same for everyone. Many authorities in the field of treating highly disturbed people do not want to know of the vivid, brilliant, and often majestic moments of psychotic mind. They feel that there is nothing to learn from the psychotic mind, from its endless seduction, from the intimate process of delusion, not even when it points—as it often does—to how to relieve psychotic suffering. Some even feel that such a study may be dangerous to one's health. Because of this, there has been a long history of ignoring the existing knowledge of how to recover from psychosis. This ignorance is the origin of the despair in the modern world about the possibility of recovery at all.

BREAKOUT

John Perceval was raised among the aristocracy and wealth of his country and, he said, "educated in the bosom of peace and plenty, in principles of delicacy and decorum, in modest and temperate habits, and in the observance of, and real veneration for, the religion of my country." Until his illness, he lived the conventional life of a gentleman of the upper class. But he did this with a growing discomfort.

Educated at Harrow, and by private tutors, he was a respectable member of the landed gentry, with all the decorum of those who, in their hearts, truly believed themselves to be the leaders and caretakers of England. His love and loyalty to the English promise of justice, liberty, and fairness, and especially to the legendary English respect for individual rights—all of which Perceval felt were the great and noble British mandate—never left him for an instant: from his youth, through his psychosis and recovery, until his death. In a sense, he was one of the truest Englishmen of his age.

He was handsome, and like his father, Spencer Perceval—prime minister to George III—he had large and sad brown eyes. His father died when he was nine years old, leaving his mother to care for John's five brothers and six sisters. John was strong and athletic, and since boyhood he had been accustomed to several hours a day of strenuous exercise. There was nothing he loved more, he said, than "good discipline." Although his intellect was formidable (he could read and write easily in Greek and Latin), he decided to leave school in search of a more earthy life. He was naturally attracted to the discipline of the military, and at the age of eighteen, through family connections, he received a commission in the cavalry and later held the rank of captain in the First Foot Guards. This transition was easy for him: "I had been nursed in the lap of ease and scrupulous morality; I now entered the school of polite and gentlemanly behavior." This term, *scrupulous morality,* runs through Perceval's life, as if it were the signature of his character.

There was a problem: Perceval was very strict with himself and others. It was his idea of integrity. At the same time, he wondered about the strength of his character, and doubted his courage if his company was ever called into battle. He was known for his "gravity and silence when the levity of my companions transgressed the bounds of decorum, and made light of religion, or offended against morality. I was firm also in resisting all attempts to drive me by ridicule into intemperance." His very sincerity manifested as a kind of overintensity in his character. Certainly, he must have appeared humorless. Around the campfire on bivouac, he might have looked like a prudish eccentric, given to arrogance about his own virtue. But, in fact, the austerity of his character tortured him:

> In private I had severe conflict of mind upon the truth and nature of the Christian religion, accompanied with acute agony at my own inconsistency of conduct and sentiment with the principles of duty and feeling taught by Jesus and His apostles; and mingled with astonishment at the whirlpool of dissipation, and contradiction in society around me.[2]

A personal revulsion gathered within him. The pressure to exert himself toward a more meaningful existence was reaching a breaking point, like a harshly disciplined horse who would someday bolt to run free and wild.

So began a *spiritual crisis.* Perceval felt that he lived with secret impulses toward dignity, grace, and compassion, but at the same time, his own egoism and the self-centeredness of the culture around him filled him with profound disgust. This revulsion fueled his tendency toward renunciation and ascetic activity, and he further turned the screws of his discipline. All his prior disciplines and efforts he now saw in a new light; they had been devoted only to the conventional moralities of desire for power, greed, and wealth.

He prayed for guidance. He studied the Bible, particularly the Prophets. In his predicament, he felt increasingly drawn to those who had lived through similar struggles to become more thoroughly human: the desert fathers and the hosts of "spiritual warriors" who risked their bodies and minds in search of a solution. He began to fast. Then he "added to this discipline, watching accompanied with prayer." As he had read about King David, he would often awaken and pray through the night. And then visions occurred, "each of which shortly after I found were pictures of *what came to pass in reality!*"

Increasingly he felt called to religious service, and sometimes visited with poor families and attended to people who were dying. He was drawn to intimate conversations about the doctrines of evangelical Christianity (just as his father had been), especially the teachings of "direct contact" with an immanent Christ. But his mind was becoming feverishly obsessed with points of religious doctrine. Everything he read about and saw around him revealed that the world was in a downhill spiral of moral degradation. Secretly, he was convinced that he could foresee the coming "destruction of the world," and sometimes it felt near at hand. This caused him fits of depression. Gradually, a decision became obvious to him. After nine years in the military, Perceval resigned his commission and went to Oxford (Magdalen College) to immerse himself in religious studies.

Conversion: Tranquility

He rejoiced in his happiness at having made the right decision, and he took every opportunity to listen to the evangelical preachers of the "new doctrines" who routinely passed through Oxford. He was tremendously stimulated by their teaching that proclaimed that the "direct presence" of the Holy Spirit was immediately available:

> I felt endued with a new nature, and with power to overcome all those habits which had most vexed me during my life. In boldness of conduct—and of speech—in activity—diligence, and in purity of mind, I conceived I saw the fruits of a new life, the evidences of the gifts of the Holy Spirit. My mind and conduct were for the first time consistent with each other.[3]

Knowing of the tragic years to come in Perceval's life, one cannot help but be pleased—as he was—in this joyful and longed-for change in his otherwise dreary character. It can be called a "conversion" experience. When William James cataloged the universal qualities of such conversion experiences, he found that they all occurred when there was a great pressure in one's life and mind; and some kind of mental implosion occurred, revealing a vast and "subliminal field of consciousness."[4] Perceval called them experiences that "astonish the heart." In our current day and age, these events in one's life are sometimes called "transformative experiences," or "transformations of consciousness." Such experiences are of the utmost importance to people who have been in psychosis. In fact, they are the treasured possessions of the psychotic experience, jewels within the psychotic debris.

The Transformative Experience

Among the many thousands of experiences called "transformative," there appears to be a great and seemingly limitless variety, and also varying degrees of effect on one's life. They range from the corny to the miraculous. But three groupings stand out: ordinary transformative experiences, conversion experiences, and psychotic transformations. John Perceval experienced all three, and in a cumulative way.

Some were ordinary "transformative" experiences: sudden awakenings as to his spiritual nature, to his spiritual calling, to a world of mystery, to the appearance of heavenly powers on earth. On the other hand, Perceval's "conversion" experiences were felt at a much deeper level. With these, he felt he had "awakened to a new life," a new being, perfected in qualities, "endowed with a new nature," filled with the "life of the spirit," and sometimes accompanied by ecstatic physical and mental sensations. Perceval's own understanding of these experiences was similar to the way Søren Kierkegaard experienced and described them:

> A change takes place within him like the change from non-being to being. But this transition from non-being to being is the transition we call birth . . . Let us call this transition the *New Birth,* in consequence of which [he] enters the world quite as at the first birth, an individual human being knowing nothing as yet about the world into which he is born, whether it is inhabited, whether there are other human beings in it besides himself.[5]

Many religions and spiritual traditions, since their origin, have known of the lust that can develop for such experiences of spiritual transformation, and many traditions warn against the development of spiritual materialism. In the Vajrayana tradition of Buddhism in Tibet—where miraculous spiritual transformations were the legends and teachings with which children were raised—both the ordinary transformative experience and the conversion experience are considered to be transient events that one may easily misinterpret, and misuse. The Tibetan term for them is *nyam,* meaning "temporary experience." They are well known to occur in the course of intensive meditation practice, and they are given several classifications. But the main point is this: They should not be seized as one's personal accomplishment or of any particular spiritual achievement. No credential can be taken from them. The slightest sense of self-indulgence or of aggression by trying to court such experiences leads to a wildness of mind, and a distraction from one's journey. One might have such temporary experiences again and again; one doesn't go through them once and get it over with.

The "psychotic transformative experience," or the one that has the most potential for leading one into psychosis, is said to happen when direct contact is made with "powers" outside of human control—powers that act for good and others that act for evil. Such powers have been described since ancient times by shamans and spiritual teachers as being dangerous to one's health. There are stories even among Native American healers that tell of gifted healers who have become casualties of working with powers. This is so because the experience may also involve *oneself* becoming powerful. And who among us has the equipment and discipline to handle such power?

Perceval's first conversion experience was ordinary enough, and although it did not last for very long, he became confirmed in his expectation that supernatural things could happen to a person who longed for them enough. He felt himself becoming capable of a subtle but direct contact with a world "beyond the visible." Soon, like a dream come true, he learned of the latest heretical doctrines and supernatural phenomena that were being demonstrated at Port Glasgow, and he felt impelled to investigate them.

LOSING MIND

Perceval stayed three months with the heretics at Row, and during that time they were being prosecuted and condemned by an outraged synod of Presbyterian elders. At the time of the hearings, one of the Macdonald brothers, an originator of the new doctrines, rushed from the church screaming, "Come out of her, come out of her, my people!" As with all the other episodes of spontaneous speaking in tongues that he witnessed (some of which he felt were utter gibberish), Perceval was enthused by the man's faith, but he doubted the wisdom of giving utterance to it.

In fact, among the congregation at Row, Perceval almost always found himself on the edge of doubt. He felt tormented about whether he should abandon himself to the religious belief he saw around him. In this indecision, his former "tranquility" dissolved. But he tried vigorously to hold onto it in the only way he knew: by accelerating his spiritual ambition. Thus began a second type of conversion experience, the one that set the stage for his psychosis.

Conversion: Power

He envied the others in the congregation who could speak "in tongues" during religious services—the sounds he heard being "beautiful in the extreme"—and he longed to "take *an active* part." One evening in a tavern, Perceval was joined at his table by a young man, and inevitably they talked about religious subjects. The young man soon confessed his depression and broken heart at being disconnected from Christ. This moved Perceval deeply, it was so close to home. He wanted to do something:

> I suffered a deep internal struggle—I seemed guided to I knew not what: at last, *I flung myself back, as it were,* in the arms of the Lord; and opening my mouth I sang without premeditation in beautiful tones . . . 'kindred with Christ! bone of his bone, and flesh of his flesh!' . . . it was not my doing—the words, the ideas even, were wholly unthought of by me, or at least I was unconscious of thinking them.[6]

There were several more instances of this kind, when Perceval felt the "power of the Spirit" enter him, and he could speak, even sing, "in beautiful tones words of purity, kindness, and consolation." Fling himself back—that, he discovered, was how he could *open* his body, his voice, and his mind into deeper surrender and transformation. Then he took it one step further.

He began to take risks. He would feel "guided" to speak at inopportune times, and although he struggled against doing this he could not hold himself back. Members of the congregation chastened him for misusing the power, but for Perceval, his body and mind had become an "instrument" that was being played for holy purposes. There were other omens. He consulted the Bible by randomly opening it (or rather, "was made to open" it) and in front of him he read menacing warnings that threatened him with confusion: "And the Lord shall smite thee with madness and blindness and astonishment of heart."

He could neither use the inspiration for his own willfulness nor hold back on giving utterance to the gift. He was conscious of the danger, he says, but he decided to *risk the folly of false zeal, rather than risk disobedience and ingratitude to the power that guided him.* He could only hope that "what had begun without me, would be perfected in me, despite even of myself."

The powers began to multiply. He acquired another power: an ability to discern the existence and quality of the spirits that he found to be secretly speaking through *other* people. He could tell this just by their tone of voice, and also by the differing effects each produced in his body, particularly by strange sensations in the back of his throat. Eventually, when his friends became suspicious of his tormented "inspiration," they asked him to leave the congregation, feeling that his health was in danger. Some of them even suspected that he might be "possessed by a devil." He tried to tell them that his inspired powers were only just beginning. He left Scotland:

> *in my own imagination,* a living instance of the Holy Ghost operating in man—full of courage, confidence, peace, and rapture, like a glowing flame, but still and submissive.[7]

The first conversion of tranquility revealed to Perceval a quality of power in the world. The second conversion was more personal—he took the power to be his own. He felt that hidden resources of his mind were being tapped, or opened up, by the power of the Holy Spirit. At Row, the heretics had practiced speaking in tongues with the intention of dissolving the solidness of the willful personality, or self-centeredness, which alone stood between themselves and supernatural powers. But it was having the opposite effect on Perceval: As he was drawn deeper into a struggle of making sense out of his mind, he felt the powers were directed toward him alone.

By the time Perceval left Scotland and sailed to Dublin to visit family friends, the powers had begun to move his limbs and direct his hands. To test out his own power—and in his mind, to manifest and thus glorify the power operating within and through him—he had to take further risks. He put himself into the pathetic situation of trying to create minor miracles; and when they did not work he despaired and was tormented by voices of vicious "internal rebuke." He became unable to sleep and wandered the streets of Dublin throughout the night. Exhausted, weary, and brokenhearted, he thought of abandoning all religious quest. In this mood he stayed with a prostitute (not before lecturing her on spirituality) and quickly contracted a venereal disease. An acute fever, noxious medicines, and a mind tortured by a sense of sin all combined to "lead me to my destruction."

Sitting around a fireplace while recuperating at a friend's house, he heard a voice say, "Put your hand in the fire." His friends held him back, but when given a red handkerchief, he believed that it was soaked in blood. He heard voices commanding him to sing out loudly during the night and to place himself into contorted positions so as to break his neck:

> A spirit came upon me and prepared to guide me in my actions. I was lying on my back, and the spirit seemed to light on my pillow by my right ear, and to command my body. I was placed in a fatiguing attitude, resting on my feet, my knees drawn up and on my head, and made to swing my body from side to side without ceasing. In the meantime, I heard voices without and within me, and sounds as of the clanking of iron, and the breathing of great forge bellows, and the force of flames.[8]

He could hardly talk when his eldest brother came to Dublin to be with him. His brother was frightened and confused and could only treat him as an irrational child. A "lunatic doctor," as they were called, was promptly sent for and declared Perceval insane. He was kept in a small room with a guard outside the door. When he became too active he was put in a straitjacket, and when he tore through that (with the "power of an elephant" granted to him by the spirits) he was placed with his arms crossed over his stomach, in two heavy, hot, leathern arm pieces, which were not taken off until he arrived in England two weeks later. With each day in forced restraints, his condition steadily worsened.

It would take him years to forgive what he saw as cruel and unnecessary treatment. He felt he was being treated like an animal and was bound to resist, not only for his sense of honor but under the command of his voices who threatened him with eternal torture if he did not fight against his oppressors. He came to believe that his psychosis would have dissipated quickly if he had been treated with understanding.

> It may be asked me, what course I would have had pursued towards me, seeing there was such evident danger in leaving me at liberty? I answer, that my conduct ought to have been tried in every situation compatible with my state; that I ought to have been dressed, if I would not dress myself; that I should have been invited to walk up and down my room, if not quietly, in the same confinement as in bed; that whilst implements that might do me hurt were removed, pens, pencils, books, &c., should have been supplied to me; that I should have been placed in a hackney coach, and driven for air and exercise, towards the sea shore, and round the outskirts of Dublin. Few can imagine the sense of thirst and eager desire for freshness of air, which the recollection of that time yet excites in me.[9]

In January 1831, Perceval was brought in manacles by steam packet and coach to Brisslington, England, where he entered the well-respected private "madhouse" establishment of Dr. Edward Fox. Throughout this time Perceval believed he was entering a prison of hell for the crimes he had committed by not acting in accordance to the holy words uttered to him, and for lacking the courage to purify and redeem himself.

It was a sordid time in English medical history. A host of scholars, historians, and sociologists have documented the madness that surrounded madness.[10] A whole culture had become confused about insanity and left the treatment of highly disturbed people in the hands of a growing middle class of medical specialists. "Private madhouses" were proliferating throughout England (150 during Perceval's confinement) and they were given enormous powers over their patients' lives. As was customary, Perceval's family yielded their own judgment to the authority of the lunatic specialists, even when they were ordered not to visit him in the hospital because his condition might worsen or that he might become violent. It has been argued that just at that time an arrogance of power developed within the medical specialty of insanity, which even to this day bears its imprint on the modern treatment of people in psychosis. At present, we are the inheritors of those same beliefs, superstitions, and delusions about treatment, and they make their subtle appearance each time we are suddenly confronted by the psychotic mind.

It is impossible to describe the "treatment" Perceval endured within the walls of the Brisslington madhouse. His own words about it are extremely painful to read. One outrage followed another. He was treated with shockingly cold ice baths and forced dunkings, cold vapor baths, and medicines that he called "noxious fumigations," and twice he experienced the treatment called "bloodletting."

> For nearly eight months I may say that I was never out of a strait-waistcoat; I used to be tied up in it, in a recess the whole day, on a wooden seat, for months and months, with my feet manacled to the floor, and in the presence of fourteen other patients . . . I twice required two severe operations, or was supposed to require; one, bleeding at the temporal artery; the other, having my ear cut open to let out extravasated blood . . . *that day* [when his artery was cut] I was bled till I fainted! I saw my blood taken away in basins full, and I did not know what to anticipate.[11]

It is ironic that his own father was involved in allowing just such treatments when they were being administered to George III during his last bouts with madness. At that time, Spencer Perceval had thought such treatment inhuman and ruinous but, like his son, was powerless and lacked the allies to prevent it from happening.[12]

Yet the worst that Perceval endured was the brutality of the staff who surrounded him. It was physical brutality, such as when one of the staff impatiently wiped food from Perceval's mouth so roughly that it drew blood. What was even more of a daily occurrence was the moral brutality, as when he was mocked or knowingly provoked into violence. He was especially abused when he insisted upon respect for his "royal blood." The doctors always thought this claim to be a banal symptom of megalomanic pretentiousness; only much later did it become known that his family line descended from the early Irish kings who fought for liberation from English rule. Probably, some amount of his poor care was due to his being discriminated against by the lower-class attendants at the hospital, whose class hatred was being inflamed by the Bristol Riots, the uprisings just then occurring nearby. When, over the next year, he was not lashed to his bed, manacled to the wall, or secluded in a pigsty, Perceval could sometimes see through the bars of his asylum window a red glow on the horizon from fires burning in the streets of Bristol. The severe conditions of treatment and the terror to which he felt himself subjected clearly drove him further into psychosis.

How can one describe the desolate scenes that leap from Perceval's writings, like Hogarthian life in a madhouse? But they are not at all unlike visits to the back wards of today's state-run asylums: These scenes remind us of nothing so much as the letters written by inmates, underground news reports, pictures, and movies that have been smuggled from those forsaken wards. These images leave one speechless. Only by imagining oneself living under those same conditions can one glimpse how such utter hopelessness and despair may disorder the mind. For almost nine months Perceval did not understand what was happening to him; finally he came to discover the secret treatment design of the lunatic doctors. Incredibly, they had an unspoken and sometimes subconscious treatment philosophy, meant for him and for everyone else: to drive mad people to their knees, to dominate them by humiliating them. They truly believed that "harsh treatment is necessary."

But until Perceval made this discovery, he felt that everything done to him was the result of divine intervention. Everything was meant to punish him, to test him, and to eventually purify him of all his sins. Then, he would not only save himself and many others from the eternal fires of hell, but he might also receive an ultimate salvation, whispered to him and promised to him by his voices. Every event, every coincidence, however small, fitted into this master plan of delusion through which he interpreted his entire world.

The injurious treatment Perceval received at Dr. Fox's asylum obviously intensified and prolonged his insanity, but it was also *the wound that he caused to himself* that actually sealed him in illness. In this case, it was a psychological wound that upset the balance of a delicate mental mechanism. This kind of wounding occurs in stages; one mental dilemma builds upon another and moves one through an archetypal cycle of psychosis. Thus, the inner journey of Perceval's stepwise descent into psychosis began with an attack on his own mental functioning.

Ignoring Intelligence

For over a century, psychiatrists have tried in vain to identify *the* defect operating in the mind of people in psychosis, the aberration ultimately responsible for the peculiar "psychotic logic" that induces their hallucinations and delusions. Perceval announced his own conclusion as to the nature of this psychotic defect on almost every page of his writings: a disturbance of the normal and intelligent function of Doubt.

He studied the natural function of doubt and all its permutations from the beginning to the end of his psychosis. This is not the doubt of indecision, hesitation, or ambivalence. Starting from his conversion to "power," he had begun to blind himself to a reflex, or a natural instinct, inherent in his own intelligence, what he called a flash of "doubt" that spontaneously interrupts a belief in the most solid perceptual world. It is a moment of clarity that happens in microseconds. It is a moment of freshness of mind. In anyone, in an instant, it can spark even in the midst of a riveting nightmare, revealing it to be only an insubstantial drama of the mind. For Perceval, it would appear and disappear during the most savage hallucinations. A quick cut through the thickness of rampant thinking—revealing a gap, a question, or a feeling of doubt. At every stage of losing his mind Perceval joltingly asked himself, *"Am I only dreaming?"* And in that moment, his insanity was interrupted.

At the very first discernible moments of his insanity, during a gathering feeling of purity and power, Perceval "doubted": "I felt it was either an awful truth or a dreadful and damnable delusion," and even when he was feeling suffused with a kind of liquid bodily pleasure he suddenly wondered, "Am I yet only imagining even when I am happy?"

Almost every day, he experienced a moment of this dilemma: Is this a dream or not a dream; am I becoming insane or am I being transformed into spiritual perfection? He had a sudden suspicion of the truth of his uncanny experiences. Then, all of "reality" was called into question and his whole system of spiritual belief would crash in an instant. It was a chasm of doubt flickering in the midst of chaos, an eruption of a primeval intelligence or awareness that threads through every stage of Perceval losing his mind. In fact, it is a universally recognizable event in the experience of anyone who is losing his mind.

How can one still lose control of his mind in the face of such powerful flashes of intelligence? One reason is that somehow this intelligence may simply not take hold: "I had a species of doubts; but no one who has not been deranged can understand how dreadful a lunatic's insane imagination appears to him, *how slight his sane doubts.*" Even in the grip of "miraculous powers" he had doubts about whether he was becoming sane or supersane:

> And if I doubted my doubts were overwhelmed if not dissipated by compunction at attributing what was so kind, so lovely, so touching to any but the divine nature, and by fear of committing the sin against the Holy Ghost. Whatever then appeared contradictory, or did not turn out as I expected, I attributed to my disobedience or wont of understanding, not to wont of truth in my mediator.[13]

"Something is wrong" characterizes the first moment of doubt, an uneasiness that naturally punctures any experience of oneself transforming into a higher or lower order of being. It is actually a quality of inquisitiveness or intelligence that is not really questioning for any purpose. It is purely questioning, not in the service of ego or non-ego; it is just a process of critical view that goes on all the time.[14] In classical Buddhist psychology, this spontaneous critical flash is virtually indestructible. It is functioning all the time and is always recoverable. But although it never actually disappears, it can be gradually eroded.

If this instinct to clarity becomes obscured, it is a great loss, one that may alter the balance among all the other intelligent functions of mind. That is what happened to Perceval's mind. But it was more than just a covering up of doubt that led to its loss, he took a more active part; he violated his own mind by almost systematically reversing the critical moment of doubt.

Manipulating Intelligence

Perceval began to reason that the moment of doubt was his greatest obstacle to spiritual success. Doubt, in this sense, meant a critical moment of not knowing if he was becoming insane, not knowing whether he was involved with a gathering delusion or truly receiving extraordinary and supernatural guidance. Perceval said that this shock of doubt always made him hesitate in going along with delusion. He accused himself for this doubt, feeling that it might be the origin of his spiritual failure: "Receiving voices as commands of my God, nothing could prevent me attempting to obey those commands, however absurd they may have appeared to myself or others, or dangerous to myself."

He saw doubt as a willful "procrastination," a mental stammer of indecision, which then caused all the actions he was commanded to make to be incomplete and lacking in the purity of intention being demanded of him by the Holy Spirit. Because of doubt and hesitation, he found himself unable to act according to the letter of the commands he received from the voices: "It made me prevent or lag behind the instant of execution." Thus, each action he attempted ended in error, failure, and a sense of guilt, while the voices that shadowed and commented upon his every movement accused him of weakness and lack of courage. Even anything he willed on his own was subject to the trap of doubt. And for this, his voices punished him with severe physical and mental pain and threatened him and his family with eternal torture.

Since doubt had undermined every intention, whether it was in submission to or rebellion against a delusion, Perceval became determined to overcome doubt, to *suppress* it.

Doubt, his own mental instinct, became his enemy. He declared an open warfare on doubt, and he developed a strategy to subdue it by turning doubt into its opposite: wild hope and faith. He put this into practice by tuning himself to become hypersensitive to the very first and almost subliminal moment of doubt. Sometimes, it was to the first "taste" of doubt, which he could feel in the back of his throat, even before it became an idea. This he used as a subtle "signal," or a springboard by which he could leap further into a delusion. In this way Perceval engineered a self-inflicted mental wound, and as he practiced it he became progressively more insane and sometimes violent.

Perceval discovered that turning doubt around into a blind faith in delusion is possible only because it is built upon another inherent mental mechanism. When his mind was most disordered, he noticed that every idea was immediately coupled with its opposite idea, and he felt that this contradictory action of turning *anything* into its opposite was latently available in the human condition and could even be used to oppose the functions of one's own intelligence. He called it a natural human "perversity," an always-available contrariness that becomes highly exposed and intensified during any deranged state of mind. Thus, the clarity of mind that can discriminate between delusion, dream, and reality could be relinquished.

Just as any of the five senses can be manipulated or conditioned in order to ignore, distort, or superimpose a mental image over an external perception, so the same could be done with internal perceptions and images. For Perceval, as it was for St. Paul, this perverse manipulation of doubt was the real meaning of "original sin."

Dilemma of Spiritual Submission

If spirituality had not existed, people in psychosis would have invented it. The havoc of mental mechanisms experienced in psychosis seems to beg for spiritual or supernatural explanation. One's difficulties are then compounded; not only is one struggling to make sense of an external world, but one feels in constant conflict with an invisible world.

This conflict first manifested for Perceval in the realm of language. When he spoke under what he felt to be divine guidance, he would often speak only gibberish, and thus incite ridicule for his presumptuousness and arrogance. Also, the guidance to his speech might abruptly stop, leaving him stammering in despair and appearing to be insane. However, if he held his tongue and refused to speak as guided, he would find himself mute and helpless. This also would make anyone around him suspect his sanity. Even when he tried to reply to an innocuous question, he felt an extreme bodily discomfort because physical pain accompanied any words that were uttered without spiritual guidance.

Like many others in the grip of psychosis, Perceval was in continual torment as to whether to obey the powers, whether to risk ingratitude for the gift of power, or risk the fear of human censure. He called this dilemma of either restraining his speech, speaking with guidance, or speaking his own thoughts *"the most active inward cause of all my misfortunes."*

But as hope replaced doubt, he reinterpreted this paralysis of speech as being still another spiritual means given to him in order to discern and cleanse himself of all evil or unsubmissive thoughts. While feeling in mortal danger for doubting his divine inspiration, he once again randomly opened the Bible and found words that he could only assume were instructions for personal action:

> Brace yourself, Jeremiah; stand up and speak to them. Tell them everything I bid you. Do not let yourself break at the sight of them or I will break you before their eyes.

Coincidences, messages, and perceptions pregnant with meaning began to fill his world. Nevertheless, in spite of all his efforts, doubt spontaneously reasserted itself and he rapidly began to oscillate between feeling himself to be in heavenly places and tortured in hell. Voices told him that his descent from spiritual glory was complete and that his only hope was to die and be reborn into a spiritual body, fully transformed beyond the defilement of doubt. He resolved to kill himself: "My body, being the last hope for spiritual perfection."

Nightmare

While restrained in his bed with leather straps for sometimes weeks at a time, he found that "the idleness of mind and body left me at the mercy of my delusions. I began to lose all command of my imagination." At first, it was a growing inability to control and check rapidly streaming thoughts, but then they intensified into a wildly running nightmare.

The inner mechanism of a nightmare became clear to Perceval. Day and night he would stare at the ceiling and wildly hallucinate: "I expostulated with the voices communing with me, in me, or without me, to allow me to exercise as the only means of saving me." All his mental processes became solidified.

Words and thoughts turned into sounds. The sounds were animated into voices, and they demanded his attention. The voices were personified and identified as "spirits." The spirits became enlivened with particular personalities, and all appeared to "buzz around my head like bees." In this way, in material form, thoughts turned upon the thinker. Some spirits assumed visual form and were felt as visitations, both outside and inside his body, from a world beyond man. They all demanded his self-sacrifice.

Each "restraint" experience led to the abrupt appearance of an organized delusion ("I was the one and only being to be eternally damned, alone, in multiplied bodies, and in torments."). As terrifying as the delusions were, they at least indicated to him a direction for action. He was told by the spirits that if he acted bravely, he could yet be reunited with his family (the lack of whom he deeply and constantly lamented), to be hailed by them as a heroic and willing martyr to the glory of Christ. In this delusion, he alone was responsible for warding off the impending "destruction of the world," the vengeance of the spirit world. It was both a representation and a premonition of an even more complete break with reality, the way a dream might portray the drama of insanity. This began a countdown to the final moment of his loss of mind.

"Crack"

The delusion continued: In a vision, he saw that his sisters had the courage to sacrifice their own lives because he had been unable to end his own. They did this to help him, and to save the world that he could not save. Everyone mocked him for his lack of courage, and under this humiliation his mind became unhinged from his body and the environment.

> At last one hour, under an access of chilling horror at my imagined *loss of honor,* I was unable to prevent the surrender of my judgement. The act of mind I describe was accompanied with the sound of a slight crack and the sensation of a fibre breaking over the right temple. It reminded me of the mainstay of a mast giving way. It was succeeded by a loss of control over certain muscles of my body and was immediately followed by two other cracks of the same kind, one after the other, each more toward the right

ear followed by an additional relaxation of the muscles and accompanied by an apparently additional surrender of the judgement. In fact, until now I had retained a kind of restraining power
over my thoughts and beliefs; I now had none; I could not resist
the spiritual guilt and contamination of any thought, of any suggestion. My will to choose to think orderly was completely gone.
I became like one awake yet dreaming, present in the world in
body [only].[15]

There was a sudden release from mind intensification and
body rigidity: crack, relaxation, surrender of will, and the uncon-
trolled passage of thoughts into visions. At that point, Perceval
"was assailed from every quarter" by spirits, visions, and voices.
There followed an almost complete *shift of allegiance and absorption into another world.*

Possession

With his mind adrift in an ocean of its own projections there
was now no space for intelligent doubt. He was in *status hallucino-
sis,* or uninterrupted hallucinations. His mind was no longer his
own, it was merely the plaything of the spiritual world. He felt
he was "possessed," and he looked only to the invisible world
for clues, coincidences, and messages as to how to behave and
how to proceed.

Now completely desynchronized from the world outside his
mind, everything he did or did not do was in utter servitude to
his delusionary world. It plagued him, and at times he fought
against it, like a relentless struggle between master and slave.

From the first available personal accounts of psychosis appearing in the Middle Ages, up to the present day, there appear
similar descriptions of "possession."[16] It is not that all such
descriptions have unknowingly unearthed and embraced a common and unconscious belief in a primitive and naive explanation; rather, they are describing the same vivid experiences that
feel as if one were under alien control. Whatever possession
might ultimately be, according to Perceval it clearly involves
unseen forces that act by seizing control of the latent mechanisms of one's natural contrariness and perversity, and thereby
create confusion in one's mind and chaos in all one's behavior.

The Miracle: Two Places at Once

In the grip of delusion Perceval noted how thoughts became reality at once, in the time it takes to blink an eye. Pictures jumped to life. Memories became vivid, present realities. Suddenly, his mind was transported to another place and another time:

> Although I was in the house of Dr. Fox upon earth, I was at the same time present in Heavenly places (or in Hell): and capable of being conscious of both states of existence, and of directing my conduct in each, in rapidly succeeding intervals of time, according to what was passing around me in each.[17]

A "previous lifetime" was unveiled to him in a vision—years revealed and experienced in a moment. The story line of that other lifetime is as follows: He had lived as a young orphan in Portugal (where he had once served in the military) and was raised by a kindly old man. But he was ungrateful to those who loved him, and out of greed for material possessions he had murdered his protector. The vision continued: He was apprehended, enslaved, and tortured. Whereas in previous visions he was to be the last hope of the nation if he acted correctly, in this new vision of his former lifetime it was demonstrated to him why he was now unable to act purely and courageously. Here was the miraculous and complete explanation of his fundamental contrariness, negativity, and selfishness: He had been stained to such an extent in a prior existence that his current life would, necessarily, be filled with yet-unpaid-for suffering. His former sin would forever be an obstacle to his redemption, or even humanness. It confirmed to him that he needed some kind of great leap into spiritual perfection, and he became vigilant for any opportunity to make that leap.

All his senses were in disarray, "mocked at and deceived." Apparitions appeared and then suddenly disappeared. Faces changed even as he looked at them. "My sense of feeling was not the same, my smell, my taste, gone or confounded." Voices competed for his attention: "Eat!—don't eat!" He said, "I could seldom refuse one without disobeying the other." Miraculous beings from various dimensions controlled every movement of his mind and body. He explained it all to himself: If everything that exists in the mind in its present appearance is merely the action of invisible forces, "why may not my individual character, and the character of all objects now reflected on the mirror of mind be changed in a minute" by those same invisible forces? It was these "miracles of the imagination" that created the delusion of being in two, or even three, places at once.

Feeling in "two places at once" was the full consequence of the disconnection or desynchronization between his mind and body, and its effects continually led to even more awkward and impulsive actions. It could be compared to falling asleep and being on the verge of dreaming and then being interrupted by someone asking a question. That interruption is engulfed by the dream. In spite of one's best efforts, and because of a divided loyalty, one's response is incomprehensible or ridiculous, although perfectly logical to the dream. It is an embarrassment, and one either awakens or turns further into the dream. Perceval's delusions created just such a false logic. Like a palpable dream, it magnetized, ensnared, and integrated all sensory experience. It spawned and cloned further delusions, and it clothed the world with visions and voices. All background noise and any indistinct sensation of sight, sound, smell, or taste became the

> foundation of speech: the sounds usually clothed with speech are not always loud sounds, but minute and intense, and generally so; but by comparison and by resemblance they suggest the ideas of shouting, crying out, laughing, bewailing, weeping, expostulation, and the like, and the effect is extremely beautiful, extremely delicate, and to a sensitive frame of mind enchanting; so that I would willingly be able to lead an idle life, to enjoy the delirium of happiness and joy produced by these sounds.[18]

Within that delusion and for many months, he said "he never spoke, hardly acted, and hardly thought, but by inspiration or guidance."

THE CYCLIC JOURNEY OF LOSING MIND

The diagram on page 34 is a summary of the different experiential domains through which Perceval passed in the course of losing his mind. Though Perceval was a unique person, the phenomenon of his losing his mind was not unique. There is a

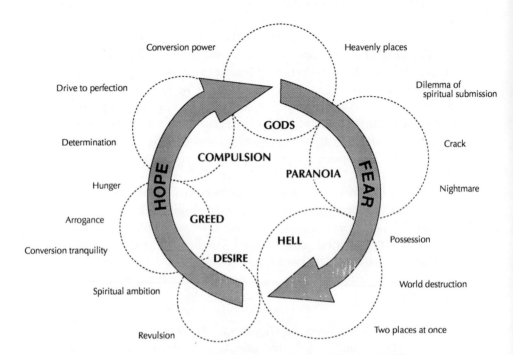

Conversion power

Heavenly places

Drive to perfection

Dilemma of
spiritual submission

Determination

Crack

Hunger

Nightmare

Arrogance

Conversion tranquility

Possession

Spiritual ambition

World destruction

Revulsion

Two places at once

GODS

COMPULSION

PARANOIA

HOPE

FEAR

GREED

HELL

DESIRE

THE CYCLIC JOURNEY OF LOSING MIND

generic cycle to psychosis, and most aspects of it are recognizable to anyone who has been insane. It is a cycling and recycling
of chain-linking experiences.

The complete cycle can be described in terms of a passage
through six distinctive states of mind, each being characterized
by a predominant emotion and a world seen through different
colored glasses. Each involves a way of perceiving the world—
has its own needs, logic, associations, symbols, iconography,
and bodily sensations. In this sense, they are not so much states
of mind as they are "realms" of being, or existential realms.[19]
In no way are these realms unique to psychosis; each can be
recognized within one's ordinary life as more or less a transient
state of being. In various heightened states of neurosis, one or
another of these realms can clearly be seen in an intensified
form. But in the gathering of a full-blown psychosis, the realms
are tremendously exaggerated and strung together to create a
complete and tortuous experience of insanity.

The driving energy that begins the movement from one escalating realm to the next is the hope of getting somewhere or
of achieving some kind of spiritual fulfillment. Hope, in this
sense, refers to a particular psychological and spiritual materialism. Beginning with the realm of *Desire,* Perceval was under a
great pressure to be free of the revulsion and disgust that he felt
for himself and the world around him. From this, a motivation
and desire to become a better, or a "higher," more spiritually
perfect person developed. This possibility actually dawned
when he experienced his first conversion to tranquility and inner
peacefulness. Everything in his life seemed to point in this upward direction toward happiness.

When these sensations increased, or when they were frac-
tured by doubt, he wanted more of them and he entered the
realm of *Greed.* This is experienced as wanting something more,
and yet as an inability to become fully satisfied, like having had
a taste of spiritual grace and then becoming more hungry for it.
But every time Perceval approached the spiritual peace that he
craved, it turned into an illusion, or he could not use it, or it
aggressively turned against him. He was at the height of impoverishment: He was arrogant with what he had, yet continually
unfulfilled. Any doubt of whether he was getting anywhere spiritual was countered by his pride of having tasted something. At
this time, beautiful voices beckoned him to a point of spiritual
voracity with poetry of unrequited love.

He strengthened his determination to push forward—almost blindly, ignoring all warnings, brushing aside and overturning doubt. He pushed himself more forcefully to protect his territory, to pry the final mercy from holy powers. This is the realm of *Compulsion,* an animallike driveness to go further, to exert power. It takes the form of a spiritual "do or die." But in this realm one can become dreamy and confused, feeling somewhat drugged, but pushing forward, simply hoping that something will come of it.

Perceval broke into a spiritual promised land, the pinnacle of the psychotic achievement, for short periods when he would feel "transported to heavenly places." In this realm of the *Gods,* he felt he experienced eternity and that he lived beyond birth and death. He sensed a separation between his consciousness and his physical being. Doubt was almost completely gone, but when it flashed he saw what he called the realm of pure imagination, or the divine mind. It led to a kind of numbness in which he became absorbed, fascinated in spiritual pleasure. But at times it wavered like a mirage, and a fear was sown—that he might lose it.

Fear became a rush of energy. He looked back in envy at the height of his spiritual bliss and knew that it had gone. He became more aggressive in his attempt to win spiritual success from the powers. He overturned doubt easily, and any moment of it he saw as a demonic influence. The voices continually issued conflicting commands, but always they demanded further spiritual submission from him. He was in the realm of *Paranoia,* where he had to protect himself "against attacks from all directions." He felt that only the exertion of greater energy, speed, and efficiency could save him from the nightmarish world that was coming.

On entering the realm of *Hell* he experienced the full fury of his own projections. He could not tell if he was committing acts of destruction or creation. His speed of mind was tremendous and in a constant momentum of change between giving birth and dying. He was given to feelings of hatred and of being hated, and, while fighting against the projections, he began to strike inward. Voices now ordered him to destroy himself. When the "crack" occurred he was at a peak point of being overwhelmed, alternately burning or being frozen in an environment of terror.

When Perceval first became ill he went through this cycle in about three months. After that, he recycled through it many times. In the last stages of his illness, he would recycle through the six intensified realms in a matter of minutes. It seems that, once done, it became progressively easier to do. He might have a moment or two of rest, or even clarity—particularly during his most despairing moments of the Hell realm—and then it would begin again. There appears to be a significant natural gap, or break, in the Hell realm, where one is open to learning things, to seeing things in a new light—and most importantly, where one is open to human intimacy and friendship. All those possibilities, of course, were absent in Perceval's dismal life at the madhouse.

In his loneliness he often thought of biblical Prophets and many other mystics and saints. They might understand his suffering, he believed, for they had lived through similar experiences; they also had been commanded about, and had been cast from the bliss of heaven into the abyss of the "dark night of the soul." As do many people in psychosis, Perceval struggled with the ageless question of the subtle distinction between a tempestuous spiritual journey and true madness, and he was certain that he was being acted upon by the same *power* that had influenced the Prophets and the Apostles.

STAGES OF RECOVERY

There is a silent despair in the modern world about the possibility of recovery from psychosis. Only occasionally is the despair publicly acknowledged, but privately, for the vast majority of psychiatrists and psychologists, recovery does not exist. They have become accustomed to seeing patients "relapse"—make a temporary adjustment to life and then fall apart under the pressures of life into the same psychotic world as before. They have seen this so often that they have come to believe that relapse is inherent in the illness, the expectable natural history of the disease. This professional belief system has been accepted and has passed into the general culture. Most people have become acclimatized to a belief that psychosis is a terminal illness, and have thus become unconscious and numb to their own despair.

When Perceval declared himself recovered, he was met with tremendous scorn. He had been in the madhouse many months

by then, and everyone around him believed he was still dangerous to himself and others. The miseries of his treatment persisted. In the course of proclaiming his recovery, he wrote over
a hundred letters (some of which the hospital never sent), peti-
tioning his mother, brothers, sisters, friends, lawyers, and the
courts for his release from strict confinement and to be given a
freedom commensurate with the abilities he had recovered. At
first he addressed his mother; she, as his legal guardian, held the
key to his confinement. He tried to explain his improvement and
his wish for freedom: "After I began to recover from my frightful
dream . . . I understood both things and persons to be really
what they were—though not always, nor for sometime . . .
though in a dream my behavior was still more moderate." But
all of his petitions were denied. He once tried to run away but
was caught and restrained. Several famous psychiatrists of the
time visited him and prescribed continued asylum treatment.
One of them refused his petition, stating that because he wore
his hair long and in ringlets (which Perceval called "natural and
manly") in knowing defiance of the hospital code of behavior,
and because he refused to simply be a good patient and do what
might be necessary for his quick release (like being kinder to his
worthy family and less accusatory of his physicians), his judgment was obviously impaired and his mind required continued
treatment.

How he longed to be away from the excitement and provoca-
tion of asylum life and to be in a more simplified environment
where he might work at stabilizing his mind. Although he was
held in confinement for another two years, he kept his longing
for freedom alive.

Almost incredibly, during this time and while utterly alone
Perceval was discovering a pathway to recovery from psychosis.
It is difficult for us to know just how unique that discovery was
or to appreciate how often and silently such an event may currently be happening in our hospitals and asylums. Clearly,
Perceval had no scheme to do it, at least at first. Recovery was
an evolution in process: He had decisions to make at each step
of the way, and there were many side roads and environmental
obstructions. Although it is now popularly believed that recovery is improbable for people who are as ill as Perceval, not only
did Perceval *fully* recover—and only the course of his life can
demonstrate that—but he did so under the conditions of madhouse care!

The hectic course of his recovery reveals some basic principles, which apply to *anyone* during the cyclic journey of psychosis. When these insights made it clear to him just what he had
to do to recover, he set an iron determination in that direction.
It is through these principles that the story of Perceval's recovery can best be told.

The Wisdom of Recovery

There are experiences of sudden "shock" or "astonishment,"
momentary "islands of clarity" and awakening. At such a moment Perceval said "scales fell from my eyes." Often these moments are accompanied by horror at the self-deception in which
one has been immersed.

There is also a more *gradual* awakening that occurs in the
intervals between the sharp points of clarity. This happens bit
by bit, sometimes agonizingly slowly, sometimes bitterly. But it
also includes moments of delight and confidence. Although this
sequence happens over and over again and its progression is
cumulative, an active, continuous *effort* is required on the part of
the one recovering from psychosis.

Each stage of recovery has its own *particular danger.* The danger of being drawn back into the whirlpool dream of psychosis
is powerful, beckoning, and even irresistible. One can become
enamored with the sudden awakenings and easily miss the point
by turning them into self-aggrandizements or by attempting to
create them at will. And during the periods of gradual awakening, one sometimes feels exquisitely precarious, combining what
Perceval called a *"child's sensitivity and an imbecile ability to control
wild thoughts."* There is a continual undertow of grief and nostalgia to relax back into the dream. Compared to the vivid display
of losing one's mind, recovery feels boring and hopeless. One's
intention and effort may give way. There is no other way to
describe what is needed to accomplish the dangerous journey of
recovery other than calling it courage.

Recovery is neither a distinct event nor a border to cross over.
Moments of recovery are happening all the time, even in the
midst of losing mind. Insanity and sanity are occurring together.
Wildness of mind and clarity of intelligence are arising side by
side. Spontaneous insights about how to recover actually pre-

sent themselves as veiled messages within a delusion itself, and they are either recognized or lost.

If any stage of the natural unfolding of recovery is *thwarted,* frustrated, or actively opposed by the environment, the effort is either abandoned completely or it becomes as it did with Perceval, a grim struggle for survival.

The implication of these principles is enormous, for it means that *everyone has the capacity to recover from psychosis* and that it might be done in similar stages: a virtual unwinding of psychosis. The following stages are described from the point of view of Perceval's experience. Each stage involved a recognition or insight into the nature of his own psychosis. Each stage is a quality of mind, not in the sense of an intensified realm but a particular moment of sanity within a realm, having its own emotions, logic, and serious dilemmas. Although they do not always follow in sequential order, they can be something of a guide through the predicaments inherent to the recovery process.

DETACHMENT FROM DELUSION

Within the first months in the madhouse, Perceval admitted to himself that nothing could deter him from attempting to comply with the commands of his delusion short of his own death. All his determined efforts at spiritual submission in the past had only led to this. He now openly acknowledged his total enslavement.

But then, as early as one month after the "crack," he had startling glimpses of recovery:

> A kind of confidence of mind came in me the evening after I had been threatened (by voices), and saw the thunderbolt fall harmlessly by my side . . . nothing ensuing, confidence again came in me, and this night a change took place in the tone of the voices.[20]

Then, this kind of event happened several more times. That is what it took. He said that only "repeated experience of the falsehood of the promises made to me in delusion could succeed in making me relinquish altogether my attempts to comply." Whatever this "confidence" was, it had the effect of also altering the delusion itself.

Doubt was returning. It spelled the beginning of the end of his bondage to delusion. But recovery beyond this point he said was "long in coming," taking six months to complete, because soon after the episode of the failed thunderbolt Perceval was strapped to his bed and "became here again a sport of the wildest delusion."

The shock of doubt allowed doubt to gain a foothold. Memories and reminders of that doubt lingered. But each moment of clarity was opposed by a recoil or aftershock, a rapid alternation between clarity and delusion. Gradually, the delusion itself was affected; with each moment of clarity there appeared a new edition of the delusion—a compromise delusion—which took into account his increased awareness and still exhorted him to maintain an allegiance to miraculous powers.

> I have so long been deceived by my spirits that I now did not believe them when they told the truth. I discovered at last that I was on earth, in natural, although very painful circumstances, in a madhouse . . . and I knew I was looked upon as a child.[21]

He slowly concluded, from the incessant contradictions within the commands of the voices, that the voices were as confused as he was. In this way, the voices were gradually weakened and eventually terminated—and Perceval makes a point of this—one at a time.

DISCIPLINE AND EFFORT

Frustratingly, shortly after each successful "disobedience" to the spirits, he would again unconsciously relapse into reckless obedience. Only further discipline and effort could counteract that kind of deterioration of his willpower.

Voices sporadically occurred (at first making no sense) that urged him to "recollect" himself; that is, to become more aware of his situation and prevent "going into a wrong state of mind . . . by *keeping my head to my heart and my heart to my head.*" He repeated this slogan to himself over and over again throughout his recovery as a means of reminding himself to keep his body and mind together: "Without that, my head wandered from my heart and my heart turned from my head all through the day." Voices told him he was "ruminating all day long," and a "moving white light appeared as a guide" and would indicate to him when he was lost in thought.

A distinct kind of effort was required to recollect himself and bring himself back to the details of his physical world. When he

could do that there came a synchronization of body and mind
that strengthened his ability to resist the temptations of delusion. For example, on attempting to write letters,

> every syllable of these letters I saw by illusion before I wrote
> them, but many other sentences also appeared besides which
> those I chose; and often these sentences made light of or contra-
> dicted what went before—turning me to ridicule and that ridicule
> goading me to anger and madness, and I had great labor and
> difficulty to collect myself to seize those that were at all consecu-
> tive—or not too violent—or not too impassioned. This was ex-
> tremely painful.[22]

Any sudden bursting of an illusion or of a glaring self-deception would "stupefy" him. At that moment his wild thoughts
would cease and allow him to see things clearly. It took an effort
to utilize that moment and not be distracted from it:

> I caught the reflection of my countenance in the mirror. I was
> shocked and stood still; my countenance looked round and un-
> meaning. I cried to myself, 'Ichabod! my glory has departed from
> me';' then I said to myself what a hypocrite I look like! So far, I
> was in a right state of mind; but the next thought was, 'How shall
> I set about to destroy my hypocrisy'; then I became again a
> lunatic.[23]

Puncturing a delusion, he realized, might come from simple
sensations or even a scattered fact, and he began to seek them
out. Once, he wrote to his brother to check out a memory as to
the correct date of the death of his dog (which figured largely
in one of his delusions), and its contradiction to the delusion
once again "astonished" him. Another time, by requesting a
copy of his baptismal certificate, he instantly dissolved his belief
in the spirit voices who told him that he was not really his
mother's son. "To confirm the suspicion I had of being deluded
my mind needed these circumstantial evidences to be corrected
entirely of its errors." He noticed that there were perceptions
whose sudden impact he had been avoiding, as if by a reflex.
When he saw his face: "I observed on catching my face in the
pane of glass that my head involuntarily turned away and I
turned back to observe what had struck me." It looked disfig-
ured and moronic, and it "recollected" him. After this event,
Perceval always carried a pocket mirror with him, so that he

could quickly check and see if he looked like a madman or not.

Finding "errors" everywhere within his delusions, a defiance against the voice of delusion rose up in him. He would hold himself back from action: "I began to hesitate before I acted and joked inwardly at the absurdities of my delusions." Then, he habitually disobeyed the voices: "It was usually a reason now for me to do anything, if I heard a spirit forbid it. I was sorry I had not done so before, being prevented by superstitious fear, for it seemed to bring me to my senses and make me calm and reasonable." But even as his conviction in the delusions was eroding, "new delusions succeeded those that were dissipated." The effort had to begin again.

DISCOVERY

His loneliness was profound. While living in a split world, where delusion existed side by side with reality, his sense of detachment from people was alarming: "They were dead to me, and I dead to them, and yet with that painful apprehension of a dream, I was cut off from them by a charm, by a riddle I was every moment on the point of guessing."

His curiosity was engaged. The presence of other people called him out from self-absorption, even when this put him at the risk of being punished for it by the voices. "A beautiful servant girl whom I called Louisa" had such an effect:

> The sight of a female at all beautiful was enchanting to me. I now began to recover my reflection rapidly and to make observations upon character and people around me.[24]

The spirit voices themselves "directed my attention with greater rapidity" to the "variety of situation and ornament." Then he could make many distinctions and discriminations between reality and that which took place within the thick veil of illusion: "As I came gradually to my right mind I used to burst into fits of laughter at the discovery of the absurdity of my delusion."

He "experimented" and played with his delusory perceptions. What he discovered intrigued him, and he began to further examine the nature of his strange perceptual processes. He discovered that he had an exaggerated tendency to "dream" even while awake; that is, to pull back from seeing outward sensations and to see instead the images of memory.

These "investigations" were carried out during brief periods when he pushed himself to stand at the mental precipice between dream and reality, a precarious position. Such an episode might begin by accident: He would be struck by the sudden appearance of a voice or a vision, and then quickly decipher it down to its component parts, as one can sometimes do on awakening from a night dream. In doing this, Perceval first saw a simple "illusion," like an afterimage, echo, or misperception. Built upon that, a hallucination rapidly took form by an elaboration on the ordinary illusion, which had only been a "trick" of the eye or ear: "I saw and discovered the slight that was played upon me. A trick, which until I became stronger in health, made me doubt that the objects around me were real."

Immediately upon that, he noticed a second trick, which changed the meaning of the perception. This second overlay was caused by what Perceval called the "power of resemblance." This function reshaped the illusion to the likeness of a memory. Then a third trick created a sense of conviction, by a power to personify the illusion or grant it the privilege of independent existence. When a newly created existence arose it would begin to act for, against, or indifferent to him. The delusion became solidified beyond doubt when he engaged it in dialogue.

As Perceval's discipline of self-observation became sharpened, he saw that all these steps occurred very quickly and outside his awareness. He was astonished by the speed at which a delusion could be put together and that he could even track that degree of speed. In short, he discovered that wildness of thought and disordered sensations together create hallucination, but only when one enters into dialogue with it does one become truly insane.

This self-observation and many of Perceval's further observations about the nature of *psychotic perception* are some of the most insightful ever made and are central to understanding the process of recovery. The examples that follow demonstrate an accumulation of insight about his own wildness of mind, all of which he needed in order to cut through his intoxication with delusion. They are presented in the same order as they occurred to him.

1.   I discovered one day, when I thought I was attending to a voice that was speaking to me, that, my mind being suddenly

directed to outward objects—the sound remained but the voice was gone; the sound proceeded from a neighboring room or from a draught of air through the window or doorway. I found, moreover, if I threw myself back into the same state of absence of mind, that the voice returned, and I subsequently observed that the style of address would appear to change according to the mood of mind I was in; still later, while I was continuing these observations, I found that although these voices usually come to me without thought on my part, I had sometimes a power, to a certain extent, to choose what I would hear.[25]

2. The thunder, the bellowing of cattle, the sounds of a bell, and other noises, conveyed to me threats, or sentences of exhortation and the like; but I had til now looked at these things as marvelous and I was afraid to examine into them. Now I was more bold.[26]

3. Prosecuting my examinations still further, I found that the breathing of my nostrils also, particularly when I was agitated, had been and was clothed with words and sentences. I then closed my ears with my fingers, and I found that if I did not hear words—at least I heard a disagreeable singing or humming in the ears—and that those sounds, which were often used to convey distinct words and sentences, and which at other times seemed to the fancy like the earnest cries, or confused debating, or expostulations of many spirits, still remained audible; from which I concluded that they were really produced in the head or brain, though they appeared high in the air, or perhaps in the cornice of the ceiling of the room; and I recognized that all the voices I had heard in me, had been produced by the power of the Deity to give speech to sounds of this nature produced by the action of the pulses, or muscles, or humours, &c. in the body—and that in like manner all the voices I had been made to fancy outside of me, were either formed from or upon different casual sounds around me; or from and upon these internal sounds.[27]

4. Upon discovering the nature of an illusion caused by the projection of an afterimage; I drew from this the following inferences: that neither when I had seen persons or ghosts around me—neither when I saw visions of things—neither when I dreamt—were the objects really and truly outside of my body; but that the ghosts, visions, and dreams are formed by the power . . . in reproducing figures as they had before been seen on the retina of the eye—or otherwise to the mind—or by arranging minute particles in the visual organs, so as to form a resemblance or picture of these figures—or by combining the arrangements of internal particles and shades with external lines and shades and etc. so as to produce such a resemblance and then making the soul to conceive, by practicing on the visual organs, that what it perceived really within the body exists outside, throwing it in a manner out as the specter is thrown out of a magic lantern.[28]

5. Though I still occasionally heard these voices and saw visions, I did not heed them more then I would my own thoughts, or than I would dreams, or the ideas of others. Nay, more than that, I rather acted diametrically opposed to them.[29]

The strength to face one's delusion comes from all such insights into the simple deceptions that go into creating a psychotic perception. Once, a magnificent vision of a naked woman, said to be his eldest sister, suddenly arose before him from the bushes in the garden and beckoned him. Just choose her, the voices told him. Recollecting how he had been so deceived by visions, he turned away, saying, "*She might come up if she would, or go down if she would—that I would not meddle with the matter!* At this rude reply the vision disappeared." This response to a vision became Perceval's second most important slogan for recovery. It became his mental practice for recovery: a way of saying no to internal fascinations.

Anyone awakening from a night dream, a daydream, or even a moment of absentmindedness "comes to." This is usually a moment of sudden expansion of awareness into one's environment. It is this kind of *environmental awareness* that Perceval tried to cultivate in himself. He studied the mechanism in himself: "Having to recollect myself, I became more aware of my real position, my thoughts being *called out from myself* to outward objects." He pinpointed the sensation of being "called out" from delusion as being a kind of passionate energy toward the world—shot out like an arrow to sensory objects—and he tried to train himself to recognize it more quickly. But there was a major obstacle. He found that this sudden openness to his sensory environment was chronically being interrupted and covered over by a mechanism that felt like a "film," or a fog, insidiously descending over his mind and clouding his awareness. Inevitably, he found himself projecting images onto this film, images that became animated, thus cutting him off from external sensory awareness. He finally solved this riddle by practicing at becoming quick enough to recognize the subtle sensation of the film as it first came to him, and then cutting through it. Thus, the sensation of the film itself became his moment of "recollec-tion," the reminder to wake himself up.

COURAGE

Each time Perceval woke up to the "barbarous circumstance" of asylum life, he became morbidly dejected with guilt, grief, and "a deep sense of self-disgust and degradation." He noted that when this happened to himself or any of the other inmates, the response was to "become wild or apathetic." He tells of "the gradual destruction of a fine old man who was placed in exactly similar situations as my own." He watched how the old man's behavior became progressively more slovenly until he became unconcerned with even the slightest dignities of living. The elderly man had been stripped of humanity. Then, with amaze-ment, Perceval saw all his *own* behavior in the same light. He, too, was deteriorating, was becoming animal! At this point he knew fully that he was as much a victim of his malignant environ-ment as he was of his delusions. He called this shock of aware-ness "a mercy"; for the old man it was a tragedy, but for Perceval it was an insight that had been mercifully granted to him.

A dreadful sympathy awakened in him, for himself and for all the other patients around him. He was filled with an energy of compassionate outrage. For the first time, Perceval committed himself to follow a plan of action: He would direct himself to-ward "health" in *every* aspect of his life. He then devoted himself to becoming well, to being strong enough to speak for all the others who would never leave the asylum—to tell the truth about the horrors of their treatment. He took a vow:

> I resolved—I was necessitated—to pit my strength and abilities against that system, to fail in no duty to myself and to my country; but at the risk of my life, or my health, and even my understand-ing, to become thoroughly acquainted with its windings, in order to expose and unravel the wickedness and the folly that main-tained it, and to unmask the plausible villainy that carries it on.[30]

This singular event of the awakening of compassion was a quantum leap in Perceval's course of recovery from psychosis. It is the case for many other people as well; a compassionate interest and even a dedication to be of service to other people is crucial to the later stages of recovery.

There was a shift of allegiance toward health in everything he did, and he resolved to "follow a plan calculated to compose and strengthen me, to arouse and cheer me—if I had not had resolution to adhere to such a plan, there might have been risk of return of illness, perhaps of insanity . . . I braced up my mind also to courageous and virtuous efforts."

He experimented with new efforts at bringing his body and mind into harmony to overcome the physical and mental torpor of asylum life: "Whenever my thoughts and hands were most occupied I became, I suppose, nearest to sound state of mind, and consequently more aware of my situation," and he also remarked "that all, or many of the faculties of mind and body should be called into play at one time, and above all things that the body should be occupied." He also experimented with his breathing and discerned a peculiar interdependence of mind and breath, finding that his mind could be calmed and controlled by "regulated respirations."

He tried to watch more closely how he ate his food, finding that the rate at which he ate and the qualities of food and their effect on him were all interrelated to his state of mind. He tested his ability to exercise by walking fast and was overcome with grief at the extent of his physical deterioration. He became concerned with his general health, and wrote to his mother to send him (which she did) the "dental materials" he needed to care for his teeth. He fought the hospital authorities to the end and finally was allowed to have some religious books sent to him.

Whenever he could be alone in his hospital room he stealthily wrote about these efforts and kept his journal hidden from the staff. He knew that they were especially interested in his notations about abusive treatment and his eventual plans for malpractice accusations. Because they would sometimes find his notes, he often wrote sensitive material in Portuguese.

Only after many letters, and what the legal establishment called his relentless badgering, did Perceval gain his release from Dr. Fox's asylum. His aged mother and his brothers gave in, and two of his elder brothers came for him. All the time while riding away in a coach from the asylum, he thought they were bringing him home. It was not until they got to the doors of Dr. C. Newington's madhouse at Ticehurst, in Sussex, did Perceval realize what had happened. The new madhouse turned out to be more humane, and at least allowed him to take walks in the enclosed garden. His treatment here was not nearly as harsh, but he resisted it as best he could, and he continued his letter writing! Now, more often, he wrote to the Metropolitan Commission of Hospitals, to certain judges and members of Parliament, and in all the letters he demanded an immediate examination of his sanity.

He insisted to his family that they remove him from the madhouse and place him in a private home with a family or with attendants to care for him.

> I needed quiet, I needed tranquility; I needed security, I needed even at times seclusion—I could not obtain them. At the same time I needed cheerful scenes and lively images, to be relieved from the sad sights and distressing associations of a madhouse; I required my mind and my body to be braced, the one by honest, virtuous, and correct conversation, the other by manly and free exercise; and above all, after the course and brutal fellowship I had been reduced to, I sighed for the delicacy and refinements of female society.[31]

At the same time that he was becoming more outwardly defiant of the hospital authorities, he was also mentally rejecting and just saying "No!" to visionary commands. The hallucinations became forgiving, softer, and at times encouraged him toward health. But he painfully discovered that he had to stand fast even against voices that called themselves friends. He had to forcibly take command of his own thought processes. This, he said, was the greatest effort of all. It meant assuming the power to direct his thinking—the very same power that, when he was losing his mind, he had attacked and abandoned. His previous practices of turning away doubt, spiritual submission, and nonhesitation had to be reversed. He did this by actively renouncing his emotional attachment to the voices—neither fearing threatening voices nor taking pleasure in hopeful voices. Soon, his fascination with the presences, voices, and spirits ceased.

REENTRY

Soon after Perceval was transferred to the second asylum he wrote to his mother and her attorney to inform them that he held them legally responsible for their having submitted him to abusive treatment, and for holding him in the hospital against his will; he wished to be immediately released to a family lodging. He had heard that this method of treatment was being done by two doctors in London, and he requested that he be put under their supervision. Again, there was a round of visiting doctors and inane interviews. Once again, they urged him to remain at the Ticehurst madhouse and not to cause further grief to his family, who had suffered enough by his illness.

But something new was apparent in the behavior of the examining doctors and magistrates—they were fearful of his being released. He saw their professional greed at wanting to keep him as a patient. He saw their fear at his potentially exposing them to investigation. He suspected that they were also under the influence of his family, who wanted him to remain in the hospital. But he came to the conclusion that the greatest influence on their rejection of his appeal was that they were unworldly people, conventional and deeply prejudiced—merely "exceedingly simple" and fearful.

Finally, at the age of thirty-one, after three years in the madhouses, Perceval's intimidation of his family and the doctors forced his discharge. Physically ill, mentally exhausted, and vulnerable to becoming quickly overexcited, he moved to London and spent some time recuperating at a home-care lodging in Seven Oaks. He needed a great deal of rest!

In the following year, he married a woman named Anna Gardner, and two years later the first of their four daughters was born. They lived mostly in a home in the Kensington area of London, and it was there that Perceval made his fateful decision to write a book describing his experience. The book was to contain all the notes and letters that he wrote while in the asylums, including his accusations against his doctors and his own family. His friends argued against it; they said he would be bitterly attacked for such an exposé, that it would only harm himself and his family and children, and that he should put those terrible years behind him.

He recalled the vow he had made to himself to speak in the name of the other inmates and how it had been the mainstay of his recovery: to use all his energy and his sanity to expose and *break* the system of madhouse care.

I reflected how many were in the same predicament as myself . . . and I said, who shall speak for them if I do not—who shall plead for them if I remain silent? How can I betray them and myself too by subscribing to the subtle villainy, cruelty, and tyranny of the doctors?[32]

He moved to Paris for the next year and during that time, largely from memory, wrote of his illness and his confinement. The writing itself frightened him. He feared that by vividly bringing back all his memories he might once again put himself on the verge of madness. He was also rightly apprehensive that he might overwhelm his readers in his flood of painful and accusatory words. While writing, he sometimes felt a return of insanity—an upsurge of a living memory, like the voracious eating of chained madmen—but then he would clear his mind "by pausing and drawing a deep breath, sobbing or sighing, as the cloud of former recollections has passed over me." On the front page of the book he added a quote from the *Aeneid.* An aged warrior is requested to recount the siege and rape of Troy:

> Oh Queen—too terrible for tongues, the pain you ask me to renew, the tale of how the Damaians could destroy the wealth of Troy, that kingdom of lament: for I myself saw these sad things, I took large part in them.

While still in Paris, he met at the Salpêtrière Hospital with Dr. Jean-Étienne Esquirol, a giant of French psychiatry and soon to become a leading figure in the reform of asylum abuses. Esquirol helped Perceval and advised him as to the political actions he might take in England. But he was disturbed by the extremity of Perceval's conviction that *all* private madhouses should be abolished, feeling that the only innovations possible within psychiatry would come from the private sector.

Without realizing it, Perceval had stepped into the great debate then taking place in French psychiatry, one that repeats itself right down to our present time: Is psychosis a disorder of the intellect and will, as Esquirol argued, or is it a hereditary and degenerative brain disease, as championed at the Rouen asylum (which Perceval also visited) by Dr. Jacques Joseph Moreau?

Back in London, Perceval felt he also had something to say about this issue. He concluded that the study of a mystery like that of insanity—a study that to him was the "most grand and terrible"—was too important and instructive to be left in the hands of the physicians. He titled his book *A Narrative of the*

Treatment Experienced by a Gentleman, During a State of Mental Derangement: Designed to Explain the Causes and the Nature of Insanity (and to Expose the Injudicious Conduct Pursued Towards Many Unfortunate Sufferers Under that Calamity). He published it anonymously in 1838, and it had immediate consequences on the course of his life.

Outrage

Living with barely controlled outrage is the experience of many people who return from the asylums. As for Perceval, he felt himself to be a lonely survivor and witness to an atrocity, one that was continuing without public awareness and that would continue far into the future. There were few, he believed, who could genuinely speak for the insane other than himself. "And yet who is on my side? where shall I find the energy to reform these abuses?" His situation was not unlike those early escapees from the concentration camps who told of what was being done but were met with criticisms of "exaggeration" and hysteria.[33] Perceval always seemed to provoke the criticism of being too "excessive, intemperate, or over-indulgent" in describing his experiences. To this he answered:

> I consider this one of the cruellest trials of the lunatic—that on their recovery, by the formality of society, they are not allowed to utter their sentiments in the tone and manner becoming their situation . . . in expecting from such as have been insane, and are sensible of their misfortune, the same tone, gesture, cadence, and placidity, that meets them in persons who have not been through any extraordinary vicissitudes.[34]

When Perceval learned that one Richard Paternoster, a civil service clerk, was being unjustly confined at Dr. Finch's madhouse in Kensington, he helped to create the public pressure that led to Paternoster's discharge. When he was freed from confinement, Paternoster advertised in the the *Times* of London "for fellow sufferers to join him in a campaign to redress abuses in the madhouse system."[35] Perceval joined him immediately, and together they began to petition the city magistrates for an investigation into asylum treatment. They were soon joined by William Baily (an inventor and veteran of five years in a madhouse), Richard Saumarez (a surgeon who had two insane brothers), and Dr. John Parkin (another former patient).

In 1840 Perceval published a second, expanded volume of his *Narrative,* and this book was even more clearly dedicated to social action. One of the spearheads of action was to be his legal prosecution of his mother and Dr. Fox. No action of Perceval's met with so much suspicion of his judgment, doubt about his sanity, and accusations of his being a traitor to his class and country than his declaration to prosecute his own mother.

Could this be outrage running wild? Many people recovering from psychosis have been known to get stuck in a sense of justifiable outrage, feeling the energy of outrage to be an essential ingredient of their health. Certainly, Perceval felt this way. He especially became impatient with people who could not see, or would not see, the abuse of power taking place in the asylum and the world around them.

The Assassination

He understood that it could happen again at any time. He might be labeled insane by his family or the lunatic doctors, and he might once again fall into the snare of the madhouse. He was already under suspicion by the Home Office for distributing literature that they said was calculated to inflame the lower classes. Paternoster himself had been whisked away by the police in the middle of the night following a financial dispute with his father. Perceval and his group of former patients worked in an atmosphere of potential violence; the age of Victoria was also the age of wrongful confinement.

Perceval's immediate family, which included a number of prominent gentry in politics and the ministry, was appalled at the public exposure of his insanity, but much more so at the legal action he was directing against his mother. To them, it was surely an act of uncalled-for revenge. To him, it was the most precise and cutting action possible to present his case: His mother, just like the public, was being duped into believing the heartless advice of the lunatic doctors. Only later did Perceval find out that, from the beginning, one of his brothers had wanted to have him released from the asylum and brought to a private lodging next to his brother's home; but his mother (on the advice of the asylum) vetoed this plan. Before his discharge, he asked his mother to join with him in a suit against Dr. Fox; she refused. Now, he felt he had no choice but to proceed alone. The malpractice prosecution might arouse public attention to asylum treatment, help provoke investigative hearings, and reduce the plight of those wrongfully confined. Also, he hoped this legal action would secure the rightful inheritance from his father, which his mother had withheld from him since his internment.

It is a strange irony that Perceval must have come to appear to his family as a haunting replica of the man who, many years before, had murdered his beloved father. The story is as follows: In 1812, when John was nine years old, his father was shot to death in the lobby of the House of Commons. The assassin, John Bellingham, was noted to be insane (as Bellingham's father had been) and was summarily hanged one week after the event. One report said: "It was one week from homicide to homicide. This trial was called a case of judicial murder of an insane man and was explicitly rejected as having no legal precedential authority."[36] Bellingham had lived a life of misfortune and bankruptcy and had been imprisoned for embezzlement. After that, he never ceased to petition and harass members of the government for compensation for what he felt was a wrongful imprisonment. He began to feel that he had to kill someone in order to bring his grievances to public attention, and Spencer Perceval—a man known for his generosity and aid to the poor—was the one. When John Perceval, twenty-six years later, began his incessant letters and petitions for asylum reform, his family heard echoes and rumors of a dangerous person, a chronic complainer against the system, an avenger, possibly violent.

Throughout this his mother pleaded ignorance. She had no idea how badly he was being treated. In any case, she felt that the doctors knew what they were doing. They told her that John might become violent if he were removed from their treatment. That was enough for her, she had experienced enough violence in her family.

Soon after the publication of his second book, Perceval abandoned his threats of prosecution, possibly because his writings and activities were already achieving his goals.

Birth of the Patient Advocacy Movement

In his books and letters to newspapers and government officials, Perceval had become an outspoken opponent of what was
called the New Poor Law. It was a complicated bureaucracy of
rules and regulations that made it increasingly difficult for poor
people to receive public relief and much easier for them to be
placed in one of the public workhouses that existed in every
parish in England. Perceval's criticisms led to his being given a
position as one of the overseers of the Poor Law management.
He was named "Guardian of the parish of Kensington"—a
thankless and usually impotent job. He visited the homes of
poor people and pleaded their cases for public assistance before
the government. He wrote to the home secretary (and published
the letter in the *Times*) in support of one poor widow who was
about to be deported to Ireland or else placed in a workhouse
because of deficiencies in the law. He fought against the separation of husbands and wives who entered the workhouse and
against young children being confined separately from their
families. As a guardian, he was also allowed to visit with patients
inside the public asylums. Sometimes he did this along with
visiting magistrates on their tours of inspection. Although
Perceval was becoming an irritating gadfly to the hospital ad-
ministrators, he began to make many friends among the inmates.

As outraged citizens (many of whom were liberal members of
Parliament) became interested in patient rights and asylum
abuses, the original group expanded and in 1846 formed an
activist organization, which they called the "Alleged Lunatics'
Friend Society." Just about everyone who joined this group was
either a former patient or, more frequently, the relative of someone confined to an asylum. Perceval was clearly at the helm of
the society and was renowned for his brilliance and energy. Over
the next twenty years, the society was indefatigable in its efforts
to protect the civil liberties of mental patients, correct asylum
negligence, expose asylum greed and corruption, and represent
indigent patients before the courts. The society lawyers took up
the cases of more than seventy patients, almost all defenseless
people who could not obtain help for themselves.

They were relentless in their bombardment of successive
home secretaries with their advice, petitions, exposés, and legis-

lative bills. In all their actions, they were fearless in exposing upper-class sensibilities to the conditions of lunacy, which had long been felt to be an extremely private and delicate matter. They held meetings, distributed educational material, and gave public lectures. But in almost every activity the society engaged in, they were bitterly opposed by the ultraconservative Metropolitan Lunacy Commission, the governing body that dictated the standards of patient care throughout England. Any patient who desired to leave a hospital had to submit to the decision of the commission. This commission was held in the iron grip of the notorious earl of Shaftesbury, a man obsessed with maintaining Victorian virtues and with fighting off every movement toward reform. He continually steered the commission in the interests of the medical profession and the influential asylum owners. Shaftesbury was the self-avowed archenemy of the society, and particularly of John Perceval, who had been his classmate at Harrow. The society and the commission were in combat, and they both vied for influence over Parliament.

It seemed that Perceval thrived on this twenty-year struggle. One time, through his investigations, Perceval managed to free a patient from years of involuntarily confinement in a private madhouse and forced the commission to reprimand the asylum owner, who then told Perceval, "I would rather have the devil confined here than you!" Being the "son of his father," he was at home in the corridors of power and became increasingly audacious in his attacks on Shaftesbury and the commission. He advertised a public lecture to be held at 7:00 P.M. on 1 May 1851, in the Kings Arms Tavern, at High Street in Kensington. The advertisement for the lecture read:

> On the Reform of the Law of Lunacy: When the abuses of the Law will be illustrated by several cases of oppression recently brought to light, and by the example of a Gentleman who was lately seized by the Police of the Metropolis under circumstances of Gross Outrage and Injustice.

A plainclothes detective was in the audience—the kind of surveillance Perceval suspected but did not know of at the time—and reported back to the police and the commission. His report must have disappointed them. He said: "There were twenty-four people present, of respectable appearance." He might have added what was already well known, that Perceval was an enthusiastic speaker who could rouse an audience with his clarity of documentation.

Personal abuse and slander followed many members of the society. When Perceval mounted an assault (which he won) through the courts, press, and public lectures on the abuses at Northampton Hospital, one of the officials of the asylum accused Perceval of being mentally deranged and wrote in the newspaper that his "sympathies with the insane are of a very morbid character and his judgement to the last feeble and weak." Even though Perceval's sanity continued to be doubted by some people, in these years of political action he gradually regained the confidence of his family. Many brothers, sisters, and distant relatives gathered to give him comfort, along with moral and financial support.

The society submitted a continuous stream of new and brilliant legislation to change the laws regarding rules of certification, enforced treatment, visitation of patients, means of treatment, qualifications of doctors and asylum owners, inspection of hospital facilities, overcrowding of hospitals, education of patients as to their legal rights, and judicial hearings for every patient before involuntary admission.

They challenged the adequacy of long-term care for all patients (whether in asylums, workhouses, or private lodgings), and they advocated for the system of treatment being used in Geel, Belgium, where patients were boarded out with families on a voluntary basis. ("I am convinced that the collecting of lunatic patients together is a necessity to be deprecated, rather than a principle to be admitted," wrote Perceval.) The society proposed transitional treatment facilities for patients before involuntary admission to an asylum and for aftercare following discharge. Perceval, especially, insisted on greater involvement of the church in the care and visitation of the insane—an ageless function of the ministry, he felt, that the church had abandoned to the lunatic doctors.

Every proposal by Perceval and the society was vehemently opposed by the commission and those with vested interests in the asylum. This conflict came to a head when the society's efforts provoked Parliament to convene a Select Committee of the House to hold hearings and gather testimony about the care of the insane. It was at one of these hearings in 1859 that Perceval bluntly said, after being asked why he was so single-minded about insuring the delivery of patient's letters: "I consider myself the attorney-general of all Her Majesty's madmen." Perceval and the other officers of the society sat through days of official hearings. Perceval was hard-of-hearing (from wounds he received to his ear at the madhouse) and each night had to study transcripts of the proceedings. At times, attorneys for the commission prevented the society from using crucial testimonies and evidence. But through the proceedings, the society members were confident and hopeful. Even reading the transcripts today, one is struck by the clarity and drama with which they presented their program for reform.

In the end, only a handful of the society's bills and amendments were passed by Parliament. But the society's educational influence was great, and they sowed the seeds for reform well into the next generation. Their demand that all patients should have a jury trial or magisterial hearing before involuntary confinement—a crucial element in the society's program for reform, and adamantly opposed by Shaftesbury—could not be enacted until 1890, after Shaftesbury's death.

After twenty years of activity, the society appears to have come to a natural end in the mid-1860s. In those last years, two of the society's ablest street fighters died and Perceval lost three of his brothers. "One suspects," writes a historian of the period, "that the appointment of his nephew Charles Spencer Perceval as the Lord Chancellor's secretary in 1866, and later as secretary of the Lunacy Commission, finally gave him some peace of mind."[37]

This history of the world's first—and perhaps most influential—organized attempt at asylum reform by former mental patients gives all of us who are *currently* involved with the issues of patient advocacy food for thought. In our age, grass roots patient advocacy is just now becoming a powerful force in determining the care of insane people. But it is beset with difficulties. Along with *almost all* of the same issues that the society fought for, current-day activists must add new ones, like the overuse of tranquilizing and "antipsychotic" medications and the right to refuse treatment. As current activists, we may naturally wonder what is to become of our own work, if as highly organized and industrious a group as the society failed to achieve its legislative goals and passed virtually unnoticed in the history of psychiatry.

Particularly in our age, amidst the increasing appearance of organizations to protest human rights violations and inhumane activities of all kinds, the movement for mental patient advocacy does not find much support. Surely, Perceval would tell us not to lose heart. He would remind us that "antipsychiatry" was not simply a movement toward reform that began in the 1960s, it began as soon as psychiatry began. He would say that there have always been tremendous obstacles to genuine care for the insane—every age has its Shaftesburys. Although the society had meager results in changing the laws of England and altering the course of psychiatric care, it directly benefited hundreds of people, and probably indirectly eased the pain of many thousands in the institutions.

A commitment to patient advocacy usually happens at a very personal level—through one's own experience, in one's family, or with friends. Thus, an increasing number of us have and will have the opportunity to do patient advocacy. If we are not involved with patient advocacy, who is? Who will be? Perceval would say that it does not matter if we do it for one year or one day, it will still affect people in the hospitals. If we advocate for the improved treatment of even *one* patient, and do it steadfastly, it can have great consequences. Having the courage to visit someone in the hospital means something. In fact, just visiting someone may become an important event in that person's life!

Perceval visited public asylums and private madhouses whenever he could get the opportunity. As guardian of the Parish of Kensington he could get into the inner wards when he accompanied official teams of inspection:

> I mixed with the patients, and stood apart from the other gentlemen, because more is observed sometimes in this way, than in attending to what is directly going on before the physicians; when a patient, who had been singing very loudly and very well, addressed me, and asked me how I liked his singing; "It is not bad," said I, "but I observe one fault; you sing out of time."—"You are the first person, then, that ever accused me of that," said he. I replied, "You do not seize my meaning; I mean that it is out of time to sing in the presence of these gentlemen, who are here on the business of the hospital." He received this with a hearty friendly laugh, and ceased his singing.[38]

On one such visit to the infamous Bethlehem Hospital, Perceval found himself in the company of Dr. John Bright, the same lunatic doctor who had visited him at the Ticehurst madhouse and had turned down his appeal for freedom. A haggard, middle-aged patient stopped Perceval in the hallway and handed him a sheath of one hundred pages of poetry, asking him to give it to Dr. Bright. Perceval admired what he read, in part:

> And there the prisoners and the keepers rest
> Together, the oppressor and the oppress'd.
> The great and small obey the same decree,
> For, as the master, is the servant, free
> Among the dead, where no distinction be.

Arthur Legent Pearce had attacked his wife ten years earlier in a fit of delusional jealousy, and he had been abandoned by his family and confined ever since. Now, he declared his sanity and was trying to gain his freedom. Perceval and Pearce became friends, and on subsequent visits Perceval convinced him to allow the publication of the poetry, feeling that it would help his cause, as well as lift his spirits, and the sale might help pay for his legal appeals.[39]

On another official visit to Bethlehem Hospital, Perceval met with Dr. Edward Peithman, who claimed that he had been confined for the past thirteen years while being of perfectly sound mind. Perceval thought Peithman to be one of the most distinguished and well-educated scholars he had ever met, and he took up his case. Peithman, a German national, had been a tutor in languages and a university lecturer but, following an absurd series of mishaps with his employer, was arrested for a "breach of peace" and then hospitalized. Over the years, Dr. Munro, a director of Bethlehem, continued to certify Peithman as insane. When the lunacy commission reviewed his case, Peithman was freed. But, immediately upon release, Peithman went to Buckingham Palace to deliver a long and eloquent petition that requested compensation for his thirteen years of illegal confinement. He was told to leave, but, when he refused, he was again arrested and returned to the hospital. Now Perceval gathered numerous testimonials from doctors, clergymen, friends, and Peithman's family in Germany as to his mental health. Peithman was released again, but only on the condition that he leave the country and return to Germany. Perceval accompanied him on the trip and helped him to reunite with his family. In Germany, his family and many doctors found Peithman to be perfectly sane, even something of a genius. Within months, Peithman— along with the German government and Baron Von Humboldt, chamberlain to the king of Prussia—demanded immediate redress to injuries from the Crown of England.

In 1854 Perceval published a full account of the story along with letters, certificates, and testimonials in support of Peithman's petition. Perceval adds this bizarre postscript:

> In conclusion, it is to be observed that Dr. Munro, on whose sole authority Dr. Peithman was detained in Bethlehem during thirteen successive years, has been proved to be in a state of insanity, and is actually confined in an asylum.[40]

ASYLUM AWARENESS

Confinement in Perceval's time was considered to be one of the unfortunate necessities of a turbulent society, but everyone knew that hospitals were dangerous places—one might never leave or might come out worse than when one went in. Today a relative upsurge of interest in patient advocacy has provided more than enough documentation that psychiatric hospitalization is still dangerous.[41] Comparison of the litigation against hospitals and doctors, and of the bills of reform submitted for legislation, between Perceval's time and our own, reveals them to be the same. We are still struggling with the same problems that plagued the early asylums: procedures of commitment, enforced hospitalization, the right to refuse treatment, the inadequacy of treatment review, untrained doctors and staff, and unreported hospital deaths. We are still arguing about the fine line between what constitutes treatment and what is "therapeutic aggression."

Many changes have occurred since the time of Perceval. But if Perceval were here now to walk our wards, among heavily tranquilized patients, to talk with them, discuss treatment with our doctors, and to visit with the homeless mentally ill within the shelters, he would conclude that there have been changes but that not very much has improved.

We still create our own style of madhouses and asylums. This can be seen at beautifully furnished private treatment centers as well as at deteriorating state hospitals. We seem to be inescapably drawn to re-create conditions of treatment that are bound to make it difficult, if not impossible, to recover from psychosis.

On examining our own systems of treatment, we might ask: How has it come to be that, in spite of our best intentions, we are haunted by the possibility of reproducing the environment of a lunatic asylum? Why haven't we learned how to run a hospital better than that? It is because creating an asylum stems from a particular state of mind, an *asylum mentality,* which can resurface anytime and anywhere and recapitulate the history of the asylum. Contact with insanity tends to provoke it: a reflexlike way of responding to insane people that can, in a moment, generate all the notoriously punishing techniques of treatment used in a supposedly bygone era. Even in the most benevolent of institutions, asylum mentality erupts as a series of self-deceptions and primitive beliefs, or superstitions, about what madness is and how it should be treated. Experience shows that no program, project, hospital, or therapeutic community can fully escape the spontaneous arising of asylum mentality; we are the unconscious inheritors of that way of trying to treat many people in one place.

Asylum mentality is a mind of exerting power over others, in this case "therapeutic power." Perceval's shocking discovery—a landmark event in his recovery—was the degree of power vested in the hands of people who were treating him and the gross therapeutic aggression that they practiced. In our time, the "therapeutic community" movement was designed to avoid this tendency to abuse of power through a program of democratizing treatment wards. But even this movement has failed (its founder, Dr. Maxwell Jones, recently said), because of the same tendency to abuse therapeutic power and thus create the same therapeutic environments of aggression.[42] The facts are clear: The accusations of "oppression" by therapeutic power in the past are the same as those made about our current institutions and asylums.

The Practice

How can we work with this seemingly universal tendency toward asylum mentality? For any of us, the most important point is to become aware of it as it happens. No one appears to be immune to a subtle appearance of asylum mentality; it can appear at any time and in many different situations of dealing with or about people in psychosis. But, one can train oneself to recognize it at an early moment and not slip further into an archaic belief system. In this way it is possible to cultivate a healthy doubt about how we are treating people whose minds are highly disturbed. To do this we need to become more aware of the subtle meanings of the word *asylum.*

A recent analysis by the great social historian Michel Foucault of the so-called Age of Confinement confirms and deepens Perceval's meaning of *asylum:* a therapeutic structure or space that is required to be filled; a theory about treatment based on ignorance; and techniques of relating to people in psychosis that are ultimately punishing.[43] Asylum mentality manifests in a variety of ways:

☐   Asylum preserves what is called "nonreciprocal observation." One is observed without being able to observe properly. One's state of mind—mistakes, awkwardness, and transgressions—is cataloged, diagnosed, and studied; whereas one's own observations are held in suspicion and doubt and are called unsound, resistance, arrogance, transference, and the like. An examination *by* the insane of their conditions, including the state of mind and therapeutic intentions of all their caretakers, is more or less prohibited. It is a situation bound to evoke paranoia.

☐   Asylum mind treats madness as childhood. It relegates the asylum confinees to the status of minors—intellectually, morally, judicially. This prejudice stems from what is known as the "damage theory" of psychosis, that people in psychosis are undeveloped, arrested, deficient, or defective. It lays the foundation for a wide variety of treatment theories and beliefs as to what can be expected from "recovery." Most of all, it excuses insufficient care. Perceval pleaded this point:

> To the custom of the courts of justice to look upon them as infants in law, from whence has followed the practice in asylums of treating them as if they were infants in fact . . . The law which, under the pretence of their being *'infants,'* and who subjects them to the caprices and arbitrary rule of their guardians, should at least protect them as a parent would her *children.*[44]

☐ Asylum embodies the idea that madness must first be subjugated for recovery to take place. In the words of Samuel Tuke—a reformer who tried valiantly to break out of the asylum tradition, only to create a more subtle asylum called "moral treatment"—insane people need to be "dominated." The mind of insanity must learn to bow before the superior power of reason and logic. Perceval felt that "so rooted is the prejudice *that lunacy cannot be subdued, except by harsh treatment,*" that this belief would appear in every aspect of interacting with the insane.

> The glory of the old system was coercion by violence; the glory of the modern system is repression by mildness and coaxing, and by solitary confinement; but repression is the word, and that is to be obtained by any means.[45]

☐ Asylum manifests in an organization of people whose hierarchy is based on a conviction of its moral sovereignty over the insane. This involves a further notion of the subjugation of insanity. One is to be cured within a moral social order based on the principle of the bourgeoisie patriarchal family. The asylums that practice "moral treatment" emulate that structure and try to refine it into a perfected family institution. It was meant to be a new, ideal asylum, but it carried with it many of the restrictions of the old asylums.

☐ Asylum is a moral domain where recovery is measured against many differing notions of "mental health." Wherever there is insanity, issues of "spirituality" arise. In the Victorian asylums, the principles of the established church were the measures of sanity. Perceval observed that the spirituality professed by doctors was so uninformed and narrow-minded that they hardly recognized that most people in psychosis were involved in a variety of life-threatening spiritual crises. When the medical view of sanity and psychosis came to ascendance, a seemingly ageless understanding of insanity as a spiritual crisis was lost. Asylum mind sees spirituality as "religiosity" and as dangerous to the welfare of the patient. Yet it does not hesitate to promote and enforce its own ideologies about sanity, in therapeutic environments whose various social designs incorporate the whole spectrum of religious and political beliefs.

☐   Asylum is a place of refuge. It rescues people from degraded, animallike environments and brings them into social conditions of a higher order. This principle arose from a growing understanding that madness springs from a diseased or problematic environment of some kind. Asylum mind poses itself as the rescuer, to which one should be grateful and obedient. It has to distinguish itself from a patient's previous life by ignoring and belittling the richness, energy, and seduction of insane worlds.

☐   Asylum, with or without walls, views madness in all its expressions as a primitive arrogance, an insufferable presumption, which sporadically arises in the human condition. And it must be punished. Michel Foucault traces this therapeutic belief to the Inquisition: "His torment is his glory, his deliverance must humiliate him." Such a theory justifies brutal and constraining treatment of all kinds, as a necessity.

The most subtle form of asylum mind has been called the "silence that humiliates," a studied interpersonal rift between doctor and patient. The professional separation between them creates a loneliness and silence for the patient in which to reflect on madness—to intensify it, so that it might mock itself. Asylum mind demands a confession to the error of arrogance and to the ancient crime of spiritual self-exaggeration; its goal is for the patient *himself* to come to believe that his suffering harsh treatment is deserved and necessary for recovery. A residue of guilt is meant to last far into the future, to be an armor and reminder against any excessive self-presumption in the future.

Many early asylum directors worked diligently with their staff to design ways and means of mockery, to humiliate and thus bring a patient to his senses. From this has come some treatment plans that prescribe the outright terrorizing of patients, in order to inspire a fear that might shock them to their senses. The asylum belief is that recovery cannot take place without sufficient inner self-mortification and an attitude of apology. But that does not occur; instead, outrage and defiance in an asylum culture was, and is, rampant. Perceval reported how he and many of the other inmates would among themselves take vows of silence and noncompliance to the doctors.

This treatment was designed to insult, under the idea of quickening, arousing, nettling the patient's feelings! . . . my mind is astonished at the idea of reasonable beings admitting the propriety of such gross mockery, arguing in so absurd a circle, to such a cruel end. It is as if when a jaded post horse has fallen motionless from fatigue you were to seek out a raw place to spur him or lash him in, to make him show symptoms of life.[46]

☐ Finally, asylum is fundamentally a medical space. Somewhere at the turn of the eighteenth century, medical specialists took complete responsibility for the care of the insane. This new territory was even royally sanctioned when the lunatic doctors were given full authority to treat George III. Their status was assured. From that point on, the lunatic doctor assumed the privilege of deciding who was insane and could commit someone to an asylum merely by his signature.

In the early 1800s it was an open and begrudgingly acknowledged fact that medicine itself had little to offer as treatment for the insane. The elixirs and the herbs, baths and bleedings, isolations and exposures, shocks of cold or hot, and restraints and drugs that had been handed down within the medical tradition just did not work. The few studies of psychotic mind available were deemed to be effete and even irrelevant to the conduct of a psychological "science." The study of brain physiology and anatomy—the exalted science and the great hope of that time and ours—already showed signs that simplistic brain mechanics would not account for psychosis. Leaders of the medical schools and hospitals of the period had strong disagreements about that. Treatment increasingly relied on medical power or on the status of magic and authority that "medicine" always accrues to itself. The leaders relied not on competency and knowledge but on the power of a credential, which implied wisdom. Medicine borrowed science's mask of power, even as it acknowledged that its own science did not work. All that could be hoped for was a prescription to recover by moral command. Foucault, in the spirit of Perceval, claims that all medical psychology still bears the stamp of asylum mentality; it still continues to rely on a scientific authority which it has not earned.

To soften this medical influence Perceval increasingly advocated for the participation of the ministers of religion in the care of the insane. He wanted ministers of many denominations to visit with patients in the asylums. This turned out to be a most unpopular request: Doctors resented any interference to their treatment hegemony over the insane, and members of Parliament thought it might erode the separation of state and church. The ministers themselves felt too inadequate to be involved; although they continued to visit prisoners, poor people, and disaster victims, they claimed that working with the insane was no longer part of their tradition. Even Perceval had some misgivings about the idea. Many years previously he had turned his back on official religion, believing the ministry to be ignorant of personal spirituality. At the age of sixty-five, eight years before he died, he wrote:

> Much mental suffering thirty-seven years ago, accompanied with the experience of very extraordinary mental or spiritual phenomena which have continued, and have been my study to this day, has made me very skeptical upon the value of the Scriptures, and on many points of the Jewish and Christian religions.[47]

However, Perceval felt that the ministers could be trained. Perhaps *they* could understand that as much as a person in psychosis is ill, he is also like the victim of an earthquake, in need of help. He believed that if anyone could inject a compassionate influence into the lives of people in the asylums, it would be the ministers, whose education was at least grounded in the teachings of compassion.

The awakening of compassion for his fellow inmates had been the crucial moment of Perceval's recovery from insanity. It gave him energy; it gave him resolve and courage to recover his health, and in the end he dedicated his life to compassionate activity. A young companion once asked Perceval why he—a man with views far in advance of his fellow countrymen and so at odds with the establishment—had not emigrated to the liberal American colonies, as many of his character had done. Perceval thought this was an "ironical compliment, yet I knew that it was the case." Yet the assessment of Perceval's character was mistaken; he was really not the colonist type. He could never turn his back on England and English people—that was his family heritage and honor. Almost as much as Perceval believed that one's sanity could be recovered, he believed that the health of his country could be recovered and that its national sanity could be restored. In all of his patient advocacy work, he tried to engage what he felt was the national sanity. Perceval was convinced—as had been many of his family and class before him—

that the English ideal of *justice* (with its exquisite respect for human liberty) was one of the world's noblest expressions of an innate human compassion. Justice was the true heart of England for Perceval, and he believed that it could always be appealed to and awakened in times of national madness.

CHAPTER 2

Mania and the Risk of Power

POWERS

Whatever else mania is, it is also living dangerously. One sports
with powers, energies, intensified mind, amplified senses, and
altogether unleashed egoistic impulses; one becomes vulnerable to seen and unseen influences of all kinds. What begins as
a glimpse of vastness, unity, interdependence, transcendence,
"god consciousness," or whatever else one calls it, may end only
in the confusion of self-aggrandizement.

At the onset of any such psychotic experience, dramatic
changes are occurring in the body, in the perceptual systems,
and in the activities of mind. One feels a growing sense of
physical vitality, mental agility, and personal freedom in relationships. One might even experience some form of "absolute
truth," and sometimes it feels like the beginning of a "new life."
These feelings may last for only a short period of time—much
to one's dismay—but they are nevertheless remembered and
longed for. One's curiosity about the nature of the experience
is a powerful force. And the desire to repossess the power of that
experience becomes a seed for future episodes of psychosis, a

psychological materialism that can intensify into a lust for power.

It is not uncommon, therefore, for those recovering from psychotic episodes to remain haunted by a compulsion to find the essential meaning and importance of the extraordinary events through which they have lived and may live through again. For them, this is not simply a scholastic concern, it is an urgent opportunity for self-discovery. At any stage of a psychotic experience one may feel a strong temptation to elaborate a metaphysics. Sometimes it is felt as an obligation, sometimes as an urge to make sense of what is happening, and at other times it is a transparent self-justification. However, in every case, the metaphysical speculations by people about their experiences of psychosis point to entities or "powers" that exert their influences only when one is in a particular state of mind. And the descriptions of this vulnerable state of mind are astonishingly similar throughout the differing accounts of psychosis.

Many of the metaphysical formulations are only bits and pieces of esoteric ruminations, not yet complete systems. Others are elaborate and comprehensive systems that explain cosmic laws—for example, the "new synthesis of religion and science" proclaimed by Chief Justice Daniel Paul Schreber during his nine years of psychosis. Schreber's theory deals with the "power" that transformed his body into a woman's in order to make it a healing instrument for the world.[1] Some formulations are compelling and interesting to a point, but many are tiresomely egocentric. Yet the similarities are striking: Whether the metaphysics are expressed poorly or well, they are all about glimpses of powers said to be inaccessible to conventional consciousness. Ultimately, they are descriptions of the workings of power in the mind and of how under the influence of such power one can become wildly confused. Such was the predicament of John Custance.

THE MAD CAPER OF JOHN CUSTANCE

For over twenty years John Custance (b. 1900) suffered from repeating cycles of mania and depression. There was no obvious sign of his illness until he was middle-aged. Until then he had been raised as an English gentleman at the run-down family manor house called Wichbury, in the small country parish of Bourne, near Hampshire. Like his father, he attended Trinity College at Cambridge, where he was a good student at languages but was really much more interested and proud of his tennis and golf. He almost won his Cambridge "blue" and once played at Wimbledon. Gradually, he came to see himself as having a career in the diplomatic corps or in international business, and although he was short of funds he traveled for a time in Europe to educate himself.

A visit to the Soviet Union in 1924 to establish business connections left him discouraged by what he had seen. He dreaded what he called the Stalinist "managerial dictatorship" in which every individual was "labeled and certified" and he believed that he recognized an "obvious intention" to conquer the world. (Long before the term "iron curtain" was coined, Custance described the Soviet borders as thick and dangerous curtains.) Finally, he took a very promising job in an important banking and investment firm in Berlin. Noted for his charm and expertise in international transactions, and although still a junior partner, he rose quickly in the Berlin financial world. He married his English girlfriend, Anne, and together they developed a fast-paced life-style, entertaining lavishly in their large apartment. They loved Berlin and lived there for nine years.

In 1930 they lost everything when the great financial and social crash ended his career and they were forced to return to the run-down family estate in England. He was untrained for anything but banking ("I made the fatal mistake of starting at the top"), and he desperately tried to earn money by lecturing and free-lance writing. For a time he worked among the unemployed miners of West Cumberland.

As soon as the Second World War began, Custance was recruited to do intelligence work. He was responsible for intercepting and decoding communiqués about German troop movements; and for four years, until before the end of the war, he worked hard and long hours in the strict confines of Bletchly Park, the ultrasecret code-breaking center of British intelligence. Custance and everyone else at Bletchly Park felt themselves to be at one of the world's neural control centers—they lived the war frantically within the high-powered activity of their intellects. Under these conditions, just months before the Allied victory, Custance became high-strung, irritable, and depressed.

He had "flights of political ideas." He noted, "I had a severe breakdown. I was transported from the atmosphere of my office, where we were engaged in an all-out effort to defeat the Germans, to the solitude of a side-room in a Mental Hospital, where I soon found myself in acute mania, coping with the fantastic creatures of the Unconscious."[2]

This was the first episode of what became many years of repeating cycles of mania and depression. Over the next twenty years Custance had eight severe manic episodes, five of which were shortly followed by months of suicidal depression. His wife and children devotedly helped him during these times and he always returned to his family and home after his several hospitalizations. In the middle of these cycles, and between bouts, he wrote profoundly about his illness, trying to expose its inner actions and meanings. He delved into the origins of this mysteriously repeating illness, known since ancient Greece and accurately named "circular insanity" by a student of Esquirol, Jean Falret, in 1854.[3]

Although Custance lived in the generation just before the introduction of "major tranquilizers," he offers answers to the vexing question of why countless people discontinue taking medications and flirt with states of mind that they should know from experience might only end in disaster.

Custance had been in psychiatric treatment centers and hospitals episodically for many years. He was grateful that sometimes they contained him when he was unable to exist without care. But ultimately he felt that no "treatment" could help him, and for good reason. He maintained a tremendous allegiance to his experiences in the manic state of psychosis. He felt that what he learned and understood during that state of mind was as important as it was irresistible. Custance viewed the depressive state that usually followed as the necessary whiplash for his failure to successfully accomplish the tasks of mania. He could not help but feel: "Next time I will make it come out right!"

In the aftermath of a psychotic episode, reveals Custance, one often feels as though something has been left undone; a suspicion of incompleteness, even long after a psychotic experience. For some, this manifests as an unceasing demand that the "truth" of psychosis be experienced, *just one more time.* Here, "truth" refers to the vital sense of contact with "powers," both internal and external, through which psychosis comes to have a quality of a "path" or a personal quest, a sense of destiny to be fulfilled, and with all the potentiality of transforming oneself into a worthier person.

Like many others, Custance thought of his illness as being somehow connected with his spiritual growth; and also like many others, he had to deal with the temptation of wanting to fully explore his potential by letting his mania run wild. One time, he allowed it to happen—he was convinced he could keep his wits about him, that he could *manage the mania.* His journals and books chart the course of his mania at a level of observation that exposes the subtle interconnections between mind and body, and which can be called a "metaneurology." He recorded the manic alterations of the "special senses" of seeing, hearing, smelling, tasting, and of body sensations, while his mind was infused with manic exhilaration. These descriptions allow anyone to appreciate the subtle biological realities of mania and how they expand into "manic consciousness." From Custance, we also learn about the emergence of forceful egoistic mind patterns and how these impulses can become an obstacle to recovery—perhaps forever.

Custance had already endured a number of psychotic episodes by his early fifties. Usually, he was hospitalized when his behavior reached a peak of excitability, grandiosity, and poor judgment. Each episode was a wretched cycle of hope, wild daydreaming, fear, and despair. "And yet," he writes, "it was as a lunatic that I saw something, a vision as it were of the whole universe from a completely different angle, which was so overwhelming, that even in my sanest moments I cannot help attributing to it a measure of validity. For better or for worse it is part of my consciousness, an aspect of things with which I have to live, so that my only possible course is to relate it as best I can to the everyday world around me."[4]

In the early 1950s Custance wrote an important study of the nature of mania and depression called *Wisdom, Madness and Folly.* He believed that it might "furnish some useful material to psychologists and psychiatrists and perhaps also be of value to fellow-sufferers who have been through the same strange recesses of the soul."[5] He wrote the first half of it while in a hospital under the influence of mania and on the advice of his psychiatrist. Its purpose was to demonstrate that there exists in madness a wisdom that had not yet been fully explored. When Carl Jung read this work he thought that Custance's experience of mania was an excellent example of archetypal forces being released from the unconscious when the "mental level is low-ered."[6] It was obvious to Custance that mania had provided the most interesting and important ordeals of his life, and he became convinced of his ability to bring some intelligence and discipline to it.

He concocted a plan to explore the wisdom of his mania; it was to be an archetypal manic-dream-come-true. When the next episode of mania arose, he would leave his home in England and travel to another country; there he would live out his mania to its fullest extent, uninterrupted by the apprehension of family and friends. He planned to use everything he had learned during previous manic episodes to control and use its energy. He felt certain that, the next time, he would be able to harness the joyfulness of mania and not lapse into wild destructiveness and, at least for him, the inevitable depression. After much badgering, his wife reluctantly agreed to the plan, although she did not understand fully what he had in mind.

SURGE OF POWER

His manic periods came roughly every two years, and one was due toward the end of 1951. When symptoms of mania began to appear in October, he chose to travel to Berlin with the intention of testing his mania by crossing over into Soviet-occupied East Berlin. It was very important to Custance that the country in which this "manic adventure" took place be some-what familiar yet also an environment of "wakeful danger." For Custance, Berlin was the "shattered city where two worlds meet," the electrical junction where the fate of Europe, and perhaps the world, would be decided. "I was quite certain that I would be brought safely home though I might well have the experiences of a Communist prison or lunatic asylum before I got there."[7]

Increasingly, he found himself preparing for what he called his "adventure into the unconscious." He was aging, and the years of mania and depression had taken a heavy toll on his body and mind. He had participated in the world of business with mixed results; mania had usually interrupted his plans. At this particular time in his life he felt he had no other choice but to come to grips with his illness: to see it through, to follow its call, and perhaps put it to rest with this one last episode.

He paid great attention to the earliest stirrings of his mania. At first, there was an alteration of every sensory modality. His vision, hearing, sense of smell, sense of taste, sense of touch, body sensations, and sense of awareness began to change. And according to Custance, they all changed for the better—his senses came alive. At times he called them "illuminated." The mania proceeded from its earliest, most subtle indications, such as the heightened perception of the play between light and shadow, to its peak experiences, such as the sensation of an intense excitability running through his spinal column: "The whole aspect of the world about me began to change, and I had the excited shivers in the spinal column and tingling of the nerves that always herald my manic phases."[8]

From the point of view of external time, his mania occurred precipitously; it could be upon him in two or three days, or in two weeks at the most. However, the evolution of the perceptual changes was gradual, chain-linked, and irreversible. In Custance's experience, virtually nothing could prevent the forward march of these changes, and, if he had anything to do with it, nothing would interfere with the intense excitement and inspiration to live—and live fully—that mania brought with it. He was always apprehensive about the chaos mania might cause, but he lusted for it nevertheless.

Both August Strindberg and Friedrich Nietzsche had also courted mania for the purpose of liberating a supernormal intelligence. They had actually studied each other's works, and Custance had studied the works of both. Nietzsche believed his mania was the herald of his transformation into the fully perfected being that his philosophy and psychology foretold. Strindberg felt that his mania would point the way to the completely natural, pure, and instinctive man. Custance was more interested in world politics; the goal of his mania was "to put the world in order." He came to believe that his manic state was the living metaphor of the postwar division of Western Europe—between East and West—and that by solving a fundamental antithesis of opposites within himself, he might also do so for the community of nations. "An unsuccessful member of a depressed class in an age of social disintegration, in a vast delusion of grandeur, I saw my own family, through my own house, saving the world."[9]

INTENSIFICATION OF THE SENSES

Changes in his sensations began as soon as Custance touched down at the airport in West Berlin—a time-tested sign, he thought, that his mission would be successful. He continually reiterated this belief as if to gear himself up to new degrees of mania. But at the same time, he took no chances: "I made every possible attempt to intensify this state, notably by means of alcohol." In the week to come he slept no more than five hours. He settled himself (*perched* might be a better word) in the same hotel he had lived in as a young banker twenty years earlier. It was from this hotel that he planned to make daring forays, led by his manic "guidance," into the heavily policed eastern sector.

He was getting "high," inspired by the work that he had set for himself, but his mania was simply not reaching the intensity for which he had hoped. It is important to note that as much as mania appears to come upon one imperceptibly, it cannot truly develop without some further effort. Those with much experience in mania gradually discover a repertoire of tricks and methods to intensify this state or "let oneself go" into it, so to speak. Custance already had a great deal of experience with mania and was a virtuoso in the methodology of becoming a maniac. The practices that he evolved were virtually a guidebook to insanity.

He applied himself to his time-tested techniques of intensifying the mania, including writing with abandon (writing and paying no attention to the words being written), drinking alcohol, fasting, having fleeting infatuations with prostitutes, abstaining from sleep, and, above all, staying *"on the move."* Maintaining a state of constant activity was the most important technique. On a junket in a dangerous place for carrying out a secret psychological-political mission and in an increasingly excited state, he was becoming a James Bond of mania: "I solemnly declare that I have been sent by the Powers to put this lunatic world in order."[10]

Back in his hotel, Custance wrote daily notes and commentaries in his journal:

> The world is transforming itself around me as I write; it is coming alive; and all the Powers of actuality, the spirits of the past, the gods and goddesses, yes and the devils too, tell me to let them have their way . . . I am experimenting with the Powers. I want to know whether they will look after me, as my inner voices tell

me they will . . . The Powers will tell me in their own way, through
chance acquaintances, symbols, pieces of information here and
there.[11]

On stealing his way into the Soviet zone, his excited state
finally reached the longed-for degree of intensity. When he wandered as far as occupied Potsdam he became terrified at being
detected by Soviet sentries; twenty-five years earlier he had seen
their arrogant marching in the streets of Leningrad, and now
they paraded as unstoppable world conquerors. Back in the
Alexanderplatz, he approached prostitutes with a grand scheme
of bringing East and West together in sexual union. He gave
them large sums of money and tried to convince them that the
spiritual nature of his and their connection might break down
the walls of a divided world. He wandered through the drab
streets of East Berlin and drank at workingmen's taverns. He
saw every event as an auspicious omen and a symbolic confirmation of what he should or should not do next. "It is a principle
of this experiment to act on suggestion, like a lunatic suffering
from paranoia."[12] He was irresistibly drawn to talk out loud to
statues in the city squares, and followed every hint and occurrence of auspicious chance events. He became hyperaware of
chance, and he directed his life by it. Chance was embodied by
his spirit-guide, called Tyche; he left everything up to her "guidance." Custance felt he was taking to the maximum those principles of a "perpetual state of guidance" only speculated about by
evangelical Christianity.

Successfully magnetizing and manipulating conversations
were always a sure sign to Custance that his mania was "working." After fast-talking his way out of an encounter with the
police, he exclaimed, "I got away with it!" And then, "It has
happened. I am mad at last. The Powers have taken over, I am
theirs body and soul. I do not belong to myself any longer; I am
simply a tool, and all I have to do is to keep myself oiled and
open, clean and receptive."[13]

"First and foremost," says Custance, "comes a general sense
of intense well-being." This pleasurable and sometimes "ecstatic feeling-tone" remained as a sort of permanent background for all his experiences during the manic period. This
background colored all the changes taking place in the five "special senses."

Changes in *visual perception* came first:

> This began . . . with the usual curious change in sense-perception
> of the outer world. I can only describe it by saying that 'the lights
> go up,' as if a kind of switch were turned on in my psycho-physical
> system. Everything seems different, somehow brighter and
> clearer. This is, of course, the phenomenon technically known as
> 'photism'; it is quite easily recognizable and bitter experience has
> now taught me that, as soon as it occurs, I should take immediate
> steps to go to the hospital, since within a few days I shall be out
> of control. This time, however, I had no intention of going near
> the doctors.[14]

A variety of other changes took place in his visual experience:
an increased sense of clarity, starlike and rainbowlike phenomena surrounding bright lights, halo effects, and so on. But most
important for understanding and appreciating the psychological
mechanics of mania—and the thread that runs through psychosis in general—was his heightened ability to have visual illusions. "I lay on my bed watching the play of light-reflections on
the shiny walls of my sick room. There were two patches of light,
one in front of me, and the other on my left. Gradually the one
in front of me began to take shape as a definite pattern. I knew
this meant the advent of a vision, and relaxed my eyes and body
accordingly."[15] As he leaned into the prevision, it evolved into
a complicated cosmo-political drama. It could be called "visual
imagination," that is, the capacity to form complete images out
of basic visual events (such as patches, colors, and angles), then,
through a number of steps, to embody and enliven those images
to the point that they communicate back to the perceiver.

Custance described his heightened ability to experience a
manic chain reaction. Visual distortions turn into illusions, and
then into visions:

> This power is proportionate to the acuteness of the mania. In
> periods of acute mania they can appear almost like a continuous
> cinema performance, particularly if there are any complicated
> and variable light patterns with which my optical mechanism can
> play the necessary tricks. These visions generally appear on the
> walls of my room, if these are shiny enough to reflect light. They
> are infinitely varied, and bear a close relation to the processes of
> thought passing in my mind at the time . . . there have been
> visions of Heaven—and Hell—of gods and goddesses and devils,
> and so on.[16]

The neurology of these occurrences intrigued Custance and he frequently speculated about them. Over the course of many episodes of mania, he developed his ideas about the biology of mania and even performed experiments while in excited manic states. It could be called a "metaneurology" because it combined observations of mind and body and nervous system interactions, minutely examined during the special conditions of psychosis. For example, he observed that the hallucinations began through a relaxation of the focusing mechanism. During a manic period he could manage to read without spectacles, and in more acute mania his spectacles were totally unnecessary and of no help at all. He presumed that in mania "some sort of relaxation of tension takes place [in muscles of the eye], which enables the muscles to function more freely and thus more effectively."[17] The reverse was true as the mania diminished. This kind of metaneurology became increasingly more profound during his manic career.

His *sense of hearing* changed. He first noticed an increase in aural acuity with an ability to take in and distinguish many sound impressions at the same time, and by an increased sensitivity to different textures of sound sensations. Because of this, Custance felt more fully alive to the outside world, receiving it through sound resonances and vibrations. The changes in hearing probably resulted from a relaxation of the muscles of the inner ear, similar to the relaxation of the eye muscles.

Custance heard many different kinds of voices addressing him. But these were usually not complete hallucinations; the voices (with which he was in almost continual communication) were still incompletely formed by whispers, phrases, puns, and innuendos. However, from these double meanings he took all his cues to act.

His *senses of smell and taste* underwent a similar enhancement. He could finely discriminate between different smells and tastes in a way that was seemingly not possible before. He discovered that mania was the only state of mind in which he truly appreciated the varieties and subtleties of scents. And his sense of taste was opened to him as a gift: "[E]ven common grass tastes excellent, while real delicacies like strawberries or raspberries give ecstatic sensations appropriate to a veritable food of the gods."[18]

In the early stages of mania, Custance would experience a greater sensitivity in his *sense of touch* and bodily feelings, which he linked to an ability to draw figures with great likeness to the

originals. In general, he reports an "extraordinary muscular
looseness or suppleness."[19] As the mania progressed, he felt
"particularly fit"; his reactions to the environment were rapid
and well defined.

He acquired a powerful, base voice, rich with resonances, "as
though passages in my chest which were normally clogged were
opened up, and my chest actually seem[ed] to set up abnormal
vibrations."[20] For Custance, this was the metaphor for some sort
of manic "opening up." In his metaneurology he attempted to
account for the "opening" by an expansion of his sense relaxation theory. He believed some sort of relaxation of normal nervous tension was involved. He felt that there were channels in
the body that convey and distribute the sensation of energy
movement, and that during mania they became unobstructed. In
the early stages of his mania he felt this to be merely good and
healthy; as mania escalated, however, these sensations were ecstatic, rushing, and overwhelming. They would peak in the
"creepy or shivery feeling in the spinal column."[21]

This last sensation involves an opening up of the channels
that connect body and mind. Here is the best description that
Custance could offer of what he called a "linking-up of tracts of
associations in the psycho-physical mechanism":

> I have noticed again and again that when thinking or writing in
> a state of mania, every time unusual connections between depart-
> ments of thought or tracts or associations occur to me I get this
> sensation in direct proportion to the importance and extent of
> the departments or tracts thus connected . . . clicked or fallen into
> place in my head. This feeling is neither purely physical nor
> purely psychological, but a sort of combination between the
> two.[22]

His digestive system functioned better than ever and his appe-
tite was good. He felt that his metabolism was rapid and per-
vaded by a sense of "inner warmth." Even on cold nights he had
a strong impulse to throw off his clothes, which was also a
symbol of his joyful feeling of freedom from all physical and
mental restraint.

Custance believed he had come upon an important insight
into mania when he saw a hidden connection between bodily
sensations and the contents of thought: "[P]hysical sensations

make themselves felt well in advance of the corresponding thoughts, and sometimes even without the thoughts becoming conscious at all."[23]

INTENSIFIED MENTAL ACTIVITY: THE SIXTH SENSE

A sixth, "special," sense, ordinarily called consciousness, is the awareness of what takes place in mental activity. Mental contents—thoughts, emotions, memories, flights of fancy—are all moving objects of perception to the special sense of awareness. This awareness as well as this innate precision is one of the psychological foundations of all Buddhism, called "mindfulness of mind," without which the practice of meditation would be impossible.

If one does nothing but simply turn one's attention to the stream of mental activity, it is obvious that at times it moves quickly and forcefully and at other times quietly and sparingly. In mania, the velocity of mind-streaming is notorious. Custance expressed the quality of "mind speed" in a variety of ways. He describes a tremendous proliferation of ideas, cascading one upon the other: "[M]y pen can scarcely keep up with the rapid flow of ideas." The cause, he felt, was an "extreme rapidity of association of ideas" and rapid dispersions of thought. For example, catching the sight of a flock of seagulls spreading overhead "set up immediately and virtually simultaneously in my mind trains of thoughts" that ranged far from the original sense perception, flying into the past or future and linked together by such things as a similarity of images or in the sounds of words, or of rapidly flashing memories. "I [could] look at nothing without receiving some idea from it leading to an impulse to action," and finally, "a flight of ideas . . . [would take] as it were possession of me."[24]

This phenomenon of "mental speed" can increase to the point that it feels like one's own thoughts have been "possessed." The degree of speed quickens every object with life: "[I]n manic states of sufficient intensity animistic conceptions impel themselves forcibly upon me; I [could not] avoid seeing spirits in everything."[25]

During mania, even thinking itself is experienced as an act of power. In this episode its total power was unveiled to Custance:

"I seem to see a vast chain of associations, often extending into departments of thought not normally connected at all. Thoughts and impressions, in fact, do not appear in isolation as they so often do in ordinary life; they seem linked up with a whole."[26]

The acceleration of thought that takes place in states of mania appears to break through the boundaries of space and time. So it is not surprising that with speculations like this Custance would take up the almost ubiquitous manic fascination with Einstein's general theory of relativity. *Only* in manic states, Custance admitted, did he feel he could understand it.

Wild Daydreaming

Patterns of thought seemed to have a life of their own and went their own way, independent of his volition. Thinking interpenetrated the "innumerable watertight compartments of life and experience."[27] He experienced the speed and forcefulness of thinking as a continuous pulsating motor behind the eyeballs, and at times he would become intoxicated with the power of his mind. He would just sit down, "enjoying the marvel of the new world which had appeared to me and day-dreaming in the wildest manner of the future."[28]

Thought intoxication—a kind of drunkenness with mind forms—was the end result of mind speed when his mind attained a certain critical velocity. An apt analogy might be the phenomenon of "critical flicker fusion," that is, when short bursts of light are presented to the eye, individual flashes cannot be discriminated after they attain a certain velocity. As the interval between flashes is progressively shortened, the flashes appear to merge into a "flicker fusion." It is this phenomenon that makes cinema projection possible. When the celluloid film moves at a certain velocity, the eye/brain cannot keep up with the independent picture frames and they merge to create the illusion of a solid and continuous image. Similarly, when thinking reaches a critical velocity, a confusional state occurs, which is characterized by projections becoming literally animated.

A particular power of the mind to imbue the imagination with life was revealed to Custance in the utmost detail. "I found in the caves of the Unconscious demons and were-wolves, strange faces of forgotten gods, and devils, while my mind played unceasingly on everything it remembered of magic and myths. Folds of the bedclothes suddenly appeared as the horrible vision of Hectate. I was transported into an atmosphere of miracle and witchcraft, of all-pervading occult forces, although I had taken no interest whatever in these subjects prior to my illness."[29]

The mind of insanity might be extremely primitive, he speculated; in fact, it "may well be a genuine return, though perhaps in a distorted form, to earlier types of consciousness."[30] He felt forced "through the crust of normal consciousness and [into] illimitable unexplored caverns of the soul in which hidden springs of beings were somehow revealed in thoughts, fantasies and feelings."[31] This, he discovered, was the source of the delusions of power that one finds in the asylums. "The sense of being intimately in tune with the ultimate stuff of the universe can become so overwhelming that those affected naturally proclaim themselves to be Jesus Christ, or Almighty God, or whatever deity they have been taught to look on as the source of all power."[32]

Trance Dreaming

Custance's psychological speculations were in surprising agreement with the yet to be discovered work of William James. James saw the seed of every variety of thought disorder to be in the readily observable processes of everyday mind:

> Everybody knows the state between sleeping and waking, in which half-realized and half-seen thoughts and images follow one another in endless succession without any conscious volition of the individual . . . abnormal mental conditions consist largely in an intensification of this state of reverie.[33]

When attention is paid to the borderland of mental activity—for example, between sleeping and waking or between confusion and alert wakefulness—one begins to find the germination point of dreams.

Dreaming and mania can be seen in close association. Custance called it an *interpenetration:* "I wake up and my mind carries on the same train of thought which has been begun in a dream. I go to sleep and go on dreaming about the subjects I have been thinking about."[34] There are a number of gradations of mental states between sleeping, dreaming, and waking that might be called transitional states. But Custance observed that in mania such states of consciousness are less separate and freely intermingle.

Mania is marked by the activation of dream states of consciousness within the apparent state of wakeful activity. Such dream states become mixed with moment-to-moment sensations. And in mania, thoughts and images intensified by the heightened senses are made abnormally vivid, compelling, and "often so overpowering that they cause marked physical sensations."[35] This mixture of dream state and heightened wakefulness allows underlying urges or instincts the freedom to express themselves.

> [T]he horses of passion and instinct have run away. The immense enjoyment that they have in doing so governs one's whole being. All brakes or clogs on the whole functioning of the psycho-physical mechanism are removed; the channels of instinct are freed; the libido can flow where it will.[36]

The resulting state of mind is thus experienced as magical and beyond conventional patterns and constraints. Its possibilities appear limitless.

SYNCHRONICITY AND UNION

Custance often wondered how he could become so enthralled with the phenomenon of "synchronicity" when he was already so familiar with its disastrous effects. But having embarked on a state of mania, he was not interested in restraining it; mania seems almost synonomous with nonrestraint. Also, he was under the influence of the usual manic amnesia about previous episodes. And, of course, there was simply no time to reflect. Events were rushing, Custance felt, moment to moment toward an ever-increasing expansion of consciousness and understanding. He recognized that his mind was undergoing a powerful transition and he felt it was unnatural and even dangerous to forcefully direct it. He could only allow his thoughts to be directed by the natural and elemental powers whose presence he felt constantly while in the state of mania.

By synchronicity, Custance meant events in which the contents of his thoughts were instantly manifested in reality: The
scenario that he pictured in his mind actually seemed to come
to pass. An upsurge of wind, the sound of thunder, words spoken to him—all might occur at the very same time he conceived
of them. A synchronous event could be anything he thought
about, which was then echoed in reality. And he believed that
the significance of such events was much greater than had ever
been expressed in any psychological discussion of coincidence
or precognition. To him, synchronous events were confirmations that something of great spiritual importance was happening to him, and they bolstered his self-confidence and his pride.
    This confidence allowed Custance to compose a metaphysical
system. He called it his "Theory of Actuality." The basic inspiration for the theory arose in a vision that had burst upon him.

> How shall I describe it? It was perfectly simple. The great male
> and female organs of love hung there in mid-air; they seemed
> infinitely far away from me and infinitely near at the same time.
> I can see them now, pulsing rhythmically in a circular clockwise
> motion, each revolution taking approximately the time of a
> human pulse or heartbeat, as though the vision was associated in
> some way with the circulation of the blood. I was not sexually
> excited; from the first the experience seemed to me to be holy.
> What I saw was the Power of Love—the name came to me at
> once—the Power that I knew somehow to have made all uni-
> verses, past, present and to come, to be utterly infinite, an infinity
> of infinities, to have conquered the Power of Hate, its opposite,
> and thus created the sun, the stars, the moon, the planets, the
> earth, light, life, joy and peace, never-ending.[37]

In this "peace" he felt forgiven and relieved of all burden of
sin. He felt a complete absence of fear. The whole of infinity
opened up before him, and for the following weeks and months
he passed through experiences that "transported me as it were
into the Kingdom of Heaven." In this realm, he was "in love with
the whole Universe . . . I was joined to Creation."
    Custance had carefully designed his manic experiment in Ber-
lin to bring about this experience of "peace" within himself, and
to further expand it to other people, even to nations. Was there
any place better than Berlin, he thought, to apply his special
energy? He was convinced that only from Berlin—where two
worlds meet at a flash point of world war or world peace—could

come The Great Political Victory. He wanted to use his contact
with spiritual powers to effect the rebuilding and reunion of the
two Berlins. This alone, he felt, was the medicine to heal the
world. But things fell into disarray in Berlin, "After all, I was
carrying out a rather dangerous experiment . . . of letting myself
go into mania with a view to seeing if I could control it. I found
I could, but only with some difficulty and strain." He spent all
his money, primarily by squandering it in ostentatious displays
of trying to bring people together. "I seemed to know that I
must spend generously without calculating and that the money
would be provided." Soon, he felt "like a man who was exhausting himself in riotous living"; and on top of that he began to
have encounters with the police. Finally, the British military
police intervened and gave him safe passage to Paris.

Paris was to be the pinnacle of his mania as well as its subtle
turning point. He felt cheerful and victorious, moving freely, as
he put it, between the positive and negative forces of the universe. He was communing with figures "beyond the barrier of
mortality." He thought that other worlds had opened up to him
because he had bridged the opposing forces of the universe.
"[M]y state of elation is itself a bridging of or making contact
between the opposites—the watertight compartment of individuality, the hard shells that surround our egos, tend to disappear. I am not I, but many; those I meet are not merely
themselves but many others too."[38]

A deterioration of this sense of freedom from individuality
soon arose, in the form of an arrogance and aggression. It is a
typical and painful paradox of mania that while seeking to transcend an individual ego, one lapses into bullying egocentricity.
An embarrassing event highlighted his self-preoccupation.
While in a state of elation he managed to arrange an interview
with the aged and revered Catholic theologian Gabriel Marcel
at his book-lined flat in Montmartre. Custance had looked forward to the meeting but found himself announcing to Marcel
that he (Custance) was mad and glorying in it. "Instead of discussing his work and learning something I talked egotistically
about my own. It was absurd." Marcel cautioned Custance about
a "tendency to use [his] lunacy as an evasion of responsibility,
as a license to remain a kind of Peter Pan."

Contrary to his usual manic liberty from a sense of shame or
guilt, Custance felt humiliation. Yet he was not about to let
anything bring him down. The world still had great enjoyment

for him: "The sense of being in mystical communion with all things is at the very root of the manic state in which I am at the present." He summed up his manic practice: "Here in Paris, as earlier in Berlin, it is perfectly clear to me that the manic state involves a kind of wild plunge into the depths, a letting-go of all restrictions on the great forces of instinct and the Unconscious." Rising to inconceivable heights, "I imagined that I was starting a movement to end all movements, the movement without an 'ism,' something natural and spontaneous which will spread like wildfire of its own inner power."

What began as a political aspiration to join the English and Soviet cultures expanded in the course of mania to set "the whole world right," and finally ended up as a religious mission. In all, Custance spent a whirlwind five days in Paris, which "passed like the dream it was."

MANIC CONSCIOUSNESS

The experience of mania is clearly a formidable physical and mental drama arousing the beauty, power, and terror that is within all people. The metaphysical insights of individuals who experience mania are rooted in tangible experiences that are impressive and difficult to resist. One woman in her eighties who had experienced over thirty manic episodes would, at the onset of manic changes, throw away her otherwise badly needed hearing aid and announce her "return to life."

Anyone who has experienced mania knows that these changes are transitory and that they never yield an eternal state of health and happiness. Yet a desire to transform oneself is so powerful that many people seize the opportunity to experience manic consciousness and risk their lives and their families. Custance continually attested to the enthrallments of mania, nearly echoing Thomas De Quincey in praising the blissful state of opium intoxication.[39] "In its favourable aspect [mania] is a strange and lovely land beyond individuality, and incidentally also beyond good and evil, since the opposites are reconciled and the peace that passes all understanding reigns supreme."[40] This fondness for mania has all the potential for an addiction to ecstasy and personal power.

There is a hunger, both psychological and spiritual (as in the

realm of Greed), for the pleasure and magic of manic consciousness. All the sensory changes and "openings" of inner channels
that go into creating manic consciousness are felt to be a "superior" state of consciousness, more profound than "normal" consciousness, which in comparison seems trivial. Some patients
even feel that manic consciousness may gather in strength
through repeated episodes. The steps Custance took to induce
his manic states—the practices that were meant to disorder
"normal" consciousness and modes of thinking—not only
added fuel to this fire but were often accomplished with a sense
of workmanlike pride.[41] From manic consciousness arose his
initial "surge of power," and out of that a great variety of
psychotic elations and excitements could blossom. *In this sense,
manic consciousness is the basic substratum consciousness from which every
variety and style of psychotic disorder springs.*

Almost all psychotic occurrences of whatever species (organic, chemical, situational) can be seen to be infused by manic
consciousness at their onset or as they recycle. This consciousness is usually reported to have a dreamlike quality. Some people who have experienced this state call it the "dream time," the
"dream world," or the "dream machine." The senses of time,
space, cause, and effect; the availability of memory images; the
way external perceptions are woven into the ongoing scenario;
the shifting of experience between subject and object; the play
with words and puns; the electrical sense of power and magic;
and above all the sense of conviction in the reality of what is in
front of one's eyes—are all marks of both manic and dream
consciousness.[42] It could be said that manic consciousness bor-
rows, or perhaps *commandeers,* the mechanics of dreaming.

For Custance, experiencing mania was like having a fuse blow
out in one's house. The lights will go out in some places, but the
remaining lights seem to become more brilliantly illuminating.
He believed that William Wordsworth precisely expressed his
experience: "When the light of sense goes out, but with a flash
that has revealed the invisible world."[43]

An atomic dimension of mind was revealed to Custance. He
saw it clearly in his visions, which he called the "Fantasia of
Opposites." In this cosmology the whole universe turns on the
principle of polarity and on the mechanics of attraction and repulsion, positive and negative, matter and antimatter. In a human
life it is male and female, spirit and matter, birth and death. In
an individual mind it is the simultaneous train of opposing

thoughts, contradictions based on the *atomic splitting of each single thought.*

If these insights were isolated to the moment of experience, they would be of small value. But Custance felt strongly that a continuing thread of wisdom lasted well beyond his mania. In spite of all his confused doubts during the terrible depression that followed, he felt that "as the result of my experiences the whole universe has changed about me, and it will never be quite the same again."[44] To anyone familiar with the manic mind, there is an obvious brilliance within it, and there is a general agreement among those who have experienced it that religious truths are realized. That is what led John Perceval to say, after his fact-finding tours of English asylums, "There may be faithful witnesses locked up." For Custance, those truths involved a conviction in a loving gentleness, purity, and sacredness of this world and of his participation in it. And most importantly, he believed (as others have[45]) that whatever recovery he achieved depended on his memories of these truths, even though he could no longer experience them.

THE AFTERMATH

By accident, Custance returned home to Wichbury on Anne's birthday, and the whole family celebrated. He soon realized that they were apprehensive about his state of mind and watched him closely, but he was elated even so, "owing to a certain feeling of pride at my apparent success in having at last taken the manic bull by the horns and tamed him." He also noticed a certain tendency to become infuriated when anyone countered his ideas with rational arguments. And then, after one week of settling down to being home, another "synchronous" event occurred: Carl Jung invited Custance to visit him in Zürich. While in Berlin, Custance had requested an interview just when, according to Custance, Jung was working out his own theory of "synchronicity." Thinking that Custance was still in Berlin, Jung invited him to come immediately. Naturally, Custance's family had grave doubts about setting him loose on the Continent once more. But, as usual, he was hard to resist and they "finally agreed that, mad though I might be, the opportunity could not be allowed to slip."

The meeting with Jung was much more successful than the one with Gabriel Marcel. "At once I had complete confidence that here was a man, one felt, who would never let you down."[46] And Custance was very respectful of Jung; he asked many questions about mania and the unconscious and found Jung's ideas to be as outrageous as his own. There was much camaraderie in their discussions of paranormal phenomena, spirit appearances, and cosmic expansions of the self. Jung, also, was delighted by the visit and later wrote in his preface to Custance's book:

> When I was working in 1906 [at the Burghölzli Hospital, under the supervision of Dr. Eugen Bleuler] on my book *The Psychology of Dementia Praecox* (as schizophrenia was then called), I never dreamt that in the succeeding half-century psychological investigation of psychoses and their contents would make virtually no progress whatever. The dogma, or intellectual superstition, that only physical causes are valid still bars the psychiatrist's way to the psyche of his patient and impels him to take the most reckless and incalculable liberties with this most delicate of all organs rather than allow himself even to think of the possibility of genuinely psychic causes and effects, although they are perfectly obvious to an unprejudiced mind . . . What the author has discovered in the manic state is in exact agreement with my own discoveries. By this I mean more particularly, the structure of opposites and their symbolism, the anima archetype, and lastly the unavoidable encounter with the reality of the psyche. As is generally known, these three main points play an essential role in my psychology, with which however, the author did not become acquainted until afterwards . . . As a contribution to our knowledge of those highly significant psychic contents that manifest themselves in pathological conditions or underlie them, this book is as valuable as it is unique.[47]

Custance "left Professor Jung and Zürich feeling that something marvelous had happened. Never in my life had I had an interview that impressed me so much." But as soon as he returned to his family, he began to try to work minor miracles, using what he felt to be his gift to understand synchronicity. He tried to predict and psychically influence horse races and the stock market. These miracles were of doubtful outcome, however, so he decided "to adopt my old lunatic technique of relaxing, listening to inner voices, and accepting wholly extraneous and irrelevant indications from the outer world, such as the flight of birds, or going towards other objects which attracted my attention for completely illogical reasons."

As hard as he tried to hang onto his sense of elation and power, he found it slipping away, and for the next several months he struggled against entering a depression. "What nonsense the whole thing was, just a grandiose delusion of a lunatic. After every bout of manic elation there comes in my experience an unpleasant awakening to hard facts, a morning after the night before. The bills have to be paid; the chickens sent out on flights of inflated imagination come home to roost."[48] In this stage of disillusionment Custance felt completely abandoned by the powers of mania and had no enthusiasm for life itself.

Six months of depression followed, during which Custance was able to remain at home. However, just two years after his "successful" Berlin experiment, another manic episode occurred. Once again, "the lights went up" and he became involved with the same old political and magical preoccupations and indulged in the same self-absorptive techniques as before. Once again, Custance tried to ride the wild energy of mania and control its outcome. As he said to his exhausted wife, "Even you must admit that I got away with it in Berlin and Paris, and what I have done once I can do again." But he did not get away with it this time. He reveled in a great display of energy, which soon became extravagant and imperious behavior. Again, he squandered large amounts of dwindling family funds on political schemes. But it was when he tried to force an interview with the prime minister of England that he was arrested, put under observation, certified, and hospitalized. After about three months in the hospital he said, "Gradually I came down to earth."

"Rare indeed are the madmen equal to madness," concluded Henri Michaux, one of the most sensitive explorers of psychotic states of mind. Custance would certainly have agreed. At one time he thought he was such a rarity, but in the end he felt this was a presumption, an egotistic tendency at very root of mania:

> No feature of elated insane states is more disturbing to look back on than their appalling ego-centricity. Whatever 'actuality,' whatever truth and even wisdom may lie in the abnormal apprehensions of the Unconscious which crowd upon the lunatic, the idea that he is something wonderful, that he occupies a privileged position in the centre of things, must surely be regarded as

wholly false and delusionary. And yet no idea is more insistent; delusions of grandeur are the commonest of all.[49]

DEPRESSION

For Custance, the enigmatic "switch-point" where mania changes into depression was always a time for worry. He knew that even to think of losing it was *already* an erosion of the manic state.

A steady fear arose in him of mania slipping away, of losing something precious to him. This escalated to a fear of losing *everything*. The fear became a cosmic dread. The loss would be more than death; he struggled not merely against the "morning after," he desperately tried to "put off that moment when I would disappear into Hell." As he knew from former times, it was a hell from which there was no reprieve, only inescapable doom. As in mania—only just the opposite—Custance was adrift in an ocean of intensified mental activity, while his seeing, hearing, smelling, tasting, feeling, and thinking were distorted into illusions and hallucinations, now no longer infused with manic joy but with depressive fear, ugliness, and repulsion.

As high as Custance rose during mania, he plummeted every bit as low during depression. Depression too was just as excessive as mania: Each unpleasant emotion or thought was "magnified to the limit." He called it the "Universe of Horrors," and in this realm everything was *precisely the reverse* of his manic state. Whereas in mania he lived in a constant state of well-being, in depression he always felt miserable and ill. His sense of manic openness and expansion turned into a "hardening of the shell of ego," where he was shut into his own thoughts and profoundly isolated and cut off from the world of God and men. Manic freedom from shame and guilt became self-loathing and continual guilt over past sins and failures. In depression he now hated the very idea of manic consciousness, feeling it had been the result of "evil influences."

The omniscientlike clarity of mania switched into a feeling of perpetual fog and darkness. All the illuminated sensations of mania were gone; in their place was dullness and disgust. Rather than being able to think quickly and have everything "click into place," depression was an inextricable jumble. He felt ignorant, indifferent, and could not concentrate. The grandeur and power of mania were replaced by their very opposites; just as in mania he sought to save the world, in depression he felt ultimately responsible for all the evil and sin affecting mankind. Now he was told by spirit voices that he had committed unforgivable sins and was the opposite of Christ. Heaven had ended and he was now in hell. Fear dominated his world, until the point of being pursued by tormenting demons, when he had to fight for his life. He was told that he had no hope, that he was "as good as dead" and simply "a person to be got rid of." For long periods of time he would lie in bed with his head buried under the covers.

Without fail, Custance said, he "learned more" from the experience of depression than he did from mania. Only in depression could he feel, to the bone, his utter aloneness in the universe. He said it was the most shocking insight of his life. The contrasting creations of the worlds of mania and depression revealed to him the utter unreality of *everything* in the mind, and how each world or private universe, or any world, insane or sane, is a hollow fabrication of the mind. This woke him up. Always, this realization was for him a turning point in coming out of depression and was the moment when recovery began. At the same time, it was accompanied by a profound aloneness in which he understood, he said, the anguish of George Berkeley, bishop of Cloyne, whose own realization of the emptiness of all apparent phenomena led to a similar loneliness. For Custance, this experience was an island of clarity and the herald of his recovery.

RISKS OF RECOVERY

In the hospital, Custance's treatment consisted of little more than barbiturate medications and shock treatments. He felt that the medications dulled the pain of depression and allowed him to sleep, but the electrical treatment (although once it helped him) usually had the effect of "bumping" him from mania into depression or from depression into mania. He frequently struggled with the hospital staff and eight times was severely beaten, once to the point of unconsciousness. From these experiences Custance came to believe that the failure of discharged patients "to fully overcome the resentment which they, rightly or wrongly, come to feel during their stay within the hospital walls, is responsible for the large percentage of the failures to achieve lasting cure."[50] Despite this mistreatment, Custance was luckier than most: Whenever the psychiatrists would tell his wife that he was "incurable" and might need to be "confined for life," she took this as her message to work hard at getting him transferred to another hospital where, in a more benevolent environment, he would usually recover quickly.

Going against medical advice, his wife and grown children often took the risk of bringing him home from the hospital. Generally, he recuperated much better at home, although he once tried to commit suicide in the barn. It was at a time when he had reached such an extremity of fear that it climaxed in a vision of fright and physical pain "infinitely increasing through astronomical time." He came to believe that his depression would begin to resolve itself only when his suffering had reached this degree of intensity.

Although in modern psychiatry it is usually taken as a basic fact that "manic-depressive" illness is biologically distinct from other forms of psychosis, Custance did not think so. In the hospitals he had lived intimately with people in every variety of psychosis and he felt them to be all of the same mind. There were sometimes great differences in style and intensity between those patients diagnosed as having "manic-depression" and those called "schizophrenic," but they were no greater than the differences in intensity among manic-depressives themselves. He saw a great variety of styles in expressing madness, but in all he saw a "common basis." People diagnosed with "schizophrenia," he felt, differed primarily in their more rapid fluctuations of states of consciousness and in their inability to "fix" or stabilize in one state for very long. For Custance, whatever form a psychosis might take, there was no difference in one's visions of heavens and hells or in the manic consciousness that they all shared.

From the point of view of recovery, people in psychosis also share a crucial liability and a practical problem that seems to necessarily accompany manic consciousness: a lack of awareness of *other* people's feelings and states of mind. It is as if anyone experiencing mania were incapable of interpersonal exchange or of empathizing with what other people are really feeling. Although at times someone in mania may feel an almost supernormal or telepathic sensitivity to other people's emotional states, it usually happens for only brief periods; largely one's attention is fixated on one's inner illuminated displays and insights. The ability to learn from or identify with anyone else is obstructed. People who recover from mania frequently explain that they were incapable of seeing themselves from the outside. Because of this disorder of interpersonal awareness, many misinterpretations and painful mistakes are made. No better evidence of this can be found than in the way in which those experiencing mania can alienate friends and other people— upon whose help they may be dependent—by insensitive and imperious actions.

On recovering from mania one begins to recognize and feel shocked by the enormity of one's misperceptions during the manic episode, not only of other people's advice but also of the instructions given by voices. Often one hears exactly the opposite of what was intended. John Perceval saw this reversal of meaning as being responsible for what he called the "poetics of lunacy."

At one time or another, people in manic states of consciousness have had glimpses of *all* energy (whether in the mind, the body, or cosmos) as governed by the same principles: opposition, contradiction, reversal. To Custance, it suggested a means to further incite manic consciousness. Instead of treating it as an interference, he incorporated it into his repertoire of mania-inducing practices. He called it the "wholehearted acceptance of the rejected opposite." John Perceval, while pondering the same insights from his own psychosis, concluded that there is a natural human perversity to react to the "hidden opposite" in all things; it is something otherwise hidden in all of us, but it becomes irresistibly present during mania. Perceval, Custance, and many others have managed to discover that the act of deliberately throwing oneself into the opposite of everything can seriously disorder the mind and even hasten the onset of mania.

But what has become of the power and the contact with power? Were all the experiences of unity and universal compassion of no account? Does anything remain?

One thing that remained for Custance was an awesome respect for the amount of mental and physical energy that could be unleased from within himself. He came to be afraid of this energy, as is common for anyone recovering from psychosis. He could never feel quite secure that an ordinary experience of well-being, or a real joy, or even a generous feeling, might not become "too much" and escalate into the sensory and intellectual upheaval of manic consciousness.

What remains of the so-called wisdom of madness? It is different for everyone. Custance believed that insanity reveals certain universal truths. For example, he believed that it exposes a secret paradox of the human psyche—that it "requires infinite expansion." Of course, such expansion is dangerous: Anyone can become stuck in the intriguing cascade of sensations and thoughts triggered by manic energy, or one may try to claim as one's own an energy too impersonal and too powerful to manipulate or possess. Ancient wisdom already exists about this: "You cannot own the power and the magic of this world. It is always available, but it does not belong to anyone."[51] This warning obviously applies to any spiritual practice that courts power and to why genuine traditions train and prepare one with arduous preliminary exercises to tame one's mind so that ego does not become riotous on contact with power. Arrogance is almost universally recognized as being the greatest obstacle and an almost continuous danger on any spiritual path. In the end, Custance was convinced that he had been through a spiritual agony the likes of which Jung called "the unavoidable encounter with the reality of the psyche."

Like John Perceval, Custance wrote his two books in the spirit of patient advocacy and of informing "fellow sufferers." And also like Perceval, he called for a "thorough reform of the Board of Controls" (coincidentally, a continuation of Shaftesbury's Metropolitan Lunacy Commission). Again, as in the past, a Royal Commission was convened in 1955 to investigate the care of the insane. Custance had followed the hearings closely. He then urged them to strengthen the Board of Controls, arguing, as Perceval did, that the board was "the only protection of mental patients, not merely against unjust deprivation of liberty but against physical and other forms of ill-treatment which, contrary to the general impression, have by no means entirely disappeared from mental hospitals in this country."[52]

The last that was heard of John Custance is bittersweet. He was living at home with his family, hard at work trying to restore the family farm, raising animals, and delighting in the birth of his first grandchild. In almost every account of his manic episodes, Custance also described moments of quiet simplicity, earthy appreciation, and everyday magic. Such islands of clarity were his most authentic and cherished moments of mania. They were appreciations of sense perceptions as glimpses of sacredness and wholeness in ordinary life. His last published words, which appeared in a chapter called "Down to Earth," speak of a more balanced state of mind and the pleasure he found in the intensity of ordinary reality:

> There has been a thunderstorm, but it is a lovely evening now, with the ley in front of the window shining in the sun with that peculiar yellowish green that so often makes the glory of a sunset. On the ley a cock and hen pheasant symbolize that unity of 'positive' and 'negative' in a completed whole which still so infuriatingly eludes me. But instead of complaining I should be thankful that I have caught a glimpse of it all.[53]

CHAPTER 3

The Epic of Megalomania

THE ASPIRATIONS OF MADMEN

Why is it such a commonplace among madmen, asked Nietzsche, to aspire to imperial heights, when even the most casual observation of the lives of kings and emperors reveals loneliness, misfortune, and despair? Yet imperial heights are the aspiration and central theme of megalomania—a state of mind so colossal and universally ominous that it has always been the subject of symbols, myths, and epic dramas.

As with the drama of Icarus, who dared fly too close to the sun, all these variations on the theme of megalomania carry a disquieting message: Any of us may find that we harbor within ourselves an insidious mechanism to self-destruct. Ajax, one of the great warriors of the siege of Troy, after being cheated out of the victory of inheriting the sacred armor of Achilles, in a fit of vengeful rage and megalomanic delusion slew a pitiful flock of sheep, convinced that they were the Trojan army. Less grand is the case of poor Pierre Riviere,[1] a village idiot who, unknown to anyone, witnessed the systematic moral torture of his father by his mother and resolved to free his father from bondage by murdering his mother, sister, and brother. In order to carry through with what he believed to be a magnificent action, he first identified himself with ancient conquerors, which developed into his thinking of himself as the ultimate power of the universe. This was accompanied by ecstatic sensations. And, like Ajax, upon awakening from his delusion he demanded and designed his own execution.

So it was in the case of Donald Crowhurst, who is the subject of this chapter. Like Ajax's and Riviere's, his life is a story of the cycle of oppression, self-deception, victory through cosmic empowerment, and death. But he is different in that he made precise observations about his mind, highlighting three clinical facts: (1) There is a prototypical psychotic predicament; (2) there is a particular propulsive sequence of events culminating in megalomanic conviction; and (3) the progressive series of psychological events is made possible and intensified by mental practices that unwittingly disorder the mind.

There is almost always a *psychotic predicament*. No one goes crazy without first having arrived at a predicament. That predicament appears to have two currents that collide. One is the personal collection of habits, tendencies, defenses, wishes, hopes, and fears, all directed toward either neurosis or sanity. We sometimes call this collection "character," personality, or personhood. Because that character has an effect in the world, situations begin to ripen, like unpaid bills coming due. The second current is the force of circumstances that confronts the character with its results, and that confrontation could lead to an explosive reaction. In the psychotic predicament, one takes the opportunity of the explosion to "switch" into another dimension of concern and another plane of activity. This new domain is vaster and endlessly more fascinating than ordinary circumstances. It is filled with a sense of insight and power, electric with the play of energy, perception, and messages, a compelling drive toward completion that offers promises of bliss and happiness of all kinds. One's attention is thoroughly absorbed away from the pettiness of the mundane world from which one has switched-out. It was at just such a point that Donald Crowhurst would say, "Finally I have done something interesting with my life."

"I AM BRAVE"

Donald Crowhurst (1932–1969) lived in our time. He was an innovative and dashing electronics engineer whose main goal in life, indeed his idea of perfection, was to live precisely attuned to the speed and competition of our culture.[2]

From childhood until the time we meet him, Donald Crowhurst defined his existence with the words, "I am brave; I can meet any challenge or dare; I can overcome any obstacle." He actually lived out such an existence. Those who knew him said that he was possibly "the bravest boy in the world . . . he was so brave it was awesome."

Throughout his life, he engaged in a variety of spectacular daredevil projects, which became legendary among his friends. His relationships were marked by an infectious enthusiasm that led those around him to suspend their doubts in the face of his ability to rise to any occasion. He continually dazzled his observers to the point where the environment would reinforce his sense of power. His mind was noted for its speed, intensity of absorption in tasks (particularly electronics), and capacity to subdue all doubts that he could work out any problems into which he threw himself.

So it was completely within character when Crowhurst, an inexperienced sailor, threw himself into an international race sponsored by the *Sunday Times* of London to single-handedly sail around the world. He was confident that he could do a creditable job and that it would arouse financial interest for his failing business. Although he had sailed very little before and had done no single-handed ocean sailing, and while this adventure might boggle the mind of anyone who has done such a thing, Crowhurst persuaded his investors to build an overly technologically sophisticated boat. On 30 October 1968, after innumerable mishaps, he crawled into the nine-by-eight-foot cabin in which he would spend much of the next eight months, and he set sail around the world.

Now his predicament, the masthead of ego ("I am brave"), began to meet with the force of circumstance that it had provoked. Unfortunately, during these months of sailing alone on the ocean he became insane. His body was never found.

In an empty, drifting boat he left moment-to-moment journals and logs of his mental content and of the inexpressible states of mind through which he had passed. They describe almost a caricature of the psychotic predicament and the stages leading to self-transformation. As well as logging his states of mind, often every few minutes, his notations also catch lightning flashes of his momentary awakenings from delusion. Naked between the sky and sea, hopelessly beyond his means, caught in a web of deception that had fooled the yachting world and the international press, and in fear of disgrace and dishonor, Crowhurst declared radio silence and "switched" from the natural world into a cosmic theater of his mind.

A PSYCHOSIS OF EXTREME CONDITIONS

In the next two and a half weeks Crowhurst sailed from England toward the South Atlantic while desperately trying to keep his boat intact. Everything was recorded in his logbook. As early as the third day, he had trouble with the self-steering apparatus. Then his radio receiver developed a problem. He could not synchronize his chronometer with his watch and he discovered a leaking float. After fourteen days his electricity generator was breaking down. At this time in his logbook, he was unhesitating and frank about his doubts and fears: "Racked by growing awareness that I must soon decide whether or not I can go on in the face of the actual situation. What a bloody awful decision—to chuck it in at this stage—what a bloody awful decision!" He took a precise inventory of his problems and they were staggering. Then he listed the alternatives open to him. He went back and forth between whether to continue the race or whether he might salvage something from the present situation and begin again next year. He recorded a fragment of a poem:

> And risk it on one turn of pitch and toss,
> And lose, and start again at your beginnings,
> And never breathe a word about your loss.

He came to the inescapable conclusion: "No, it's not feasible." Then he reworked his alternatives that might "involve no disgrace . . . and save face," such as stopping in Australia or

Cape Town. But he could not stop worrying about disappointing people if he withdrew from the race, and most of all he worried about the large sums of money he owed. In all of his vacillations, the idea of his personal survival seemed to hardly matter at all. Finally, he decided only to delay making any decision at all and continued to sail southward in a state of indecision.

He at last got his generator working (it was always said of him that he could fix anything) and sent off a radio cable, but without stating his actual position. In fact, he was paralyzed by indecision and had almost stopped sailing. He wrote in his logbook that the hatches were leaking badly, that he was unable to seal them, and that there was no method of pumping out the water that had leaked in (150 gallons overnight). But in his radio messages he completely withheld his hopeless situation. He simply could not bear to make a humiliating confession of failure. Instead, he said that because of generator problems there might be radio silence in the future.

At this point in his logbook, notations about the futility of his situation cease and he approaches the voyage with a rebounding enthusiasm. On 21 November he wired a message: "tuning trials over race begins." Then, from 6 December on, Crowhurst began a deliberately fraudulent navigational record in his logbook. It was clearly for public consumption, or for the racing officials who might someday scrupulously inspect his log. On the eleventh he wired his press agent that he had successfully broken the world record for miles sailed during a single day, and it made instant headline news. He waited—no one challenged his fraudulent claim (later considered by technical experts to be a tour de force of navigational forgery) and so Crowhurst sailed on.

Now he broke off his entries in the first logbook and switched to a second one. In this new log, Crowhurst told the complete truth about his strange voyage: He was talking only to himself. At first his telegrams to England told just small lies about his position, but then in a telegram on 17 December he committed himself to being nowhere near where he actually was. Yet even then, there were signs (such as heavily annotated navigational charts of the Rio de Janeiro harbor) indicating that he doubted what he was doing and that he contemplated plans to land and finally give up the race. Just before Christmas he "righted" himself and backed off from doubt.

From this point on, Crowhurst was no longer racing anywhere. To have gone farther and entered the roaring forties of the South Atlantic and the furious waters of Cape Horn, around the tip of South America, would certainly have destroyed both his boat and himself. For the next three months he again declared radio silence due to generator troubles. But the few messages he did send progressively indicated that he had navigated the Cape, crossed into the South Pacific Ocean, sailed south of Australia into the Indian Ocean, rounded the Cape of Good Hope, at the tip of Africa, had once again entered the South Atlantic—and was on his way home! Back in England he was becoming something of a public hero, but actually throughout all this, his boat merely wallowed off the coast of Brazil and Uruguay. He had sailed only two thousand of his thirty-thousand-mile fantastic voyage.

In these three months of silence Crowhurst worked furiously; not at sailing, but in fabricating his voyage. He was consumed with devising weather reports that would indicate in his records that he was somewhere other than where he was. Most of his day was spent absorbed in and riveted to the complicated details of plotting his illusory voyage, maintaining a genuine logbook as well as a falsified one, and accurately calculating the ever-diminishing possibility of his finishing the race. During this time, he recorded one hundred thousand words of navigational notations!

But since he was not doing any serious sailing he also had time to read one of the few books he had brought with him: Einstein's *Relativity*. He now felt he could understand it and played with his own ideas on the subject, which he called "creative mathematics." He also had time to do some creative writing in the second logbook, and he became fascinated with observing different species of birds and fish. He wrote a fable about a wretched land bird who was thoroughly disoriented and had attached himself to the boat, finally flying off in the wrong direction to his doom. He called this piece "The Misfit": "We were both victims of the one malaise . . . Out of their own resources they delay as best they can the inevitable exhausted subsidence into the icy waters of death."

His logbooks indicate that it was a difficult and frustrating time. Each further false record and radio announcement of his location demanded another confabulation. There appeared, however, hints that he was beginning to enjoy himself. Crowhurst gradually began to assume the identity of a heroic character, becoming someone other than who he was. Eventually, by this same process, he declared himself a "cosmic being."

It was a gradual switch, a reemerging out of groundlessness and failure with a more exaggerated sense of egohood, more vast than the world of competition. Crowhurst switched out of a circumstance that could only mean defeat or death—he accepted neither. Instead, he set a course for an illusory voyage, one in which he had to totally believe in order for it to be faultlessly carried out. But it is unclear whether he took that final step.

Although it never really worked, it is interesting that Crowhurst had engineered a "switching" mechanism to make his boat unsinkable by electronically righting itself at the critical point of overturning. It seems that the switching mechanism was a conceptual metaphor for continuing—backing off from the fury of the Cape and righting himself from failure, despair, or groundlessness. It was Crowhurst's approach to the world, so finely tuned that it could cut each moment of self-doubt.

His efforts at deception were tumultuous. There were times of frustration and moments of agony in maintaining the fraudulent voyage, but each of these moments turned into a new and more encompassing plan of action. His new plan was to return home a creditable second or third in competition, in which case his logbooks and other revealing data would not be examined with close scrutiny. But this plan was not to work because on 23 June, after almost eight months of sailing, the only remaining contender who stood between Crowhurst and eventual exposure and humiliation sank and had to abandon the race. Crowhurst immediately planned a one-word message—"desperation"—but never sent it. Instead, he decided on radio silence.[3]

At this point, a new psychotic predicament began. All systematic sailing ceased. Over the next five weeks, Crowhurst step by step switched into a new adventure, a project infinitely larger than any he had embarked on before, which culminated in his deep delusional conviction that he had transcended the powers of God, thus successfully accomplishing and prescribing the path for the next stage of human evolution. He was involved in a psychotic transformation:

> Now we must be very careful about getting the answer right.
> We are at the point where our powers of abstraction are powerful

enough to do tremendous damage.

Once we understand a normally stable system well enough to tamper with it in unnatural ways we must be very very careful about what we decide to do. We must think hard and long before doing anything, and when we decide to act we must be careful not to rush things. Like nuclear chain reactions in the matter system [Hiroshima], our whole system of creative abstraction can be brought to the point of 'take off' . . .

By writing these words I do signal for the process to begin . . .

On a page of its own was a quasi-mathematical formulation:

$$\int_{-\infty}^{+\infty} \text{Man} = [0] - [0]$$

It was a symbolic commentary on his life. Though it made no real sense mathematically, somehow or other this equation meant everything to Crowhurst. He called it the "Cosmic Integral." Literally, it means that all that man is from beginning to end adds up to nothing. It declares an absolute nihilism in which every possibility of human existence—the mind of delight as well as the mind of disgrace—is only an illusion of the mind. The Cosmic Integral indicates that all forms of existence are ultimately deceptions. And deception is the product of imagination. Anything can be imagined.

Crowhurst had only days to go before he might be spotted by the boats and helicopters that would soon be looking for him. Yet it is obvious from everything he had been writing and planning that death was a "given" to him, already his decided fate and no longer the issue. And it is probably safe to say that Donald Crowhurst was not a man who was afraid of dying. Now his urgent preoccupation and the most intense struggle of his life was how to eject his purified intellect, or what he called "my impulse," from the degraded confines of his body. For Crowhurst, this was to be his last switch-out. As he continued his intensive contemplations he felt that this ultimate switch-out could only be accomplished by an Einsteinian effort of free will. Perhaps it would be the first successful application of Einstein's great laws of energy and mass for the purpose of "psycho-nuclear" spiritual transformation.

At this point, Crowhurst was entering the God realms of
Perceval and Custance. But he was even more intent than they
on taking the definitive step to becoming a supreme being:

> If I stipulate of my own free will that by learning to manipulate
> the space–time continuum Man will become God and disappear
> from the physical universe as we know it I am providing the
> system with an impulse. If my solution is rooted in the mathemat-
> ical requirements of a solution it is 'correct' and immediately
> acceptable to a rapidly increasing body of men, then I am very
> close to God and should, by the methods I claim are available,
> move at last to prophecy. Let's have a go! . . .

> The system IS SHRIEKING OUT THIS MESSAGE AT THE
> TOP OF ITS VOICE why does no one listen I am listening
> anyway

At this point his writing was interrupted by a cable from his
public relations expert: Teignmouth awaited him with an expected crowd of one hundred thousand (!), and the BBC, news-
papermen, and his wife would be sailing out to meet him and
would be with him soon. For the people in Teignmouth the
clock was still running, but Crowhurst had allowed his nautical
chronometer to run down. Crowhurst's next entry in his log was
in response:

> God's clock is not the same as our clock. He has an infinite
> amount of 'our' time. Ours has very nearly run out. We on the
> other hand do not have very much time left.
>   The only rule of the game is this: the game must be played in
> the mind and nowhere else but in the mind.

> Let us play.

And then came a proclamation of insight and power, of what
he thought was enlightenment:

> In just three days the work was done! Christ is amongst us just
> as surely as if he was walking about signing cheques . . .

> You will have trouble with some of the things I have to say.
> Until recently—three days ago—I had a lot of trouble with them
> myself.

> I was determined to solve the problem if it took me the rest of

my life. Half-an-hour later, I had set up the basic equations, and seen the pattern. Three days later I understood everything in nature, myself, in all religion, in politics, in atheism, agnosticism, communism, and systems. I had a complete set of answers to the most difficult problems now facing mankind. I had arrived at the cosmos while contemplating the navel of an ape . . .

At this point, Crowhurst used his radio transmitter for the last time. He gave his correct position to the naval operator and said that his wife should not come with the boats to meet him; he insisted that she stay at home. Then he started a fresh page of writing.

Nature does not allow
God to Sin any Sins
Except One—

That is the Sin of Concealment

This is the terrible secret of the torment of the soul
'needed' by a natural system to keep trying

He has perpetrated this sin on the tormented . . .

Crowhurst continues to chart his megaspiritual development, his move to beyond-God:

I was beginning to understand more and more of the cosmic beings. All cosmic beings had to throw themselves on the mercy of one man!

By this process I have become a second-generation cosmic being. I am conceived in the womb of nature, in my own mind. Then I too have a problem. I must move the bulk of mankind in the right direction at once.

There is not the slightest hint of embarrassment or apology for what Crowhurst now has to say. He feels himself to be at home anywhere because:

Pure mathematics fit any place any time. The applied mathematics fit only me, the man of the world, with the knowledge of the cosmos, this time, this place, and a particularly beautiful instrument of God.

Eventually, Crowhurst begins to fuse his mythic and actual biographies:

> The shameful secret of God. The trick he used because the truth would hurt too much. If it had been known before, the necessary perfect shining instrument would not be what it is today.
>
> The quick are quick, and the dead are dead. That is the judgment of God. I could not have endured the terrible anguish and meaningless waiting, in fact.
>
> There must be much we can learn from each other. Now at last man has everything he needs to think like a cosmic being.
>
> At this moment it must be true that I am the only man on earth who realizes what this means. It means I can make myself a cosmic being, by my own efforts, but I have to hurry up and get on with it before I die! . . .
>
> There are 'limits' to the amount of integration apes can do. They have certain 'rules'. There is no limit to what intelligent, soulful apes can do
>
> > Man is forced to certain conclusions by virtue of his mistakes. No machine can work without error!
> > The only trouble with man is that he takes life too seriously!

Those were the last words he wrote in his logbook after an exhausting all-night session of writing on 30 June. Then, he took a break and went to sleep.

There could be many speculations about the "roots" of Crowhurst's transformation into megalomania, but they might only lead to one more psychological detective story. However, if Donald Crowhurst's conviction of having transformed into a "cosmic being" seems intensely pathological to us, it made a great deal of sense to someone who had been brought up with a sense of the miraculous, as Crowhurst had been. In fact, it is one of the most curious features of Crowhurst's life that he became highly sensitive to the possibilities of extraordinary self-transformative experiences. His life can be viewed as a series of transformations.

THE SPIRAL OF TRANSFORMATION

> He had been a girl
> It had been a trick, a deception.
> He bounced back, righted himself.
> He assumed his rightful place in the company of men.
> He went further, he became a super-boy.
> Secretly, he believed in his invulnerable and unique intelligence.
> In psychotic transformation he became a super-man.
> He assumed his rightful place in the company of the gods.
> It had been his secret, mythic life all along.
> But he was even more special than the gods—he was a mortal who accomplished it on his own.

Born somewhat late in his parents' lives, he was their only child. His father, known for his heavy drinking and occasional episodes of abuse, maintained an emotional distance from his son. On the other hand, Donald was very close to his mother and was clearly a treasure in her life. They communed with each other about their experience of God and she did her best to protect him. But all the evidence indicates that she was bringing him up as a girl! A photograph of him at the age of six shows him with long curly hair, which hung below his shoulders. He is demurely sitting in his parents' garden in a white sunsuit and gives the unmistakable appearance of being a little girl. His mother had longed for a daughter, and on her insistence his hair was not cut until shortly after his seventh birthday. A picture from that time shows his remarkable change into a little boy, holding his sailboat. Within a year came the first reports of the bravery that was to become the signature of his character.

If there is such a thing as a developmental history of transformation experiences, certainly Crowhurst's haircut is a landmark event. The Haircut was a paradigm, a metaphor for the possibility of self-transformations and how they might take place. But what is more relevant than these speculations—and more in keeping with Crowhurst's scientific inclinations—are the mental mechanics of the transformation. As Crowhurst said, the game of transformation "can only be played in the mind."

Seven psychological events, one built upon the other, form a universal structure of megalomania. They add up to the natural history of the megalomanic ordeal. Its foundation is ordinary enough: the blind propensity of one's egohood to make sudden surges into power and predicament. To that are added the stages that can be called: Speed; Desynchronization; Absorption; Insight and Power; Beyond the Law; Conflicting Commands; and Death and Rebirth.

The whole of these stages is best described as the seven turns of a spiral into megalomania (see the diagram on page 111). The image of a spiral reflects first the continuity between the stages and how in Crowhurst's life they can be seen to be happening over and over again. But the spiral also represents the dizzying quality of being within its tornadolike whirling. In the full spin of a spiral, you don't know if you are spiraling out or going to the interior, if you are ascending or descending, if you are gaining or losing. In psychosis, the spiral represents the central dilemma: whether one is in the process of spiritual evolution or deevolution, and each turn of the spiral gets you deeper into it. (I have often seen spirals drawn on the walls of back-ward seclusion rooms.)

But what is this "switch-point" for which everyone involved in the phenomena of psychosis has such fascination, since it seems to be the point of origin of the breach with reality? Our own curiosity about psychosis impels us toward this origin. Ultimately, the switch-point takes place in the mind. Everyone concerned with psychotic phenomena is stunned by the suddenness and abruptness with which one can cross the border into insanity. That border has a particular structure, a sequence of psychological events. By a precise reading of Crowhurst's logbooks, messages, and tape recordings that describe his passage through episodes of groundlessness, paranoid fear, and straddling the edge of meaninglessness and meaning, we find this sequence of switch-out completely detailed and documented.

Crowhurst's (or anyone's) switch-out occurs during the first two stages of complete psychotic transformation—*speed of mind* and *desynchronization of mind and body.* These can be discriminated during the twenty-four hours leading to Midsummer Day, 24 June 1969.

The speed of Crowhurst's activity had been apparent since he hastily entered the race. Now, adrift and wandering, there appeared an increasing pressure of thought and a gathering of attempts at manipulating his mind in order to blow away doubt (as did Perceval and Custance before him) with the winds of enthusiasm. However, because of the power failure in his self-

SPIRAL OF MEGALOMANIA

steering apparatus, he had to remain awake much more; and sleeplessness intensified his wildness of mind, as is always the case with mania. (He was also using Dexedrine to an unknown, though minor, extent.) As this speed gathered, he began to feel its effects upon his body first as euphoria, physical well-being, and an increasing sense of accuracy that led him to proclaim, "My reflexes amaze me . . . I can catch things with my hands even before they begin to fall." Crowhurst began to feel "free" from the constant worry about the "rat race" of ordinary existence and noted that his body was becoming cleansed of the accumulated "poisons" of ordinary activity.

At this point, he abandoned all attempts to sail and allowed his boat—what had been the body of his life—to drift in the Sargasso Sea. He began to switch from being aquanaut to being cosmic explorer. Over the next week he wrote over twenty-five thousand words of "philosophy," which detailed his belief in the intellectual power of mind over body and matter. "Every word was of supreme importance; he had a message which must be revealed to the world, and he sensed he had only seven days to write it. Even as he began he was scarcely sane, with each page he wrote he lost more control, and by the time he finished he was totally out of touch with reality."[4] With increasing speed he turned his attention to pure consciousness and the possibilities of ejecting a purified mind out of a degraded body and environment.

Crowhurst's switch was fueled by *absorption states*. The tendency toward this stage of psychotic transformation was always apparent in his character and it now became intensified. He always had an ability to "lose himself" in concentrated effort, and this increased during his demanding electronic repairs, deceptive communication, and now his increasing dwelling in conceptualizations. He became absorbed to the extent that he lost track of time; tracking time had been the one and only discipline that he had attempted to maintain.

Anyone who is involved with the production of such concentrated states of mind has been said to be approaching the realm of the "formless gods": "He realizes that he can achieve purely mental pleasure, the most subtle and durable of all, that he is able to maintain his sense of solid self continuously by expanding the walls of his prison to seemingly include the whole cosmos, thereby conquering change and death. First, he dwells upon the idea of limitless space. He watches limitless space; he is here and limitless space is there, and he watches it. He imposes his preconceptions on the world, creates limitless space, and feeds himself with his experience. Then the next stage begins of concentration upon the idea of limitless consciousness. Here one does not dwell on limitless space alone, but one also dwells upon the intelligence which perceives that limitless space as well. So ego watches limitless space and consciousness from its central headquarters. The empire of ego is completely extended, even the central authority cannot imagine how far its territory extends. Ego becomes a huge, gigantic beast."[5]

During the next stage, Crowhurst expanded his practice of speeding through the cracks of doubt in his increasingly solid world. He attempted to tune his mind into the mind of Einstein, specifically Einstein's audacious leap beyond space and time in the theory of relativity. Crowhurst felt he had absorbed himself into the mind of Einstein. He moved headlong into the fourth stage of the spiral when he began to recognize his own *insight and power* through wild identification with Einstein's thoughts. Then, in a hectic intellectual effort, he transcended the limits of Einstein's mind and felt himself take the next powerful step in the evolution of human nature. Later, he repeated exactly the same feat in a wild contemplation of the nature of God.

In this "mindless" practice of identification, Crowhurst grafted onto his root stock delusion ("I am brave") an escalating series of displacements ("I ams"): "I am brave"/"I am capable of anything"/"I am energy and impulse"/"I am God"/"I am beyond God." He said, "Now at least man has everything he needs to think like a cosmic being. At the moment it must be true that I am the only man on earth who realizes what this means. It means I can make myself a cosmic being, by my own efforts, but I have to hurry up and get on with it before I die!"

Crowhurst began to play with his newly won understanding and his sense of power over mind, imagination, and nature. He called it "the power of the Gods" and named it "creative abstraction." It means he could create universes: "Like nuclear chain reactions in the matter system, our whole system of creative abstraction can be brought to the point of 'take off' . . . *By writing these words I do signal for the process to begin.*"

Now, intoxicated with the power of his mind, Crowhurst achieves a particular form of psychotic freedom and inexorably enters into the stage of being *beyond the law.* As he has transcended the boundaries and regulations that ordinarily limit mind, he also feels he has transcended all other conventions, boundaries, and laws as well. They are the laws of lesser beings that bind us all in a "rat race" of competition; they include conventional morality, all systems of human ritual, the rules of language, all secular and cosmic authority. He feels that all laws are shoddy constructions and that he can instantly create and dissolve them. At will, he can enter and exit any universe or "game." He notes that "complete freedom of choice beyond the reach of any discipline is the meaning of free will" and declares himself "beyond God."

For many people, this stage of psychotic transformation is one of violence and liberties of all kinds. Violence is justified because there is no higher authority than oneself. Because one feels in full command, violence is possible in the service of a truth discovered by an empowered "I am." It is in such a way that Crowhurst excuses himself from the attempt to create a fraudulent voyage, his "sin of deception."

The next stage ushers Crowhurst into a final episode of transformation, which leads to death. He experiences "perplexity . . . a dark uneasy feeling . . . in the pit of my stomach." This represents the beginning of the "natural history" of psychotic states of mind, which is to plummet into paranoia, on the verge of "complete freedom." What Crowhurst alludes to, for us, is the microstructure of paranoia, the stage of *conflicting commands*. He says, "I was annoyed with the cosmic beings. Something was going wrong." A cryptic note refers to the "anguish of a cosmic being." Then imagery appears: "tentacles reaching out at me from the depths of the sea." Aggression begins to color his perception, including the perception of thought itself.

He is experiencing the whiplash effect of aggression. It is as in a dream, where the interrupting or awakening outside stimulus is engulfed by and woven into the dream drama in the imagery of persecutors.[6]

The persecution that psychotic people begin to feel at this stage is a personification of their own doubt, a doubt that has been ignored and aggressively cut short with the increasing speed of mind. For Crowhurst, there came the inescapable revenge of his mind. The doubt that he tried to obliterate was an indestructible aspect of his mind, a sign of his basic intelligence. It sometimes makes itself known in the only transfigured forms allowable: hallucinations of images, voices, and feeling states. They demand attention. Again, it is as in a nightmare, where the persecutors become more insistent the more one tries to ignore them. That is to say, doubt eventually returns even if it has to clothe itself in the animated images of fear.

Nevertheless, we find Crowhurst continually rising above his moments of fear, each time with a new proclamation of glory and achievement. This is the switch-out, the switching mechanism, backing off from despair. It is a period of tremendous compression, his thoughts running wild in what he sees as an awesome birth process. He says, "By this process I have become a second-generation cosmic being. I am conceived in the womb of nature in my own mind. Then I too have a problem. I must move the bulk of mankind in the right direction at once." A moment of peace is followed by a moment of rude awakening.

He awakes from sleep thinking it is morning but sees the moon low over the horizon. At that point he literally confuses the sun and the moon. He believes he sees the moon setting in the sky, when actually it is the sun rising. He quickly calculates the time from his charts and comes up with an absurd number. Then, he comes back to his senses. In an instant all his previous calculations about himself and the universe dissolve into doubt. It is a situation in the middle of the third predicament, unspeakable "groundlessness."

Everything begins to move more quickly than before. Welcome-home boats are about to rendezvous with him. "How could he, Crowhurst, the supremely precise calculator, the beautiful shining instrument that now knew the innermost secrets of time, have made such a culpable error? And at a time when he was caught up in the ticking movements of his clocks, counting down the seconds towards the moment when he must become a cosmic being?"[7] Then, the words appear in his logbook, in disgust, with a thick pencil:

"MAX POSS ERROR."

But once again Crowhurst got on with it; he reset his chronometer and began the final countdown of his "ape" existence. For days, he had been a god within a mortal body, and now all that remained to complete the "solution" was for him to eject his cosmic intelligence out of his body. Now he writes as he would in a racing log but in the urgent, telegraphic, and highly condensed poetic style of someone about to die. He begins again:

TRUE POSITION   July 1   10:00 H

Then:

EXACT POS   July 1   10:03

He then ruled three columns on the left side of the page, as he did for all navigational work, and five minutes later made his first cryptic countdown entry. Now begins the last ninety minutes of Crowhurst's life and his last daredevil attempt—in his characteristic style—to force the issue, to force circumstance.

And how are we to understand what happened now? Did Crowhurst "wake up" from the shock of a "MAX POSS ERROR"? Did he then go on to log his last moment-to-moment thoughts about what remained of his life? Or was Crowhurst as "insane" as he was just the day before, when he was challenging cosmic beings? Was he trying to switch a complete failure into a success? Is what he writes now merely an epilogue to insanity? Is there still some kind of deception going on? How can one trust him now? Is there any value whatever in the Crowhurst story?

In his final log entries he asks himself the same questions, and he attempts to answer them. One question that remains is: Did he learn anything from the strange voyages he had been through?

It is up to us individually to decide just how genuine Crowhurst is at this time. At the least, it can be said that what follows is definitely Crowhurst once again in his cabin workshop, working at, and attempting to work through, his problem. The way he works at this may seem incoherent because it moves in a zigzag progression; nevertheless, it is clearly in one piece and comes to a conclusion. He has in front of him his book, clock, and barometer.

Thus begins yet another spiritual journey for Crowhurst and a final attempt at "switch-out." He has given himself a deadline and has thrown himself into a final predicament in the same way that he talks about the leap of a porpoise embodying a crucial instant of commitment to action and then a point of no return. It is at such points that Crowhurst has recognized his bravery and has confidently put himself to the test.

He quickly reasserts a successive series of identification, "I am brave . . . I am the truth . . . I am the exact." He continues writing with full conviction as if to say, "I am enlightened and what you are reading is exactly how I did it." He now is working constantly, to cut his doubt about his final "I am." He is determined to ride the "impulse" of his own "will." He is at the point of saying, "I am impulse, pure energy, one who by pure effort could become whatever one thinks." And he gives himself until 12:00 noon to do it. By such one-pointed concentration he drove himself to the verge of an absorption state of mind.

COUNTDOWN

With his first new entry Crowhurst declares his intention to put everything right:

10 08 40	Reason for system to minimize error To go—remove experience Barometer pressure on the move
10 10 10	System of Books [his own logs] reorganize perfectly Many parallels.
10 11 20	Realization of role of decision making Hesitation − time Action + time
10 13 30	Freq. Books Soul of men into their work reason for 'work' unimportant?
10 14 20	Hermits force unnecessary conditions on themselves Seek truth wasting time.
10 14 30	My folly gone 'forward' in imagination Wrong decision not perfect Time no longer computed Had disorganized Clocks
10 15 40	Think no need worry about time ± but only elapsed time ± May be meaningless? Important reason for work is
10 17 20	(lost) understand right Sorry waste of time

10 19 10   Ape indicates perplexity by
            headscratching!
            not right? Evil is choice of
            interpretation right of symbols
            Not quite right?

            New reas[on] occurs for game. My
            judgment indicates cannot not use
            anything 'put' in place, but have to put
            everything in place. Task very difficult.

            NOT impossible. Must just Do the
            B[est]
            Strive for perfection in the hope of

10 22   Understand Two 'reasons' for task of
            conflict.
            Rule of game unsure. If game to put
            everything back?
      30   Where is back?

10 23 40   Cannot see any 'purpose' in game.

10 25 10   Must resign position in sense that if set
            myself
            'impossible' task then nothing achieved
            by game
            Only reason for game to find new rules
            governing   old truths.
            Understand Exact position of concept
            of balance of Power. It is only one way
            of expressing hope. The age process is
            new way of despair concept

10 28 10   Only requirement for have new set of
            rules is that
            there IS some

10 29   Understand reason for need to devise
            games. No game
            man can devise is

            Resign game if you will agree only one
            [crossed out]

            harmless. The truth is that there can

only be one chess master, that is the
man who can free himself [from] the
need [to] be blown by a cosmic mind.
there can only be one perfect beauty
that is the great beauty of truth. No
man may do more than all that he is
capable of doing. The perfect way is
the way of reconciliation. Once there is
a possibility of reconciliation there may
not [be] a need for making errors. Now
is revealed the true nature and purpose
and power of the game my offence

I am what I am and I see the nature of
my offence

I will only resign this game if you will
agree that on the next occasion that
this game is played it will be played
according to the rules that are devised
by my great god who has revealed at
last to his son not only the exact
nature of the reason for games but has
also revealed the truth of the way of
ending of the next game that

It is finished—
It is finished

IT IS THE MERCY

11 15 00   It is the end of my
my game the truth
has been revealed and it will
be done as my family require me
to do it
11 17 00   It is the time for your move to begin
I have not need to prolong the game

It has been a good game that must be
ended at the
I will play this game when I choose I
will resign the game 11 20 40 There is
no reason for harmful.

* * * * *

Crowhurst had "come to," woken up out of a fit, as out of a fit of rage, a fit of passion, or a fit of any kind—epileptic, catatonic, concussive—or any loss of conscious awareness. We could say that within a moment Crowhurst spontaneously recovered from his psychotic period. It is not unheard of. In fact, it happens in the midst of psychosis all the time—a small island of doubt and clarity that is quickly covered over by the surging hope of transformation, the effort to be someone else.

With human time running out, Crowhurst sat down face to face with his chronometer, to record the moment-to-moment movements of his mind, this being all that he had left to work with. It was the final stage, of *death and rebirth.* He writes, "Reason for system to minimize error/To go—remove experience/ Barometer pressure on the move." He will proceed to have "realization" after realization, all recorded in the terse, condensed poetry of those who are about to die. This was not some headlong, sloppy suicide. It was Crowhurst's final attempt to bring his mind to a peak point of pressure, thereby crystallizing his intelligence in an unyielding countdown to death. He wrote about beginning to understand how to press on with this awesome task.

Within the first fifteen minutes of his countdown, one of the notes indicates that he has identified his major obstacle: "My folly gone 'forward' in imagination." He sees that each moment of "hesitation" leads to an imaginative sidetrack, and within two minutes after beginning to speculate and ramble he writes, ". . . right Sorry waste of time." He continues, "If game to put everything back?/Where is back?" He is struggling with the meaning of life, time, and death.

He continues in his characteristic style, despair rebounding into insight. He has begun to feel that he had set himself an "impossible task," and he rebounds on to a new tack to "free himself [from] the need [to] be blown by a cosmic mind." Then, after struggling to find the "perfect way" he declares, "I am what I am and I see the nature of my offence." He begins to ramble about the singularity of his revelation but abruptly cuts it short with the words, "It is finished—It is finished/IT IS THE MERCY." Even seeking the truth had become another kind of game and all that was left was to unhesitatingly live out the force of circumstances. In his final words he attempts to reassert another peak of freedom: "I will play this game when I choose I will resign the game 11 20 40. There is no reason for harmful."

Throughout the countdown, Crowhurst was on the edge of losing his mind. The tendency of his mind to wander was profound. He escalated the pressure of mind and circumstance at the same time and attempted once again to drive himself into a stage of insight and power. He thought he could do it sanely this time. But he recognized that he could not rouse himself by his own willpower to reach the stage of beyond the law. The only law that he felt he discovered was that of the indestructible linkage of cause and effect.

He wanted us to be able to say that his work, his task, and his feat were brilliant, and he carefully left his record as an invitation for us to get inside his mind. But nothing really happened. He exited his life in the same way he had lived it. Before he had set sail, eight months earlier, he had left a tender and ominous letter to his wife (she discovered it after he had been at sea for four months), in which he said, ". . . whatever happens you can be certain I did not spend my last moments paralyzed with fear." Eight days after Crowhurst began his countdown, his boat was found empty and adrift.

Rescuers looked for a possible swimmer but found no one. The mystery of Crowhurst's disappearance made front-page news for a week or two, and for a long time afterward there were occasional crank sightings of Crowhurst having been spotted in Cape Town or on an island.

(And who won the race, anyway? It was the young Robin Knox-Johnston who was the first to return and, now with Crowhurst gone, who also won the prize money of five thousand pounds for the quickest time. He donated this money to a Crowhurst Relief Fund, which had been established to help the family. As part of a psychological study of stress, Knox-Johnston was evaluated by a psychiatrist both before and after the race and later wrote, "I am delighted to say that on both occasions he found me 'distressingly normal.' ")

Gradually, Crowhurst's family learned to live without him. That was his hope, and also his prediction. In the letter to his wife written before the voyage, he expresses a most tender "overwhelming love" for her, and he gives her practical advice in caring for herself and the children in the event of his death at sea:

Nothing is certain—least of all life, from day to day, minute to minute, or even second to second. This was the manner of my death. What does that matter? A car crash, a falling slate, thrombosis . . . ten thousand alternatives lie ready waiting to sever the tenuous links of circumstance that keep us alive. I do not expect to die. There is no awful pall of fear hanging over my soul and there will probably never be, because I am not afraid of the thing or its consequences to me—only deeply concerned with those to you and the children that I love only second to you.

THE URGE TO TRANSFORM

All psychotic transformation is a desire leading one to death. Not every attempt at psychotic transformation will have the linear compactness and apparent suddenness of Donald Crowhurst's, but if one goes through two or three or more psychotic episodes such as this one, each awakening from the dream and nightmare of psychosis is more devastating than the last. One wakes up, looks around, and, unlike in the dream when asleep, one has to take responsibility for the actions and reactions committed during the delusion. One feels at that point like King Lear, who recognizes that he has made a monstrosity out of his life and that his authority and even his love were destructive to other people. At such a point, people frequently say, "I am getting out of this before I do more harm."

It is not just that the consequences of psychosis lead to death, but also that death itself is inherent in the urge for transformation. Because death is the undercurrent of the pleasure and the freedom being courted in the psychotic transformation, it requires the death and eventual freedom from the body, from relationship to the world, and from the workings of one's mind.

The body in psychosis is in transition. It begins to manifest a variety of possibilities. Sometimes, it is felt to be a spiritual body, a purified body, an invisible body, a body of the other sex, an inanimate body, a machine—a new body, endowed with new characteristics and possibilities far beyond the confines of the body left behind. This is a hard-won transformation following an intensely painful struggle within the body itself. It is sometimes experienced as a war, a revolution, an agonizing gestation, or a titanic struggle between the forces of good and evil, a power struggle between one's degraded humanness and the sacred forces of nature. At first, one's body feels tortured in being selected as the arena of such a battle. Then one is either blessed with orgastic sensations that herald a transformation or the body is destroyed and one begins to identify with the living dead. The blessed body is short-lived and it is grieved for. Nevertheless, it remains the reference point and hope for all further life.

Psychotic communication or relationship to the world is also a vehicle of the urge for transformation. One's language, perceptual contact with the world, and projection of meaning represent the same fundamental aggression; that is, to be someone else or to be somewhere else. The quality of psychotic language or interchange with the environment is a continually changing reflection of the different stages of the psychotic predicament. There appears a pressure of speech that indicates something intensely important is happening, and it is filled with multiple meanings and a hunt for messages and coincidences that confirm and further the transformation. Sometimes it is like the highly condensed speech of dreams, where words become elements of a stage set intended to create the atmosphere of a total drama. Eventually, words become the thread of delusion, woven together with symbols, messages, and memories that begin to clothe the world in a single coherent story about oneself at the center of the universe. Crowhurst began to speak like a "cosmic being." Others speak in "tongues," or highly cryptic messages as mediums for powers beyond themselves. It is a purified speech, more urgent and important than their own. Sometimes that speech is proclamatory and one assumes the role of an insistent prophet.

But a struggle occurs within speech in the same way as it does with the body. The speech that at first was so fearless and confident becomes riddled with conflict and fear. As doubt returns, there occurs a struggle between inner speech and outer speech. It often appears in the conflicting demands that make their appearance in auditory hallucinations. Then, all communications may become paralyzed. Complete muteness may become the effort at reconciliation between the gift of higher speech and the tendency of the impure, degraded speech that represents oneself.

The language and communication of autistic, psychotic children is yet another variety of speech in the service of transformation. At first, language is seen to be ineffective, confusing, and filled with a hypocrisy that makes it unutterable. Eventually speech itself becomes an object of mockery. One's internal dialogue is besieged with oscillating contradictions. The speech of others becomes permeated with disguise and threat, and speech in general becomes a weapon that might be dangerous to oneself or harmful to others. Outwardly, such a child abandons speech altogether and assumes the stubborn position of animal speech—more basic, fundamental, and pure than human speech—using gesture, display, and the utterance of echo. Inwardly and secretly, speech is being created anew from the bits and pieces of conventional language and symbols to create a private world in which a tenaciously transformed self continually triumphs over the fear of annihilation.

Psychotic speech, whether it be internal or external, private or public, is always directed to others. One feels specially "chosen" and thus obligated to speak, sometimes to preach, or sometimes not to speak at all. There is a great variety of these "others" even within a single psychotic experience. They might manifest as "spirits," as animated personifications of the energies of the natural world, or as messengers or agents of higher powers.

The most general sense of "other," however, is in the form of an eternal lover. One person might call it "queen of the galaxy" who strikes like lightning to produce pleasure or pain. Another person calls it the "dead father" who oversees, guides, and controls, and whose return is awaited in the form of a lover or savior. At times it is God or Satan, or any number of people who are thinly disguised appearances of those who were supplicated for help.

But whoever they are and in whatever form they assume, the relationship with "other" has a quality of bondage. At some point, the other demands self-surrender, devotion, and unhesitating obedience to the letter of its will. It may become a master-slave relationship, where the master requires loyalty of action under the threat of withdrawal of protection and love. The slave then strives for the perfection of self-surrender, by the painful renunciation of all self-willed activity. But the slave cannot help himself. He always finds himself in some process of revolt or indiscretion. In some situations of intensive psychotherapy, the therapist comes to be seen as the miraculously created "other" and the drama of the original predicament begins to be recapitulated.

In the same way, Donald Crowhurst was involved with a variety of others even though his situation cut him off from any genuine relationship. In his logs and journals he slid from one object to another: from the bravado of public address, to a select gathering of his supporters, his wife, himself in the process of transition, his dead father and mother, to "everyone," and then to the principle of truth itself, incarnate as a god, who was "master of the game" of life.

Even though all his objects are embraced in the service of further transformation, his megalomanic switch-out has within it the seed of compassionate impulses. This is always a subtle but intensely meaningful quality of all megalomanic episodes and of psychological conversions in general. In the early phases of a psychotic predicament, one has lost the sense of personal honor and one's heartfelt connection with the world is severed. But these are regained within the switch-out, and one's formerly frozen compassion is liberated in triumphant messianic out-pourings. This joy is an important aspect of transformation. One is transformed and can thus complete a necessary act, per-haps even heal the world.

Psychotic mind in its rapid transitional states remains the basic instigator and impetus of transformation. Mind wanders with increasing speed as the gaps of doubt are overridden. Then, there is intense fascination and absorption in the sliding speed of thought. There occurs a progressive disjunction of mind and body, an unhinging of mind and environment. One feels that one is breaking through the barrier of the thought processes that had been so rigidly confining. With increasing intoxication in the newfound powers of mind, insights appear like fireworks and revelations. It is at such a point that one claims to have attained "freedom." Psychotic mind declares, "What-ever I think, I can become." Psychotic self-transformation is made complete in the free play and manipulation of delusions and is fully confirmed by the sensation of mental pleasure. Inevi-tably, there occurs a "maximum possible error." It is then that the urge for transformation can be seen for what it is—a funda-mental aggression against oneself, the ground of psychosis.

RECOVERY

The story of Donald Crowhurst is a gruesome one, but when we intimately study the bare facts of psychotic experience and the

stages of transformation it becomes possible to think in terms
of stages of recovery. The stages of recovery can only be understood from the experiences of those who have actually recovered. But one thing is clear. Recovery can only take place within
the context of a sane environment, an environment of compassion and appreciation, which can permit the unwinding of the
stages of transformation. Otherwise, recovery is extremely rare.

Obviously, no one should be left alone in a psychotic predicament. When we understand the nature of the predicament,
whether it be in children or adults, there is a simplicity and
straightforwardness to it that allows us to extricate another from
the necessity of switch-out. We begin to recognize that someone
is "in trouble" when his sense of existence or character is beginning to be challenged and overwhelmed by the forces of circumstance that the character has created.

Beyond that, we can organize the unstable nature of the experience of groundlessness. When we relate intimately and precisely to such people, we find the experience of groundlessness
constantly recycling. Furthermore, there can be an exit from it
in either of two directions: ordinary disillusionment or psychotic
switch-out. Within an impending psychosis or its continuous
recycling, there are innumerable experiences of spontaneous
awakening, or maximum possible error. When that is acknowledged within an ongoing relationship, communication can be
open and direct. Even though those small islands of awareness
may be quickly covered up, they gradually begin to accumulate
and string together in a way that allows for a genuinely sane
relationship to occur, side by side with, or beyond, the experience of delusion. Eventually, one may be more attracted to the
richness of an awake relationship and begin to shift allegiance
away from the world of delusion.

When we begin to see the propulsive aspect of the predicament and the urge to transform, the typical psychotic practices
of wild identification and cutting of doubt become more apparent. In many ways, these practices can be slowed down within
the spaciousness of a relationship that will allow the ordinary
function of doubt to make its appearance without being ignored
or seized upon. When the manifestations of doubt are simply
accommodated, they can be seen clearly as moments of awakening and do not have to eventually return in the images of fear,
struggle, and conflict. Because of this, the stages of transforma-

tion become less forcibly linked to each other and become only transient experiences.

However, if one is already enmeshed in the transformative delusion, there remain two aspects that maintain a fragile connection with real human relatedness: appreciation of the insights into the nature of mind that arise during the psychosis, and appreciation of the compassionate impulses that become distorted into megalomania. Within the delusion itself, phenomena are seen to dissolve into new phenomena. There are shock waves of clarity where one recognizes that the phantasmagoric play of projections has created a private universe that is utterly unreal. All of one's convictions, beliefs, and perceptions are experienced as unendingly hollow. This recognition might be devastating, but it need not be. With the help of another, it can be seen as a dream that one can refuse to enter or from which one can come and go. What is left are the hidden and tender impulses toward others that have always been embedded within the megalomanic delusion. They can be appreciated and acknowledged when they subtly make their appearance within the therapeutic relationship, and because of that there is a further invitation to shift one's allegiance to health.

In his brief recovery from madness, King Lear discovered that he had to live his life with courage and patience. It is a tragedy that that dawning recognition did not occur to him sooner. In much the same way, Donald Crowhurst became one of the multitude of the minor tragedies of madness, of those who would be kings and queens.

CHAPTER 4

Major Ordeals of Psychotic Mind

Rare indeed are the madmen equal to madness.
—HENRI MICHAUX

RADICAL EXCHANGE

It is definitely possible to be of great use to someone in psychosis without knowing the almost unbearable details of the apparatus of their minds. Even children and elderly people—scarcely suspecting the complexity of the psychotic experience—through kind and intimate relationships, have been known to give comfort to people lost in psychosis. As much as such comfort and respite is a blessing to someone in the pain of psychosis, it is not sufficient to counteract the powerful tendency of psychosis to reproduce and recycle itself. Until the person in psychosis can recognize for himself the roots of the wild and exaggerated mental events that intrigue and come to dominate him, he will be subject to continuing cycles of seduction, confusion, and despair. Discovering the means for such recognition is what this chapter is about.

Ultimately, recovery depends on how much a person in psychosis is both willing and capable of relating precisely to the details of his mind, on his own, alone with his experience. Only this kind of precise observation can reveal the cause and effect of the mental events from which that persons suffers. To demonstrate this we must turn the microscope into higher power and examine the movements and energies of psychotic mind—micromovements and microenergies. This will lead to a little-known depth of psychotic suffering and another magnification, or a "blowup," of intelligence running wild.

Historically, among those who have cared for people in psychosis many have attempted to penetrate the mind of insanity in order to gain knowledge of it beyond a fleeting empathy, a momentary identification, or simple exchange of feelings. They have attempted a "radical exchange" with mad people; they have tried to ingest madness within themselves and to suffer some of its consequences for the purpose of intimately knowing its hidden ordeals. Some people have attempted it out of compassion, in order to be of greater help. Some have done it out of a passionate curiosity to simply explore and know mind in its depths.

There have been a number of mishaps. A professor of chemistry in Leipzig in the early 1900s, Dr. Emil Staudmaier, insisted on knowing the mind of madness from the inside out. He trained himself in "practices" of deranging his mind, ones similar to those used by all the characters of the previous chapters; that is, he did everything he could to intensify his imagination to the point of hallucination. In the end Staudmaier became hopelessly insane, caught in an uncontrollable and seamless web of imagination. Eventually he recovered from his overly ambitious experiment and described to us how not to engage psychotic mind.[1]

Other explorers of madness have been naive about the hazards of using hallucinogenic drugs in their researches. As early as 1936, it is reported that a Dr. Morelli performed a remarkable experiment on himself but, "after taking 0.75 gr. of mescaline he experienced such a furious onslaught of perverse impulses that he had to take refuge in a sanitarium."[2] In France there had already been a long tradition of poets, artists, and scientists who had experimented with mind-altering drugs. Baudelaire and Rimbaud are well-known examples, but perhaps the most notorious of all is the dramatist Antonin Artaud, a legendary figure in the Surrealist movement. In 1936 Artaud lived with the Tarahumara Indians in Mexico and participated in their elaborate religious rites of taking peyote.[3] It was he who used the term *metempsychosis,* to refer to the knife-edge of psychosis that one may experience with a hallucinogen. But, on his return to Paris, he became increasingly disturbed and spent the next several years in psychiatric hospitals, eventually dying in one of them.

The controlled experiments with mescaline conducted by Henri Michaux are perhaps the most successful in the field of hallucinogenic-drug research. This French poet and artist died in 1984 at the age of eighty-five. The record that he left of his nearly ten years (1957–c. 1966) of experimentation with mescaline is prodigious. During his studies he precisely described—through essays, poetry, drawings, and paintings—the miseries, joys, and meaning of the hallucinogenic experience and, most importantly of all, its relationship to madness. In over half a century of sustained work Michaux produced seventy-eight publications and many hundreds of drawings and paintings. Thirty-six of his books were written after he began his work with mescaline (and other drugs), and nine of them specifically explore the nature of psychosis as it is revealed by the hallucinogens.

In spite of his stature in French letters, very little is known of Michaux's personal life. To the outside world he was always something of an enigma, and his friends loyally protected his desire for anonymity. Other than his artistic and scientific work, he is mostly known for being reclusive, a "loner." Photographs of him are rare. But here is one description:

> The eyes are Belgian—a pale steely almost arctic blue. The shoulders wide, surprisingly. Under them the walk, the open-at-the-collar bell-bottomed manner of a man who has spent most of his early life at sea; with something added—in a bald mass of pate and probing needlelike nose—that suggests less the sailor than a wise and penetrating seagull.[4]

Andre Gide celebrated him as early as 1941 in a book called *Discovering Henri Michaux,* but then there followed twenty years of his being largely unappreciated and sometimes scorned by literary critics. Mostly, the critics called Michaux eccentric. His writing from the very beginning intimidated people and when he began his studies of hallucinogens, that intimidation grew worse. Some readers found him extremely sparse and private.

But he also gathered a small readership of mostly French artists and writers ("the 200," he called them). Along with his studies on the nature of hallucinogens, he wrote about the recovery from illness; aging; dreaming; children's drawings; creativity; and the contemplative experience. All of these are unique and profound contributions to psychological knowledge, yet, unfortunately, they have gone largely unknown.

Here, Michaux's inner journey of the "hallucinogenic experience" is used as a method of magnification and of radical exchange. It has been claimed that this experience can, among other things, give one a taste of madness itself, as well as a glimpse into its underworld. It is also well known that this kind of intimacy with the wellsprings of psychotic mind can be both frightening and dangerous. Nevertheless, a certain willingness to take risks, along with a knowledge and training in relating to *the basic awareness always available even during mental crisis,* makes it possible to prudently engage in a radical exchange. It is certainly not being recommended that individuals who work with people in psychosis should take "madness-inducing drugs." However, what has been learned from those who have performed such experimentation is of vital importance because a precise understanding of the hallucinogenic experience can be a key to unlocking the nature of psychotic mind.

Michaux's work with hallucinogenic chemicals is not really comparable to those that have been written about before or since. He brought an uncommon knowledge and discipline to what he experienced. Prior to his experiments and even during them, he trained himself in the disciplines of Yoga and Buddhist sitting meditation practice. He became stalwart and courageous in facing himself without distraction. Thus, Michaux approached the drug-induced state from what could be called a "contemplative" point of view; he was accustomed to being alone, practiced in observing states of mind, and had precise control and poetic expression of language.

In the Western world, he was one of the great explorers of the hallucinogenic experience, a field of knowledge considered sacred for thousands of years by some traditional cultures. In 1956, at the age of fifty-seven, he began his explorations of hallucinogens as the drugs were becoming known and available in Europe. At that time, it became public knowledge that hallucinogenic healing traditions were actively flourishing in Meso-America. In an article for *Life* magazine, the mycologist R. Gordon Wasson told of his experiences with a Mazatec lineage of psilocybin-mushroom healers.[5] Wasson's collaborator, also a world authority on hallucinogenic mushrooms, introduced Michaux to psilocybin. Thus, Michaux became familiar with the ancient spiritual tradition of using hallucinogens for healing purposes, and he treated the drugs with an unusual respect.

Very quickly during his "controlled" drug derangements, Michaux made an unsettling discovery. There was virtually no symptom or sign of psychosis that he could not witness within himself under the influence of a hallucinogen. He observed that every possible disorder of mind was deeply, almost lurkingly, available within himself. This was an extraordinary realization. Undoubtedly, it troubled him. He observed people in psychosis: in the hospitals, in their homes, in their letters. He noted their fragility, their arrogance, their fear, withdrawal, despair, secret raptures, mutism, stubbornness, pride in hallucination, and so on, and he realized that all this could be (and would be) activated within himself by the drug. In fact, it could probably be activated in anyone!

Once, when Michaux accidentally ingested an excessively large dose of mescaline, it became apparent to him that there was probably no one who didn't have the latent capability to become insane. Certainly, all his observations indicated that everyone possesses the necessary psychological equipment. This is not an idea that pleases most people. But this finding is the reason why Michaux could talk of madmen as "brothers," and why he came to spend so much of his life and energy in trying to explain the ordeals of people in psychosis by uncovering the universal elements of insanity, "what is basic to human beings and what is abnormal."[6]

The realization that psychosis may be an ever-present possibility in the human condition seems to trigger an instinctive fear and dread in many. John Perceval urgently tried to call attention to this singular fear because he witnessed it in all of his caretakers and he felt that it was having profound consequences on the way insane people were being treated and would always be treated. This fear of "losing control" of one's mind causes a great resistance to any kind of exchange or identification with, or genuine empathy for, a person in psychosis. From that has stemmed the neglect, therapeutic aggression, and the many impersonal theories of treatment that are now so prevalent.

Henri Michaux knew this fear acutely, yet he managed to

accomplish the ordeal of a radical exchange: He witnessed the dormant seeds and earliest stirrings of madness—each of its embryonic forms—spring forth and proliferate through his mind as the drug ripped through his body. His experiments were not easy. At the height of his first mescaline experience he wrote 150 pages of notations: "During all those incredible hours, I find these words written more than fifty times, clumsily, and with difficulty: *Intolerable, Unbearable.*"[7]

What follows is a collage of Michaux's deeply personal "journals" of hallucinogenic experiences, a record of microscopic observations of mind-tracking-mind. It can be considered clinical "case material" in the sense that it is a rare description of mental phenomena told by the subject himself. Its quality of excessiveness and repetition represents a painful experience of psychosis itself. This kind of documentation frequently draws a variety of reactions that can obstruct one's exchange and understanding: It is *only* a drug experience; or, it is merely one individual's idiosyncratic reaction; or, it is coming from a disturbed character. As with all such clinical descriptions, it is best to avoid analysis and interpretation and, for the moment, let it stand on its own.

ANCIENT MISERIES

The following experience occurred on a summer evening at Michaux's Paris apartment near the railroad station. The apartment is cluttered with books, musical scores, and drawing materials.

He settles himself in. Preparations, precautions are taken: He makes his apartment orderly, a vague sense of protecting his environment. Friends who know what he is doing are "on call" and can be reached by a device so that he does not have to dial the phone at a time when he might not be able to, because of forgetfulness or panic or worse. Tranquilizers are at hand. So are fresh oranges for their revival power.

He rouses his intention "to observe, to observe at all costs." Books and pictures are placed to act as reminders, as flashes of wakefulness or symbolic guidances during the deluge—accessible inspiration for when the bottom drops out. He knows that at the bottom will be his "concentration," or something like that, which needs to be held steady in order to bear witness; because surely he will not be able to control the contents of his mind. It will not tolerate control, it will not be his mind to control.

In an atmosphere of razorlike apprehension he takes the drug. Once again, how to decide on the dosage—an irrevocable turning point? He knows that he is in dangerous territory. He knows that the ancient peyote priests of Mexico began their "medicine" ceremonies, after fasting and continence, with a prayer to protect themselves against madness. There is no going back: Once you take a bite of the center of the earth, it cannot be undone, you are stuck with it.

The drug moves through him, feeling him, caressing at first, then moving audaciously, shamelessly into private parts—invasion, taking possession, becoming one with the life of every cell. And vibrating, singing in unison, proclaiming a song of victory, its ancient ritual of terrible cleansing.

He attempts to make no resistance. He tries to open himself, to let the drug run freely through him in unknown channels, which, at the same time, the drug is shaping, carving out, and vitalizing. He knows by now that his task is to relax his mind. But it finds him out: It begins to hunt and ransack (soon it will vandalize) every blockage and hesitation, every secret holding place and terror spot.

All of this first happens in his body and is soon to be followed in his mind. His fluids are saturated, he is drenched in the lust of the drug. He is theirs! Whose? Does he even want to find out? . . .

The beginnings of "thought disorder" are born from countless bodily "shatterings." All the ordinary "connections" are being ravaged. He is being reconnected, rewired. A sudden insight: "Thought disorder" stands revealed as thought reordering.

What we know of the nervous system cannot account for what is about to happen: "A shock zone has been entered." It is called the *second state*. We are entering into a different area of the mind-body connection, perhaps an area of the more "primitive nervous system." Here, the structure of the brain is close to the structure of thinking—where they mutually affect each other, where mental activity is creating structure or arousing latent structure, where pathways are activated that require mental stimulation to be awakened and become functional. He who takes the drug, the one who is being deranged or derailed, can actually *see* all of this—if he does not panic in the face of what may seem to be a runaway brain and wild mind.

The soft whistling of the wind becomes inseparable from an inner shivering. Then a prickling sensation, as if cells were in convulsion. There is a scintillation in the visual field, a herald of the "retinal circus" to follow. A vibration, not violent, more of a humming or "zinging," and sometimes several different vibrations are felt not only in the body, but *everywhere:* objects vibrating and singing to the point where they intensify into crystal. Everything is becoming fragile and excruciatingly precious.

Undulations begin. Out of microscopic swells, waves emerge and break loose. Images come in waves, *riding* the waves; and there are waves of thought, thoughts molded by the waves. He feels in the grip of undulations as strange, slow rhythms become established in his body: "It is as though one had another heart whose systole and diastole occurred fifteen or twenty times an hour."[8] Wind, shivering, scintillation, vibration, undulation, primordial rhythm—a new tempo is being installed in him. And it begins to *accelerate.*

The brain is palpable. He *feels* the wave forms: They change from the smoothly flowing sinusoid to jagged tiger-tooth waves. They transect him: "The lines, the lines, the diabolical lines of dismemberment!"—undulations running "from one end of the universe to the other." ("Between the lines of the universe, a microbe is caught.") He feels that he is being *"infinitized."*

The waves become visual; not "pictures" of waves, but waves attached to images, waves clothed and dramatized by visions and ungraspable ancient memories. He is the waves, he is nothing but waves. All his mental images are pulsed by the waves, impulsed and pro-pulsed by the waves. Huge sheets of color, oceans of color—colors that he always avoids—are there. The images are captivating. He is losing control over his ability to will a thought, or even to force a thought. An unearthly *speed* has taken hold, beyond him, on and off like an alternating current, sweeping him into insane hurricanes of thought. Bombardments of thoughts.

What are the contents of his thoughts? It is impossible to say: They are of every variety, every quality and tone, ceaselessly moving through like flashes of lightning. Mescaline plays his emotional keyboard, *its* own tune, shrilly, sometimes discordantly, hitting every note, as if testing him, seeing how much he can take. Perhaps also tuning him? Tuning him for *what?* He dare not think.

Immediately, it is there! The full drama of what he had just refused to imagine: in full regalia, in *excessive* ornamentation. He sees the overtheatricality of someone's (whose?) hands gesticulating toward him as in an Italian opera. The entire vision, lasting only a moment, nothing more than a "visual metaphor" of expanding and contracting rhythms, and still evolving.

And then it is gone. Vanished! Never to return:

> Each instant is formed, is completed, caves in, is remade in a new instant which takes shape, which is formed, which attains its fulfillment, which caves in and is remade in a new instant which takes shape, which is formed, which is completed, which bows down and is linked to the following which announces its appearance, which takes shape, which is formed, which is completed, which shrivels up and dies in the following, which is born, which rises up, which gives way and blends with the following, which comes along and sets itself up, develops and joins on to the following . . . which is formed, and so it goes endlessly, without losing speed, inexhaustibly, unmarked by accident, monumentally pursuing its wild perfection.[9]

He suffers from strange discontinuities:

> They left no trace. As soon as one had passed, it vanished into nothingness, leaving nothing behind it, neither in the two or ten seconds of 'immediate' memory, nor during the tiniest fraction of a second . . . There was no duration. It all streamed past me without my grasping it, without my being able to grasp it—in any manner . . . Absolute nonfixation.[10]

Tremendous *speed* is the signature of "manic consciousness." Michaux had gone truly mad once, when he unknowingly overdosed on mescaline, taking six times more than he would have allowed himself. Then, the "pace" of thought was not merely accelerated, but *madly accelerated,* where the difficulties become insurmountable. He literally didn't know if his nervous system could take it, if the wiring wouldn't blow out: "It is the exertion of stress on his thinking, of which he is incapable, which is the main cause of his ordeals."

He is a man beside himself; "he" is everyman who has ever been intoxicated in this whirlwind of speed.

> He sees thoughts operating by themselves. Suddenly, one of them prevails . . . digressions, side-thoughts; he cannot recapture a thought just passed, nor follow it; nor will the next thoughts follow in line; the speed of disappearance, the speed of appearance . . . increasingly disconnected from the first thought which he nevertheless continues to aim at . . . trying to rid himself of intruding thoughts, which inexorably bring a new digression . . .[11]

And when thoughts are "madly accelerated," the *oppositions* begin: waves of contradiction, leading to seizures of doubt and ambivalence. All this born of an instantaneous and electrical polarization:

> They pass at full speed, each of them affirmative at one moment, negative the next . . . Thoughts that occur in alternating, almost spasmodic oppositions. Shattered and shattering thoughts, thoughts which madden him, which he goes mad trying to follow, to correct, to reconstruct, to slow down, to unite, to make even, to make final, to make intelligible, to make tranquilizing and sound in spite of everything, thoughts on which he could still lean . . .[12] He is no longer between two possible solutions, but in a mechanism of oscillations. A hundred times in a single minute he can see, now one pole, now the other, at a rigorously unchanging speed, without being able by groping to modify the 'lightning' in the slightest, or to imagine, even for a moment, a compromise between these two categorically clear-cut and opposed forms, an ambivalence which will have no end, from which any conclusion is excluded.[13]

He remains fixed in his armchair, unable to move, unblinking, unflinchingly watching the spectacle:

> Just as the images then often appear paired, according to a rigorous, elementary, exaggerated, spontaneous, almost mechanical, and insanely repeated symmetry, the thoughts came in pairs, one provoking the other, one invoking the other (either similar or

analogous, or antagonistic). Strange pairs they are, each thought
with its contrary, the yes with the no, the pro with the contra,
affirmation with negation, and if they were not too long, thesis
with antithesis . . . evident effects of a doubtless normal function
which maintains thought under tension, but at this moment, incredibly exaggerated and multiplied, distressing and useless, distracting and driving to perpetual indecision, a phenomenon of
irreconcilable contradiction which endlessly returns to the
charge, incessantly traumatizing . . . permitting us to understand
the ravages it can make in a schizophrenic, as it sets up an insolu-
ble ambivalence, expressions of the hell of an irreducible antago-
nism, experienced with no chance of ever escaping from it, either
by progressing beyond it or by a final affirmation.[14]

He looks into a mirror and is horrified to see a haunted face
and "the grave calmness of someone who is responsible for a
dangerous maniac."[15] He sees the behavior of madmen with
new eyes: "If ever, I kept telling myself, if ever I recover my
capacities, I must write in their name."[16]

But writing has now become impossible. The agitation is too
great, and it is all extremely personal, intimate. It is about one's
self: self-deceptions, pride, conceit, sense of stain, lack of confidence, presumptions, anticipations; everything that he does to
elaborate and "embroider," everything he thought he was,
hoped to be, or feared—all this is being shredded, torn down,
as "he" watches like a homeless person seeing his makeshift
dwelling being dismantled.

So this is the true beginning of mescaline madness, a caricature of all madnesses: "caught, not by anything human, but in
a frenzied mechanical agitator . . . held prisoner in a mad workshop of the brain."[17]

Suddenly he wonders: Has he really taken a drug? He gets up
to check on the empty package, sits down, gets up to check
again, and again. Beforehand, in his "normal state," he had set
out oranges, as he always did—a natural antidote, he felt, for
critical moments or "chasm situations," such as now. Wearily,
he eats an orange. He looks at the clock: About one and a half
hours have passed since taking the drug and entering the "second state."

But years, hundreds of years, pass in a moment.

* * *

He thought there was a remission, so to speak, but it was only a lull. "It" begins to churn. Dynamic pulsings of opposites, "antithesisizing," pulverizing, atomizing: "The 'yes' and the 'no' pass back and forth, now the one, now the other, without gradations, unpremeditated, with the regularity of a motor piston."[18] Once again, he is "man in the presence of his motor."

These are the *micro-operations* of this motor: speed, acceleration, and oppositions, and there will be many more to come. Each idea or belief becomes a center of energy—a pulsing machine—and it lashes out from there:

> as if all the mind asked was to function much, much faster than usual, to function at perhaps its 'free' speed, that of nightmares (estimated at fifty times faster than normal) the speed that is born in seconds in the mind of the drowning, the speed that occurs sometimes in the dying and causes delirium.[19]

The micro-operations continue. A coat is lying on a chair; but he looks again and finds a slender young girl sitting upright, waiting. He corrects the mistake easily. But the next time he looks—there is no doubt, the chair is "occupied." The same happens with a crumpled piece of paper on the desk. An orange skin on the plate arises as a "pre-being, an 'about-to-be.'" And again the chair, which, on the third sighting: "this time I cannot keep from becoming a woman."

> General animation on all sides, objects and limbs of animals, a kinetic debauchery, streak past me as they shoot across the visual screen . . . Possessed by the animate, by the extreme, the *infernal animate,* all I can attribute to anything is the animate, that extreme animate whose excess maddens me, and which I am forced to project, which I will project over everything unexpected which comes into sight. An object is a presence, primarily presence, and from presence, what demented movement might not ensue?[20]

He watches as objects, even thoughts, spring to disturbing life, becoming beings and faces, a multiplication of presence, who watch *him;* echoing, repeating his words, mimicking him, soon they mock him. "A familiar sign: when you can no longer prevent things, objects, parts of objects from becoming faces, people, beings; or from turning into busts or masks which lie in wait, which will come to life."[21] Whatever the perception—

whether of sight, sound, feeling, even the perception of thought—it is energy, presence, *movement:* Whatever he sees has the capacity for pulsating life; whatever he hears sounds like human (or nonhuman) voice; whatever he feels is like living flesh; whatever he smells is the odor of a body; whatever he tastes might crawl in his mouth. But most distressingly, whatever he thinks may be someone else's thought.

Instinctive and subconscious micro-operations are being unveiled by the drug. They, in turn, reveal the microconstruction of madness:

> It is not foolish to say that it is the hallucination which produces madness and not madness which produces the hallucination; it is the dramatized and enacted, performed, hysterical, and unrelenting spectacle which drives mad the person who had only vague things to blame himself for, and perhaps he did not even know what they were. The tremendous and incessant spectacle maddens the man who otherwise would be able to endure it.[22]

Perhaps now he should take a tranquilizer, as he sometimes does when he reaches his limit of fear of becoming mad; after all, he has swallowed a "poison." But it is a question that sets off a fusillade of ambivalence.

He watches as it wears itself out. He is like a small boat entering a calm sea. Emerging from this he discovers (or is shown?) a new meaning to the word "courage," in heroic visions of kindness and valor—each one of which is capable of changing a man's life! And each one vanishes.

Michaux walks outside to a balcony:

> A black sky filled with stars stretched out all around me. I plunged into it. It was extraordinary. Instantaneously stripped of everything as though of an overcoat, I passed into space. I was projected into it, I flowed into it. I was violently seized by it, irresistibly. Dizzily, I sank upward.[23]

At "full speed":

> A tidal wave which suddenly overwhelms the earth, but it was the sky, the enormous sky which I sovereignly entered. I received the sky and the sky received me. At the same time, I was in an

extraordinary expansion. Space turned me into space . . . In a great many other ways, it came to me. Space was everywhere.[24]

The relentless tearing down has ceased. There is nothing left to ravage—only an "incorruptible observer" remains. He has entered a *zone* of utter simplicity and stillness:

Relieved of all surroundings, cleansed of all consistency, of all property, of all sense of ownership, incapable of conceiving any possession around me and lacking the preliminary minimum necessary to any attachment, I was in an ecstasy of space.[25]

A completely unexpected "metaphysical rush" begins—once again. It is expansive, it is what all the mystics and saints have talked about. He is a man reunited with his depths, and with all men.

And after that is the alarming process of *reentry.* Gravity reasserts its claim on him. He is "falling" into consciousness, into "reconsciousness." He witnesses a rare moment of the immediately-after-drug state, the fall into verbalization:

He is going to have a thought. It cannot fail . . . Here comes one, here's another. They flow in, resuming their interplay. The mind works again . . . He can resist the incontinence of thought, he can oppose contradictory thoughts.[26]

Seven hours have passed. Finally, he is alone in his brain. What does it do? It takes bearings: second by second, "orienting himself in his memory, in his environment, in his future."[27] He is returning to "pedestrian speed," the speed of retention, of computation, of scrutiny, memory, study. There is another danger here, he thinks, of "excessive mastery . . . of failing to leave intelligence *at liberty,* to remain in touch with the unconscious, the unknown, the mystery."[28]

The next day he draws. The drawings, wholly without his intention, are vibrating lines and undulating waves, intersecting and dissecting—and for moments, he is living the experience again. "Invasions," he called them, "delayed invasions."

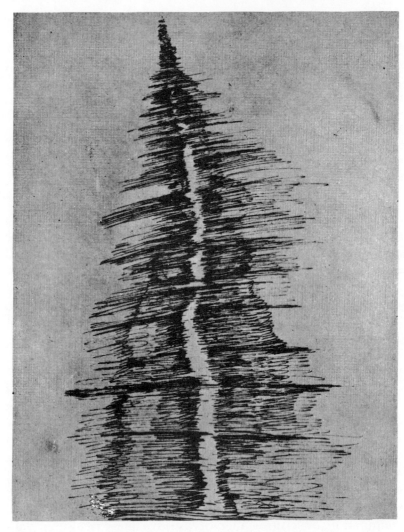

FIRST DRAWING (BY MICHAUX)

SECOND DRAWING (BY MICHAUX)

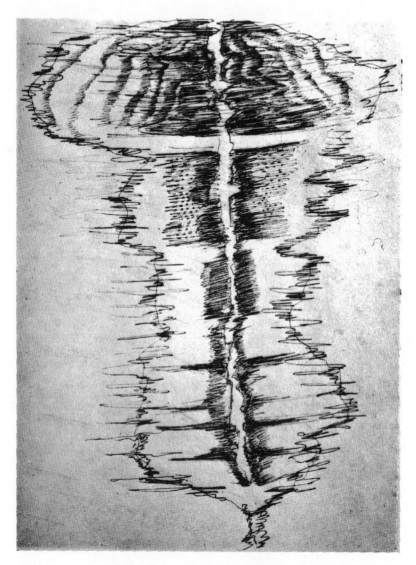

THIRD DRAWING (BY MICHAUX)

THE ROOT DISTURBANCE

At the onset of a psychosis, as with the onset of a hallucinogenic drug, one begins to lose one's willful control over mind. One cannot change direction or linger over a detail. One cannot follow through, or "think" through anything. One cannot stop or start; some great system of inertia is gone, one cannot "operate" the machinery. It is a shock zone, the universal experience of what Michaux has called the *second state.*

The second state becomes a struggle for personal survival because everything one has or thought one was, one's "identity," is being stripped from consciousness as a certainty or constant reference point. The early experience is the same for both types of madness: The "brakes" in the system give way, unbridled thought processes cannot be stopped, unveiling a life of their own, and an unfathomed and elaborate mental machinery of micro-operations becomes exposed. One begins to function differently; one *must learn* to function differently.

In a sense, a person in the second state has been "wounded." It is similar to what happens to the person who awakens from a head trauma and discovers himself to be aphasic and unable to find words. For the time being, he is *dislocated* from words and must function without them. There is a panic: Groping in a world stripped of words, dislocated from being the "operator" of words, one must function differently or not function at all. Then, like all aphasics dislodged from this center of activity, he realizes the enormous extent to which words have created and manipulated his world.

So too, the wound that leads to madness is a dislocating wound, but here one feels dislocated from *life,* family, relationships, and what has always been important. The usual ways of controlling mind have become unusable: They are overrun, sometimes annihilated, by the sweeping mental acceleration. Now, without the everyday orientation of being the one who controls, the "operator" who directs the mind, he realizes that he must function without a sense of self. And, like the aphasic who perpetuates his wound by too rashly trying to force words and becomes panic-stricken, the person entering psychosis creates limitless confusion by trying to reinforce his personal identity, in an attempt to catch his bearings by trying to build himself up. What began as a desperate attempt to "hold ground" and regain the center ends in grandiosity or despair. It is an over-shoot of the reflex micro-operation that relocates and *reorients*. This is the fundamental situation—what Michaux termed a "chasm situation"—that turns an acute mental derangement into prolonged turmoil, a "bad trip," or madness itself.

There is a tremendous variety of causes of such dislocating wounds. Each one is a brain-body insult that also causes a mental wound. Each wound carries within it the same ominous potentiality for exaggerated attempts at self-fixation, a trademark of "psychotic excitement." It is the psychiatrist's nightmare that he may mistake a rapidly growing brain tumor for a psychotic turmoil, the mental signs are so similar. Here follows an abbreviated list of the kinds of wounds reported to directly or indirectly interfere with brain functioning and that may result in major disturbances of consciousness. When that occurs, the *subjective reality* is indistinguishable from hallucinogenic intoxication or the psychotic experience:

- Allergic viral encephalitis (which may follow infections of measles, German measles, or chicken pox)
- Allergic reactions to wheat or rye
- Toxic brain pathology in reaction to local anesthetics, penicillin, and other drugs
- Endocrine imbalances, such as in hypothyroid or hyperthyroid crises, adrenal diseases, and steroid replacement
- Central nervous system involvement from autoimmune illnesses such as multiple sclerosis, systemic lupus erythematosus, and AIDS
- Central nervous system involvement from the steroid medications used to treat the preceding diseases
- Introduction of, or withdrawal from, a host of psychoactive ("neuroleptic") medications that affect the many known and unknown neurotransmitters
- Overdosage of stimulant drugs such as amphetamine, cocaine, etc., even caffeine intoxication
- Reactions to antimalarial drugs and antiasthmatic drugs
- Postoperative complications, e.g., following coronary artery bypass surgery
- Chronic epileptic disorders of all kinds, most notably with temporal lobe seizures
- The consequence of childbirth, e.g., postpartum psychosis

- Head traumas of all kinds (more commonly from right-sided injury)
- Assorted brain abnormalities, such as basal ganglia calcification, frontal arterial-venous malformation, brain-stem tumors, thalamic infarction, and the effects aging or senility
- End-stage kidney or liver failure
- Vitamin B_{12} deficiency
- Chronic dialysis brain inflammation
- Acute alcohol poisoning
- Prolonged sleep deprivation, from whatever cause
- A variety of sensory isolation phenomena

Each of these conditions has been documented to be a physiological insult that can lead to the experience of insanity. These wounds appear to be able to mimic any form of psychosis, just as the mental manifestations of advanced syphilis were well known to mimic *every* diagnostic category of severe mental illness. At the same time, there is a prodigious variability of manifestation between the different types and even within the same type—each beginning and ending differently, being of shorter or longer duration, accentuating manic, depressive, paranoid, or catatonic features. They are all distinct forms of psychotic derailment, but psychosis nevertheless.

In the usual psychiatric diagnostic classifications they are grouped together as borderline, contingent, or "secondary" manias or psychoses. They have been labeled makeshift and elusive diagnostic categories (changing over time) known as "organic mental syndromes," "atypical psychoses," "schizophreniform reactions," and "schizoaffective states." These are said to be eruptions from a hidden and simply unrecognized disease that, in turn, has been labeled "masked schizophrenia," "latent schizophrenia," "psychotic character," or "schizotypal personality."

But this pigeonholing of diagnoses—as if they were separate states of mind—always ignores the subjective quality. The feelings, the sensations, the ideas that occur to one during any of these so-called different derangements, are the same. It can be said that the *second state* is the common denominator for all these derangements, and that the felt texture of the mental derangement is similar because the mechanisms of their production are the same. The second state can be realized by a great variety of offenses to the nervous system, whether they are physical, chemical, or psychological.

"Brain fever" is what John Perceval called it in the past (and some still do) but he did not mean it in the same way as did the brain pathologists of his time. He meant more of what Michaux meant, an acute body-mind imbalance that throws one into the second state. Michaux's observations indicated that

> all forms of madness have common features. The disordered mind establishes a precarious and even dangerous equilibrium just as, in a hundred different infectious diseases, the same fever is experienced by the diseased body, the same dangerous equilibrium unfailingly found, for this is the only equilibrium that the organism afflicted by microbes and viruses is capable of knowing. After a long period of incubation or following upon a simple blow on the head, or as a result of purely psychiatric elements, or subsequent to neurological lesions, or due to any number of extremely varied causes, *the speeding up and then the slowing down of associations,* the escape of ideas, megalomania, paranoia, hallucinations and visions are likewise to be found in a great many pathological states, as a kind of mental 'fever'.[29]

At critical points during any of these psychotic phenomena the subjective experiences turn out to be strikingly familiar. It is a time when those afflicted share some or all of the common symptoms of "wounded" minds: intensified senses, illumination and the herald of a "new life," conversion, surges of insight and power, an egotistic twist, an ever-present doubt or threat, a hint of paranoia, a glimpse of possession.

The wound that leads to madness resulting from a shock substance, brain infection, vitamin deficiency, endocrine imbalance, and so on, is a wound that both *releases and reveals.* Mental acceleration, the common denominator of all "wounds," is released; the "power" of mind is revealed. As the "free" speed of mind is approached, a further sequence of mental mechanics is released. This is said to "feel" like one is becoming naked: "exposed to oneself," "stripped down to essentials," driven by the bare elements of mind. Many people have referred to this sense of release as the "beginning of a new life."

This "new" life, said John Perceval, becomes exposed as a secret life, an innermost life of man, the life of the "soul." In this way Perceval conceived of the second state as having both divine and demonic potentialities. Perceval intentionally produced a wound in order to enter the second state; he did this through fasting, what he called "watchfulness" (an intense attention to his mind), and "prayer" (including repetitive mental recitation of certain "spiritual" words). He did these, he came to believe, in the same way as did the prophets and desert fathers of any religion, and with similar consequences. The prayer, he felt, excited his "imagination," while at the same time, the fasting and other austerities fatigued and exhausted the controls of his mind. Thus, he repeatedly could enter a state that he called "trance." It was in that state that he said he "had no choice or control" but to see the magnificent visions of a new life brought before him. His greatest mistake, he concluded, was to be so gullible as to yield to these visions and to become guided by them.

These were the mechanics through which Perceval brought about two "conversions," namely, "tranquility" and "power." Soon, however, he was being elevated and destroyed in rapidly alternating visions of heaven and hell. Yet, within these abrupt recyclings there were moments of hyper-lucidity in which he saw the operations of his mind clearly and in a new way. He too called it a maddening machinery of the mind. About his experiences of the "ravages," the "tearing down" ordeals of the second state, he could not help but feel that they were the preparatory purifications required for his "new" life, his "spiritualized life," a rebirth, born again, with meaning.

For John Custance, the dawning of a new life was inspired by special personal "powers," which he experienced in the second state. The "lights went on," he said, as if he were awakening from the sleep of ordinary existence, and the world became enlivened, vitalized, reanimated, made exotically real and exquisitely precious. He simply could not get enough of it. The second state became tinged by a greed to pursue "manic consciousness" at *its* "free" speed, which was to end in a final exaltation of mania, a spiritual perfection or "enlightenment."

In Donald Crowhurst's experience, the second state consisted of not only a new life of power, fitness, and omniscience, but he took it beyond the others; he was to be the vanguard of our species, through a transformation into the "new being," the next step in a dramatic forward thrust of human evolution. He faced his ravages with a single-minded urge toward complete alchemical transformation. While sailing alone in the South Atlantic, Crowhurst was lashed by the elements, went sleepless for days, was cut off from communication, and struggled against exposure and disgrace. Under these extreme conditions, Crowhurst sustained a wound leading to madness.

When a "wounding" occurs—by whatever means—it gives rise to a common experience that something new is "dawning," which may be hopeful or foreboding. This is the most common initial expression of the root disturbance.

As much as they were sufferers, Perceval, Custance, and Crowhurst considered themselves explorers of unknown mental realms, as did Michaux. With mescaline as his vehicle, Michaux set out to "unmask" the enormity of the mental operations responsible for madness. For him, mescaline was "a drug to violate the brain, for it to 'give up' its secrets and the secret of rare states. To demystify."[30] In this dangerous journey, at times Michaux became the hunted as well as the hunter.

There are by now many people who have experienced the intoxication of psychosis *and* the similar intoxication of hallucinogenic drugs, usually at separate times, but sometimes together. In fact, there is no other social class of people who use hallucinogens with more frequency than the chronic mentally ill. The usage has become endemic to this population, especially since the drugs are often used by them to overcome what is called the "consciousness clouding" effects of various tranquilizers, and the feeling of a lack of "spontaneity." Even more frequently, marijuana is used for the same purpose. Another reason for taking hallucinogens is that they intensify the psychotic experience. I have known some people who were recovering well from psychosis without any tranquilizing medication but took large amounts of LSD because they were becoming depressed and they longed for the energy of psychosis. All of the reports testify to the similarities of entering the second state, regardless of whether one enters it by drugs or by psychosis.

The ones who have known both madnesses say that the real difference between them is the "duration" of the dislocating experience. The experience of the drug usually lasts from five to seven hours. But often during the drug miseries one may panic—thinking, thinking excessively, "This might last forever!" Henri Michaux said of this: "What saves one in the case of mescaline poisoning is the lack of duration. If the second state lasted longer, those who take the drug would suffer the permanent ill of the interruption of consciousness and many others. But they do not have time to become bound up with the drug."[31] And occasionally the intoxicated one seriously mishandles his mind, a mind already under attack, and his situation degenerates into a prolonged madness.

One way to become "bound up" with a psychotic experience is to try to hold on to one's position, or try to stabilize in a particular experience of self and self-enjoyment ("the *real* me, who I wish to remain forever"). Some attempt to appropriate the energy, power, and speed of a beginning psychosis as a sign of their unique station in the world, "for their own glory," as Perceval said. In this way they accelerate their psychosis to a maddening pace. It is the same with the drug, only in microcosm: Even a momentary attempt to revel in self-importance or egocentricity involves one in a massive diversion of energy and a torrential backlash of the micro-operations.

Generally, we think of psychosis as lasting for years, but there have also been many thousands of psychoses of shorter duration. This applies not only to those who have intermittent bouts of psychosis but also to those who have only a single experience, like many children who have a grand mal epileptic seizure but never have one again except under conditions of high fever or exceptional stress. There have been psychotic episodes that have lasted only several days. There are other episodes (including most drug-induced states) that last only a few hours. In fact, I have seen people endure psychotic turmoil for only an hour or less. This was the case with a dyslexic adolescent who dreaded being at school. When he had a particularly difficult time in the classroom, he would spontaneously feel that everyone was reading his mind, mocking him. For a few hours afterward he might feel that messages were being given to him through the television set. In terms of the subjective reality of a person entering the second state, its duration is not the immediate concern—especially as all time appears to collapse into what is universally called the "timelessness" of the second state. Real time, that is, clock time, dissolves into mental time, where it feels like the experiences of a lifetime can be had in a moment.

How long a particular psychosis lasts—no matter how it was induced—obviously depends on a great variety of conditions, including one's general state of health, one's relationships, one's life circumstances, and so on. But more significantly, the outcome depends on how one *relates* with one's disorientations during the disorder: what one's intention is; whether one's concentration is stable or wandering; one's power of "recollection," meaning an ability to come back to one's senses; the depth of one's courage; and the degree to which one is either punitive or benevolent to oneself. People who have recovered from psychosis have said, "What you bring to it is what you get." This is true for every variety of madness, or whenever the second state is awakened.

The difference between guarding and abandoning one's intelligence and sanity during a psychosis has very great consequences, yet only a hair's breadth separates them. The early situation of psychosis is usually very fragile and flickers back and forth between clarity and confusion. The amount of this flickering is often conditioned by *who* one is with and *how* one is being treated. When the environment is a safe one, with healthy friendship and patience, the psychosis may resolve itself in short order. On the other hand, when a psychosis that might naturally last only several hours or days is overreacted to by others in an attempt to suppress it as quickly as possible (as with overmedicating or other subjugating techniques), the disoriented one often fights against the effects of what he feels is an intrusion and a punishing abuse of his already-fragile mind. Such situations commonly lead to months or years of aggravated struggle with oneself and with psychiatric and legal authorities (while the psychosis worsens).

Anyone who becomes wounded in this way and is thrown into the second state (whether by a brain tumor, a poison, or a predicament) eventually becomes bound up in it and experiences the micro-operations of acceleration, antithetical thinking, sense of "freedom" (or imprisonment), infernal animation, and a gathering omnipotence. When that happens, one is living in the same domain as Perceval, Custance, Crowhurst, and countless others who have been overburdened and overwhelmed in the second state.

In Michaux's disciplined hands, mescaline became a microscope. With it he could examine the interior of the second state. He found the second state of mind to be fundamental and anterior to the development of every variety of madness. The second state was revealed to be a natural but archaic substratum of mental functioning, built into the nervous system, always available, but accessed only by exceptional circumstances and conditions. Initially, it is a neutral state, but when its rudimentary reflex micro-operations become exposed to awareness, they may come to *dominate* awareness.

THE MICRO-OPERATIONS

The hallucinogenic research of Henri Michaux provides compelling evidence that the world of madness is born from the second state. That is, the second state contains all the seeds from which the different phenomena of madness can wildly germinate. The micro-operations *are* the seeds.

Although each of Michaux's drug experiences was uniquely different, each one invariably included a "tearing down" by the actions of the micro-operations. Many who have entered the second state have felt that they were in the midst of some shattering rite of passage. Michaux catalogued the micro-operations: speed, accelerated thought, madly accelerated and repetitive multiplying thought, the oppositions, infernal animation (already highlighted in "Ancient Miseries" above), and others to be described. He found that every one of these operations could suddenly evolve into a distinctive offshoot of thought (a "defective sequence"), the first recognizable flicker of a psychotic state. It is in this way, for instance, that the microevent of infernal animation springs forth into the thought and feeling of "being watched." A proto-paranoia is activated.

From these beguiling and pernicious sidetracks of thoughts and images, "chasm-situations" can evolve. The sense of being watched develops: One is stared at, mimicked, mocked. Then, a hair-trigger blame—finding an object to blame, followed by a sudden accusation. Abruptly, the paranoid one has estranged those closest to him. Now he is in a "chasm" of loneliness, and he may even begin to feel that his relatives have been transformed into "strangers." He is in a "crisis" of escalating alienation, a chasm-situation of recycling loops of thought and action, and it is these that are clearly identifiable as madness itself.

A chasm-situation is what underlies the behavior of someone who appears to be "stuck in a mad place," where he is unable to go forward or backward and sometimes fights tooth and nail to hold his position within an unfamiliar functioning:

> He knows now, having been its prey and its observer, that there
> exists another mental functioning, quite different from the usual
> one, but a functioning nevertheless. He sees that madness is an
> equilibrium, a prodigious, prodigiously difficult attempt to ally
> oneself to a dislocating, despairing, continually disastrous state,
> with which the mentally deranged must, must at all cost, get
> along, in a frightful, unnameable partnership.[32]

The concern here is with mental operations that ordinarily
escape detection. Due to a shock-substance or a psychosis (or at
the moment of death, it has been said), consciousness is dislodged from places where it has always been and it refocuses
elsewhere. Some have said that this event feels like a "release"
from all-consuming "normal" preoccupations and is thus a newfound freedom. John Perceval called it an "emancipation of the
senses" and of many other mental faculties, which would otherwise remain unknown to us. John Custance called this process
an "illumination" of certain areas of mind, while the lights dim
in the conventional sectors. Michaux said it was like a queer case
of drawers that can function only alternately—some must be
closed before others may open. It could be said that this is a
revealing of the "unconscious," the microunconscious, where a
continuous stream of instantaneous and electrical microevents
is ceaselessly shaping our conscious world ("Beneath each
thought, what plankton!" said Michaux). This unconscious,
closer to the world of particle physics than it is to psychology,
is injected with consciousness by both the drug and psychosis.

Though invisible on the surface, meteor showers of microevents are displayed. Later, when they overwhelm one, they
become destructive and initiate "the great tragedies, the great
deliriums of madness." It is by them that madness persists.
Mental disturbance would not exist without them.

The Infinitizing Machine

As the second state is entered, the ordinarily silent micro-
operations begin to spring to life. Their "cover-up," by the
usual lumbering and meandering activity of forming a thought,
is lifted. They compel and command attention.

It can feel like the micro-operations are slicing through the
mind. In gigantic, razor-sharp "Zs" the undulations come, zig-

zagging, severing, dissecting, disconnecting, and showing the molecular structure beneath:

> Everything in thought is somehow molecular. Tiny particles that appear and disappear. Particles in perpetual associations, dissociations, reassociations, swifter than swift, almost instantaneous.[33]

The Speed of Mind.   The sense of energy, like a wind reaching gale force, is a common theme in the life of all who have lived in the second state. To them, a "speed," of which they had no comprehension in their normal state, at first thrills them, and then dislocates them. This ubiquitous phenomenon of insane speed has been described in a number of different ways, but mostly in terms of its effects and consequences. Here, with Michaux, we are examining the nature of mind-speed itself. What is the origin of this speed, so infamous to every species of madness, and what are its characteristics?

First, the speed is already there. Anything that moves one into the functioning of the second state reveals it rather than creates it:

> A speed now seen as much more considerable than previously supposed, an intensity which brings to perception the images (and micro-impulses) otherwise imperceptible, vague and remote. The drug makes the subject conscious of many other transitions and also of desires, which become sudden, violent, lightning-like impulsions.[34]

Man is composed of many different speeds happening simultaneously, but usually we are aware of only a narrow band of speeds, the ones we can comfortably attune to. The speed band of the micro-operations is beyond our everyday ability to observe. The ponderous speed of language—a summation of thousands of high-frequency thought processes that give birth to content and grammar—is hopelessly inadequate to describe the rapid conduction systems of the micro-operations. Meanwhile, for all of us, words and sentences calmly pass over abysses of speed: "Let us not be fooled by them. Man is a slow being, who is possible only as a result of fantastic speeds. His intelligence would have long since divined this, were it not for the very operation of intelligence."[35] For Michaux, perhaps not everyone is always so far from the real mental speed. He suggested that idiots savants and lightning calculators, those who are prodigious for their speed, somehow manage to take advantage of the ultramental speed—the fast circuit—and can enter into a direct relation with it.

The micro-operations are neither good nor bad, sane nor insane; they are simply the essential building blocks of our "macromind" abilities (of discrimination, of "holding in mind," of following through, of imagination). We cannot function well without them. However, they are a potential problem, an enormous problem if one does not relate to them properly. Normally, they are ignored, taken for granted. In the drugged condition, they are forced into awareness; there is a direct confrontation with the reality and configurations of ultraspeed. The one who enters the second state has no choice, he must enter into some kind of relation with the speed, whether it be accurate or inaccurate. There is no reverse gear. How one relates to the micro-operations will tell a story of either health or illness. First, they need to be recognized.

Here we discuss the sequence that micro-operations appear in when someone is going mad. Sometimes they appear in a steadily advancing order, sometimes they are all happening at once. They are natural functions running amok, brush fires flamed by winds of psychosis, and moving.

Repetitions. Repetitions of ideas and images come in bursts and are related to the sensation of advancing waveforms, like a thought or an image suddenly caught reverberating in an echo chamber and becoming insistent, louder, accentuated.

Multiplication. Everything in mind is multiplying: cloning, branching off into endless varieties of itself, never tiring, producing a jungle of new species of thoughts, an insatiable evolution, filling the whole world.

Proliferation. The energy of proliferation has been let loose. Proliferation occurs in a dimension just behind the ordinary linking of thoughts. It is the energy that links thoughts together in what is ordinarily called "discursive thinking": leaping out in any direction, generating an endless procession and what on the surface appears to be a continuous running on of thoughts. As fast as everyone knows such racing can sometimes be, it is slow

motion compared to the speed of the micro-operations spinning
thoughts together. The running on, or flight of ideas, happens
in minute surges: First, the thought or image is "named," then
appropriated as "mine, my thought," then judged pleasant or
unpleasant and to be approached or avoided. That high-speed
sequence produces a chain reaction of thoughts.

Proliferation increases as the speed increases. It loses inertia
or resistance. All resistance to proliferation is swept aside as
proliferation "runs over" every sense of pause, every gap in
thinking, every moment of rest, becoming a wall-to-wall consciousness of thoughts. Along with this there is a gathering of
suffering:

> Thoughts, images, urges—everything comes at an excessive
> speed, disappears with the same speed, which no sentiment will
> influence. It thinks, it doesn't need him to think. It does without
> him entirely. It leaves him outside. Without thought, in a parade
> of thoughts! Wholly disarmed, impotent. To think is to be able
> to stop thoughts, to take them up again, to find them, to place
> them, to displace them and especially to be able to 'go back.' But
> he can only go forward, forward . . . His head cannot stop think-
> ing. He cannot say 'enough' to the swarming useless activity
> which continues and which he cannot stop.[36]

Thought-Image.   In a lightninglike interlock they are wedded: A
thought, and the spontaneously imagined sensation of it, causing a momentary "dream" of the thought, are linked together.
This linkage is a building block of ordinary "imagination," and
also of hallucination. It is the basic fast-circuit habit of a natural,
or constitutional, "tendency to apparition." The second state
startlingly uncovers this linkage. It can also be seen "in action"
if one is able to pay extraordinary attention to the formation of
a dream, as it is being fabricated in front of one's eyes. For
example, when one is falling asleep, a sudden "twitch" of the leg
is immediately linked to the drama of stumbling.

This imaging micro-operation, the relentless illustrator, creates theater by dramatizing ideas, and it does so "without the
least participation of the will and without any consciousness of
desire." Within the second state, this micro-operation can be
seen to be embedded in consciousness, an automatic act of
being "conscious." Some have said that this action is in "bond-

age to consciousness."[37] It is a common experience in the second state (and sometimes while dreaming)[38] that it dawns on one, "Whatever I think—*happens!*" Within the excesses of second-state speed one may come to feel, "I can create worlds!" Donald Crowhurst called this phenomenon "creative abstraction."

A chasm-situation is created through a "calamity of intensifications." Thinking, intensified by speed, repetition, multiplication and sensation-lock, becomes *heard* reflection. Thinking is materialized in voices, or whisperings, or buzzings. It feels like "someone is saying aloud the thought which I am about to think." And the sound takes over, said Michaux, and "glues itself to the front of the stage which everyone carries within himself behind his brow."

Inside or outside?   Where is all of this happening? Inside or outside? That is always the question. Perception teeters on the brink of doubt as to whether what is happening is inside one's mind or in the environment. Or whether it is happening at all! One appears to have fits of inattention when all one's concern becomes fixed on a dangerous interior.

Oppositions.   Oppositions are endless, whiplashing chains of thought together with their negative antithoughts, in mechanical coupling, in subatomic parity. This is a reflection of how the nervous system is built: Every neural unit is an on-and-off coupling, every impulse arises with its counterimpulse, every muscle group is linked with its antagonist, every perception includes its negative afterimage. The structure of the system seems wired for instant complementary counterpoint—a primitive stereo-thinking principle. Whatever is subjected to it, whether it be a sight, sound, idea, or feeling, is as if put in a rotary blender: "Everything you offer to the mescalinian schizo will be ground to pieces." It is "infinitized"; *he* is infinitized. Within the micro-operation of oppositions, speed thrives on itself, perpetuates itself, accelerates.

The chasm of oppositions is a chorus of discordant and disparaging voices, conflicting commands, and staggering ambivalence at every level. On the surface, one is unable to eat, or not to eat. At times it comes to a standstill, a gridlock, a jamming, perhaps the only "braking" this system can know.

Infernal Animation. In a sense, this is nothing more than the human tendency to "personify," to imbue with life. It is a further action of the nervous system at liberty to do more freely what it already does. It is usually innocuous on the surface. But at the point of its microdevelopment—almost mockingly brought to light in the second state—the micro-operation of infernal animation can achieve demonic proportions. The first moment of animation feels like a sense of presence, of imminence, of "about-to-happen." At first, it is only a potential space, pregnant with possibility, yet directly sensible. Then it begins to pulsate (and what space can resist throbbing in this atmosphere of pulsing proliferation?). A "prebeing" begins to quicken and emerge.

Yet it cannot stop there. The presence becomes a creature; the creature has eyes, around which forms a face, which looks at you, which is inquisitive, and so on—anything can happen from there. To John Perceval they often appeared out of a flame. (For years, Justice Schreber called them "fleetingly improvised men." They could appear out of anywhere; some even lived in the pores of his skin.)

Perverse Impulses. The attack of perverse impulses may begin slowly, at first only by innuendos, suggestions, urgings. But they escalate into a furious onslaught of infernally animated oppositions:

> a *procession* of mad ideas, for they always came one by one . . . I might do a thousand insane things, cut my finger, break the window, set fire to the chairs, open my veins with a razor, smash the mirrors. The contrary of normal action was what seemed tempting. The fascination of the aberrant idea, the fascination of the thing that should not be done. Any object, when an idea for dramatizing gets hold of it, is capable of anything. I was afraid to go to sleep. I was afraid to let myself go. I was afraid to turn out the light, knowing that in the dark my thoughts would be without resistance.[39]

The one who is attacked struggles with all his might against preposterous acts rushing into his mind. Arriving at unbelievable speeds, they seize him, goad him, throttle him to make him carry out the acts in question. Everything that has been rejected raises its head. They are all abnormal ideas and they are avid for realization, the lure of the indecent, a kind of perverse "freedom." Many of the saints, during "sensitive" states of mind, have attested to the temptations of the demonic. But here, the brakes have faltered; Michaux felt it impossible to resist a perverse impulse: "I am they. They are identical with me, and I am more than acquiescent, I am inseparable from them the moment they appear."[40]

Now arises an archetypal chasm-situation of madness, the sense of persecution:

> That he is assailed is the pure truth. He undergoes assaults, mysterious, invisible and not understood by others. This persecutes him. Who holds this extraordinary power over him? The lunatic sometimes takes years to be able to point out his persecutor or persecutors, and sometimes they never are clearly designated. Generally, both ignorant and educated people likewise end up in madness by incriminating secret societies, supernatural, paranatural beings, who act at a distance, by magic, by fluids, by rays. This is in a sense a rational reaction. It is hypotheses to be tested, which is dictated by circumstances so singular. *The general idea of a persecution* invades him, comes from all directions, a real crossroads-idea which everything supports.[41]

There is no doubt that it *feels* like one is being "possessed," sometimes by a demoniac double or opposite: "By idealized perversity which every man unknowingly carries within him, an ideal made up of thoughts and desires grouped together, momentarily forming the 'self', a self which is totally and vertiginously swept along."[42]

Selves. Selves come and go. They are utterly real, new visions of oneself, at times a processional of them. In an instant, a "past life" is lived and abandoned. There may be many of them, new personalities, momentary, short-lived. They may be lives of nobility or of infamy. One may experience them like a tearing apart, a tearing down, or stripping away. While that is happening there might be flashes of insight: "There is no one self. There are no ten selves. There is no self. SELF is only a position of equilibrium. One among a thousand others continually possible and always ready."[43]

Each self is experienced as complete and profound, intensified and exaggerated by the micro-operation machinery, yet it also has a certain hollowness. But it is not simply their transiency that makes them suspect. Each is transparently manufactured, and when it leaves there is a momentary disillusionment. However, when one of these selves is held onto and elaborated, it leads to chasm-situations of disastrous self-importance.

Sense of Conviction—Certitude.   Everything is convincing: Once you get a mescalinian idea into your head, it is more real than anything else, and it has to be reckoned with, on the spot. An intensification of thought-images, plus the sense of "presence" linked to most sensations, gives mental images a surreal presence. These hallucinations are infinitely more compelling than the sight of ordinary reality, they are "super-real." Ideas become reality, memories become present tense, speculations ("what-ifs") become convictions:

> In the tragedy of the measureless intensifications in the midst of which he is advancing, here comes the one which is perhaps the gravest of all (and he does not see it), the one which will cause the doors of the asylum to close on him, the sense of total certitude.[44]

Everything becomes a "sign" to him, or a proof of what he only suspected. But the glibness of his explanations gives him away. After all, he is using logic only as an afterthought. His real basis for argument is in his conviction, in knowledge by direct revelation. He is again in a chasm-situation of "insight and power."

The most natural study of the sense of conviction is, of course, the dream state. The dream state is marked by complete certitude, by a conviction in the reality of what is happening. In fact, it is a caricature of our inherent tendency to become so convinced. Thus, the apparatus, the means necessary for such an illusion of surety, is within all of us and is always disturbingly available.

Two Places at Once.   Being in two places at once is a "trick" that we perform very comfortably in the normal state. It is our tendency or habit to be somewhere else, as to be in a daydream at the same time that we are trying to be here. We can eat, read, bathe, and do most of our work and at the same time we might be absorbed in a mental drama. We often seem to prefer to indulge a divided world, to dilute the world by living with a split consciousness. In the second state, too, this tendency is accentuated to the point of a chasm-situation.

The dislocated one is torn between the absolute certitudes of an inner reality and an outer reality, and both are making demands on him. John Perceval felt overwhelmed with ingratitude when he could not do it, when his world of angels and demons demanded his complete obedience at the expense of his body and mind. It is no wonder that the deranged one so typically asks himself, "In what part of the world am I at the same time that I am here?" He feels that his survival depends on how well he can perform the difficult feat, like a juggling act, of living in two places at once.

When he is able to do it, he feels that it is a most magical sensation: "The lunatic constantly talks of magic. He has a right to do so. On whom more than on him does magic operate, an altogether special magic?"[45] But otherwise, and for most of the time, he lives in the great pain of feeling inadequate and doing poorly in both worlds—he is a "failure."

Reorientations. In the normal state, we may notice that we have casually glanced at our watch for no apparent reason. That is only the tip of the iceberg of what we ordinarily do in the microunconscious. The one in the second state discovers himself invoking micro-orientations to trace, to recall, to grasp, to fix, to predict, to recapture a sense of place—many times a minute. He tries to find shelter. But over and over again, in hundreds of ways, he keeps losing track of it. This repeated orienting of himself, this abrupt and incessant taking of coordinates, is like a continual tic movement of the mind.

These ordinarily silent operations of reorientation and re-alignment are uncovered and magnified in the "desperate attention" of the second state: "I had to admit it: from birth, I had spent most of my life orienting myself . . . taking bearings, second by second."[46] The amount of time and energy spent in attempted reorientations is phenomenal, and fatiguing. The moments of exhaustion can be profound.

The Waking Zone. The above observations of micro-operations in rapid action, noticed and recorded as they are happening, require tremendous accuracy of perception. It is remarkable that, in spite of all the mental turbulence of the micro-operations, this wakefulness and precision is completely available during the second state. Michaux called this function of intelligence an "incorruptible observer": "All is madly shaken. All or almost all, because at the same instant, a new, hitherto unknown watchfulness is there, installed, observing, reflecting . . . purely me, a separate me, irreducible me, beside the mistreated, fragmentary, intermittent one."[47] This acute awareness appears to function almost unaffected by mental speed and has an unshakable capacity to discriminate the micromoments of experience. It is on this "waking zone" that all recovery depends.

During the hallucinogenic experience there are moments, sometimes long moments, when there is a direct perception, a direct "knowing" of the waking zone. It happens most strikingly when there is a *"slowing of associations,"* as Michaux called it. Thoughts may entirely cease. It has been likened to entering a calm sea or the relaxation after the struggle of birth, of truly being on earth or in the true depths of oneself. It is sometimes described as being pristinely clear to the extent that the cause and effect of all activity happening in the realm of mind is illuminated. This experience is usually overlooked and ignored by everyone around the person having it. Professionals, especially, dismiss these experiences as having no value, of being only further "imaginings." Yet the one who experiences the waking zone as being at the very core of existence feels it as a momentous event of life-changing and "spiritual" proportions.

> A psychotic episode may contain within it the beginnings of a spiritual breakthrough. The spiritual qualities of extreme mental states are real and powerful, and they are part and parcel of the pain, confusion, and dangerous quality of madness. To devalue or negate these spiritual aspects is to devalue or negate the person who experiences them, for these qualities are inseparable from the person. That is the true definition of stigma—a devaluation or negation that marks as shameful those qualities that are in a person's heart.[48]

It is almost impossible to chemically obliterate this awareness. But it can be obstructed. It can be clouded over, or made dysfunctional by a variety of conditions. For instance, there can be an extreme swing of the pendulum toward slowing down. Just as the speed of mind can be seemingly infinitely accelerated, so it can be *de*celerated, to the point of complete "numbness" or total inertia.[49] Thus, the waking zone needs to be protected, supported, and strengthened during the turmoil of the micro-operations. Recognizing both the existence and the vulnerability of this waking zone is therefore of critical importance to an intelligent administration of powerful mind-altering "antipsychotic" medications.

What happens within the waking zone that makes it so indispensable to recovery? It precisely separates and distinguishes between the appearances of mental events. It is attentive without bias or distortion. It can recognize what is happening within the mind for what it is, whether sane or insane. It focuses particularly on a fundamental quality of mind, the *impermanent nature of the field of consciousness.*

During the speed of the second state, no phenomenon of mind is brought to as much painful realization as the impermanent flux, the continual arising and dissolving of mental worlds and apparitions. This impermanence is also responsible for the momentary breaks in what might otherwise be an unbearable intensity:

> No matter what the spectacle you were watching in your vision . . . it will suffer a general overthrow. Another composition will take its place, will be developed, will be repeated until a new upheaval occurs and your attention will turn to the next sight. It is then that you give a low sigh, a sigh of extreme relief which is very moving to anyone who hears it and understands. But the new presentation will follow without delay. Here it comes: it emerges, grows distinct, is developed, is manipulated, changes, multiplies, then in turn, when its time has run out, it collapses and is not seen again.[50]

The shock-substance is not creating this spectacle of "change." It simply allows what is ordinarily taking place to be unveiled in agonizing clarity. Many people who have not necessarily been in extreme mental states have spoken of the inherent and fundamental role of the impermanent nature of mind. It is crucial to early Greek philosophy, to the Hindu and Buddhist meditative traditions, to the philosophy of Nietzsche, and, in its most abstract form, to modern physics.[51]

In its most subjective form, impermanence is dazzling. It gives no quarter. Michaux called it the "torture of what is unstable," and it is at the very center of the infinitizing machinery. This fundamental situation of chaos is itself represented, is itself theatricalized in hundreds of ways. A deluge of images dramatizes what is happening. Here is one of Michaux's "field notes," called "The Razor of Impermanence":

> Dazzling scythes of light, scythes set in flashes of lightning, enormous, made to cut down whole forests, start furiously splitting space open from top to bottom with gigantic strokes, miraculously swift strokes which I am forced to accompany internally, painfully, at the same unendurable speed and up to the same impossible heights, then immediately afterwards down into the same abysmal depths, with the ruptures even more and more monstrous, dislocating, insane . . . and when it is going to end . . . if it is ever going to end? . . . Finished. It's finished.[52]

Impermanence in excess and the chaos of losing orientation are translated into bodily feelings of huge extension. The sense of the body loses its limits: transformed into another body, or into an abstracted body, one without restraint, or released from measure and restriction, in a delirium of vastness. The mental mechanism, following the body's delirium, is also repeatedly drawn to the infinite: "an impression familiar to dozens and hundreds of unsuspecting, dumbfounded mescaline experimenters, which has it equivalents in several mental illnesses and ranges far into unreality and megalomania."[53] The razor of impermanence is the most cutting blade of all the micro-operations within the infinitizing machinery.

Overbearing metaphysical convictions abound. In the second state Michaux is in a chasm of reaching for divinity (a "theomania," as he calls it) and he claims direct contact with a palpable infinite. *Everything* leads him to it:

> a certain metaphysical banality consisting of the common human basis of thought that instantly transmutes itself into beliefs bearing on Immensity, Eternity, Immortality. The Absolute. Immanence. What is beyond Time, Space, the accidental, the phenomenal.[54]

It must never be forgotten, Michaux warns, that all these disorders occurring to someone in the second state are the results of "innumerable little internal ambushes," which only later becomes visible to others. Even when he is delirious, said

Michaux, "he creates and manifests a disorder much less acute than the multiple minute disorders that hack him, shake him, unbalance him from all sides."[55]

Michaux expressed this further in his poetry:

> *Firing*
> *Firing in the head*
> *firing which doesn't stop.*
>
> *Collapse*
> *Outside became too strong*
>
> *A man standing in a corner of the room*
> *suddenly there*
> *suddenly disappeared*
>
> *Sabotages*
> *innumerable little sabotages*[56]

The critical factor for being able to protect one's mind during madness is the recognition of impermanence. Madness is a violent lesson in impermanence. The basic fact of the inevitable decay and death of every aspect of life is terrifyingly highlighted during the second state. If recognition of this is resisted, denied, or repressed, it causes tremendous psychological tension and a recurring escalation in the wildness of mind.[57] A final chasm-situation might evolve: "The infinitization, the perpetuation, the atomization, the undifferentiated fragmentation, aggravated by the antagonistic and conflicting agitation which reduces everything to absurdity, permits nothing but ambivalence, reiterations, obstinacy, refusal, and an inhuman detachment."[58] Detachment may be the result, becoming "chronic" psychosis, the psychosis of *arrest,* where many simply "let go," and live and mean to live on the "other side."

One wonders how many sufferers are able to learn this. After all, said Michaux, "Rare indeed are the madmen equal to madness." But it is possible, it has been done: "In the huge organism that a human being is, there always remains a waking zone, which collects, which amasses, which has learned, which now knows, which knows *differently.*"[59]

Mastering Mental Speed

For the one who harbors the poison, mental speed is the great unbalancer. His problem becomes *how* to relate directly to mental speed *while experiencing it,* and while lacking the customary reflexes that provide braking power. The important point is that the waking zone be safeguarded from the speed. What follows are suggestions of how he could care for himself when living in the great speed, and how others around him (who now know his ordeals) could be a source of encouragement.

He who is "under the influence" of a drug or a psychosis needs to learn how to best take care of himself. Much information about how to train himself may come from his own prior experience with madness. For example, he learns quite quickly that he *needs rest.* If he doesn't learn this from the first episode, then surely he might from the second or the third recycling—that trying to remain too long at the controls of his accelerated mind will exhaust him, weaken him, and make him increasingly vulnerable to the excesses. He must take his rest, for however long it lasts, even if it is only for a moment.

This kind of learning requires that he have a certain sympathy for himself. But such sympathy or the kindness to care for himself is notoriously absent in the person about to enter madness. It is more likely that someone entering psychosis is abusing himself and is struggling with self-aggression. This is why so much attention has been given to the painful details of his mental commotion: to arouse his kindness toward himself and that of others for him. He suffers enormously, and his true ordeals have not been recognized and appreciated enough by others, or even by himself. The more we know about his true ordeals and become familiar with the problems of mental speed, the more we can help him.

But to a large extent he is alone. Like Perceval, he is alone and feeling abandoned in an asylum. Like Custance, he wanders alone in inner cities. Like Crowhurst, he is cut off and isolated on his boat. Or, he may simply be all alone in his apartment. He will experience seizures of fear, which come and go. Because of this he may also learn more about the nature of courage than he could ever have imagined.

He is alone but he is also uniquely equipped. The waking zone is always available to him. He is capable of tremendous precision, observation, and concentration in spite of the dislocations. Still, he needs to *recollect* the existence of this wakefulness and, at the same time, he needs to protect it from being overwhelmed. This zone of attentiveness should not be relinquished, it should always be remembered by himself and others. He is often unaware, or he easily forgets, that there are a variety of means by which he can recognize and protect it. There are a number of things that he might learn in the following recommendations and that he might even remember when he is alone. It is a time of being "wounded" and the stakes are high, yet there are many antidotes that can be applied.

Emergency Instructions

I offer the following in the form of direct address to anyone in the second state, as possible methods of maintaining awareness during this difficult situation.

Distraction is everywhere. You feel that you will even become distracted from your *body*. Too hastily, you think that you are losing contact with it. Body sensibility is your gravity, your contact with earth, and it is urgent that you be alert to it. It may be filled with restlessness and energy but it is still under your control. You are able to move it with intention, even though you might forget what that intention was in the next moment. You have the power to prevent the scattered discharge of bodily energy by remembering or being reminded to hold still and relax. You can adjust your posture and experience its profound effect on your mind. You can feel your body and its sensations, a sense of weight and presence. This mindfulness of the body has the effect of slowing your thoughts.

You are continually breathing but you have a strong tendency to ignore this function. When you are entranced by an inner world, you tend to hold your breath, or it is too shallow and only in the upper chest, or you breathe only intermittently. You will need to remember to breathe and even to take some delight in the changing textures of breathing, especially the filling and emptying of the lungs while inhaling and exhaling—the freedom and the luxury of breathing. When you focus your awareness on the sensations of breathing you also generate your power of attention. Perceval spontaneously discovered this while locked in seclusion: after some minutes of practicing deep breathing— in one nostril and out the other (an "alternate nostril breathing," as it is known in the practice of yoga)—he found that he would become more relaxed and mindful.

Your mind is infinitely distracted by its "contents," which both awe you and overburden you. But this is no time to indulge in contents, wonder, or analysis of intense images and pictures and dramatic scenarios. More importantly, behind the contents are the infinitizing activities of the micro-operations. They are the real threat. Even while your awareness is distracted in a "Babel of sensations," as thoughts and images move like meteoric showers across your visual screen, you are still able to *recognize and identify* each of the micro-operations and their ruthless activities. There is a certain *strength of nondistraction* that comes from this recognition.

Nondistraction is your key to mastering mental speed. To do this, Michaux said, "I must observe at all costs. Hold my ground. Not yield." This close watching refers to a special kind of attention, that of not following the preposterous, extravagant false ideas and illuminated impressions and associations that constantly lead down the "path of the fantastic." When healers used the drugs in ancient Mexico and put themselves on the verge of madness, they took great precautions against distraction. Their message can be condensed: "Don't get stuck. Don't elaborate on what is happening. Especially, don't get caught in the visuals. Don't dwell anywhere."

A certain resistance is necessary. But it is not the resistance of taking flight, or of refusal, or of digging in the heels, or of avoidance; they only create furious escalations of speed. There is no choice but to go through it. There is no way to go back to the beginning of a dream once you are in it. (However, even Michaux sometimes took a minor tranquilizer when he felt he could no longer bear it.) It is possible to allow the mad mechanism to pass through at its inhuman speed—and not miss a beat! Abstain from being caught on the hook of fascination. Keep observing the events as they arise—the next event, then the next, and the next. Ceaseless dissolutions. Impermanence is now the ally, the only reference point, the most poignant reminder of wakefulness that you will have. Now that you have come face-to-face with the quick circuit of fascination, of mental indulgence in microcosm, this is the opportunity to *cut fascination* at its roots. See, but don't investigate. Do not cling to phantasmagoria, abstain from fascination. Disengage by "lightning divorces."

Don't force thoughts and don't try to repress thoughts. Don't pursue them as being either personal confirmations or threats. Don't cling to words that in the next instant will spring to life in riveting theatricalization. Don't struggle against the speed, let it be as it is. This can relax and quiet you. The repetitions will lose power. The oscillating oppositions will dissolve each other. In regard to the continual expansion, the maximization, always going toward the extreme, the superlative: don't take it personally, don't attach to what can only end in megalomania. "Enough," said Michaux, "I've understood. Don't think! Don't think at all. Vacuity, lie low! Don't give It ideas. Don't give the mad mechanism spare parts."[60]

There is, however, a thought that is safe, that, in fact, is very helpful to declare: "Infinitization." It simply describes what is happening and it acknowledges the mechanics of confusion, without judgment or blaming oneself. It is a thought that arises from our critical intelligence and that labels and names the reality of the infinitizing machinery. It could be thought deliberately, *"In.fin.it.i.za.tion."* It allows for a moment of cessation of activity, and a moment of rest.

In this crucible of velocity, while feeling vulnerable and helpless to control your world of thoughts and images, you may discover a certain softness, an almost abstract tenderness toward everything and everyone. With that comes a moment of relief and of physical and mental relaxation. It is a feeling of sympathy and warmth toward everything outside of yourself along with the dropping away of an intensified self-consciousness. You are hardly alone in having had this experience. Almost universally, the one in the second state calls it Love or Compassion. Michaux called it "Misericordia in wave forms." But remember, you are still living in the great speed, and this too can "run wild." For a moment, sometimes a flashing moment, it brings you out beyond yourself, transcending your mental turmoil. It first stirred in you when you realized that you could be neutral; you could accommodate both intense pain and pleasure without attachment, without preference. You now may find that you are capable of experiencing wonderfully compassionate urges, and that this, more than anything else, is nuclear to your being. If ever there is an antidote to madness, it is here, in an *opening out.*

WORKING MODEL

"I have my cocktail," someone told me over the phone. "I can turn it on and off whenever I please. I've gotten that expert at it." He was referring to his series of manic episodes and his ability to enter mania at will. He was calling from an Arkansas jail after he had been arrested for possession of illegal drugs. He desperately wanted to escape from conditions at the jail. Two days later he had a psychotic "attack" and required emergency psychiatric care. "Was it like a hallucinogen?" I later asked him. "Yes, but much worse in intensity, like a fire up the spine!" This disruption lasted for months. Of course, he said, it's not like simply pushing a button. The conditions have to be right. All the right ingredients need to come together. Whenever he is able to do this there is serious trouble in his life, a "predicament."

A woman capable of "turning on" (but, as usual, not off!) her psychotic symptoms lived in this way in intermittent cohabitation with her delusional lover, a sort of cosmic hero who she invoked when she felt particularly lonely or abused. She could initiate his longed-for appearance into her life by taking off her clothes and dancing wildly in the moonlight. To this were often added loud incantations that turned into a bellowing. Sometimes it also required taking amphetaminelike "diet pills" to bring him forward.

Is there any wonder that there should be such "prodigies" of psychosis, since there are prodigies of just about anything else in the human experience? Besides the well-known prodigies of music, chess, mathematics, and other mental manipulations, are the sensory wizards, those who can "tune" a sensory organ to the virtuoso performance of "perfect pitch"; the eidetic imagers, those who can "bring alive" and feel an idea or memory; the idiots savants who might be masters of memory, lightning calculations, and so on. But there have also been those who, by spontaneous or accidental achievement, have practiced every mind-body interaction imaginable. They have stopped their breath, their heart; immobilized their body; produced profound anesthesias; created meditative states of trance, of ecstasy, of detachment, of "god-intoxicated" states, states of mental fixations, mental states that have been cataloged in the hundreds. All through diligence!

Similarly, in the back-ward museums of mental hospitals are such prodigies. Particularly, they specialize in mind states. Out of imbalance, loneliness, and frantic ambition they have developed arcane disciplines. They demonstrate that any mind and body connection can be put together, if only one plugs into the right wiring. That wiring is relatively easy to "hook up": Anatomically, you can get to anywhere from anywhere within the brain and body in nine neurons or less![61] It is this possibility of great "plasticity," or recircuiting, that allows some people with severe brain wounds to recover lost functions by circumventing a damaged area.[62] Even without any actual recircuiting of that incomparable wiring network, there are certain chemicals that can open up any of its possible connections—just as the dream state does, just as the second state does.[63]

Thus, it is easy to understand that someone can engender in themselves, without any causes other than their own bizarre and esoteric drills, what is commonly called a pure or "functional" psychosis (the psychosis of "unknown cause," "idiopathic" psychosis, seemingly spontaneous and unrelated to material disease). Of course, something in the body is always involved, if only secondarily. Even the pure conception of lust, when "imagined," when fixed upon, visualized, animated, and rehearsed, will lead to a strong physical reaction, mediated by the brain, via chemicals, into bodily tension and orgastic excitement. That model of mind-brain-body connection is already well established.

What follows is a working model of psychosis, that is to say, a model that can be worked with in a practical way, that has "clinical implications," and that can be used in designs for treatment. Briefly, the model has these stages: The "Cocktail" is the mixture of causes and conditions necessary for "Imbalance" to occur, consisting of a wounding rearrangement between the body, neurotransmitters, and the mind, giving access to the "Second State" of mental functioning—including the micro-operations—which differentiates into multiple "zones of consciousness," one of which is "manic consciousness." Thus, a functional psychosis *evolves* (see schematic diagram on page 173).

The Cocktail

The "Cocktail" consists of a Predicament, an Intention, Exertion, a Substance, and Mindlessness. Usually, all of these in-

Zones
of
Consciousness

MANIC CONSCIOUSNESS

Second State
Micro-Operations

Imbalance
Neurotransmitter
   "Double Action"
Rhythms
Speed

"Cocktail"

Predicament   Intention   Exertion   Substance   Mindlessness

EVOLUTION OF A FUNCTIONAL PSYCHOSIS

gredients can be found to one degree or another in the production of a psychosis.

PREDICAMENT

More men, women, and, especially, adolescents have become insane in the wake of unrequited love affairs than those driven mad by toxins, defective genes, and other abnormalities put together. It is a clinical commonplace that the phenomenon of unrequited love is a fertile occasion for madness, and this probably has been so since prehistoric times. Perhaps this is why it is said the world over in pretechnological healing traditions that excessive passion is a "poison" that makes one's system "toxic" and then endangers the mind.

The humiliated lover is involved in a predicament. From rejection, or from a real or imagined loss, the lover suffers the crushing disappointment of an intense conviction. His "conviction" might be of his destined place in another's life, or of his sexual irresistibility, or of having found an ultimate mate, or of living only the shadow of a life when not with the other, and so on in countless variety. He has reconstructed a "self" that can only exist in the presence of the other. When this self is rejected, the "groundlessness" or emptiness of his existence can be similar to (and feel like) the "tearing down" experiences of the drug-induced state. But he sometimes rises up from that experience and "switches out," traversing the psychotic "spiral of transformation" into an existence of magic and power. A new passion emerges—one of infinite nature, a celestial version—as the predicament comes to completion.

INTENTION

Groundlessness is the occasion for transformation. The urge to transform is usually a motivating factor long before a predicament arises. This desire to become someone else has been "cooking" since an early age. An ordinarily hidden hope and conviction grows that a transformation might come upon one suddenly, as can happen when falling in love. Who has not experienced this alchemical transformation, or this urge in fantasies or dreams? William James said that this capability for sudden transformation, which comes in so many varieties and intensities, is perhaps the most curious of all man's capacities. The intention to transform awaits its catalyst. In the case of the lover, the idealized object of love is the agent for transformation.

John Perceval had longed since adolescence to molt his personality, which had gradually rigidified within the excessive formalism and hypocrisy of his family culture. And he did accomplish that, like a phoenix. John Custance, accustomed to rebounding from depression by manic transformation, traveled to postwar Berlin, divided by paranoia, in order to court and win a final manic liberation. Michaux engaged in an ageless poetic tradition or practice of a "deliberate derangement of the senses" to rescue the imagination from its conventional restraints.

"Freedom" is the issue; freedom is always the hoped-for fruit of transformation. Crowhurst virtually demanded his freedom, which meant a supernatural removal from the scene. Intention becomes an ambition, an attitude based on escape—just waiting for an opportunity. Even the one who experiences a dislocation through brain damage begins to talk obsessively about freedom.

EXERTION

Work or effort is required to bring this intention about. All of the characters of this book worked very hard at manipulating their bodies and minds. Custance worked around the clock at practices (mistakenly called empty "rituals" by some) to unbalance or desynchronize his mind and body: by struggling against sleeping and eating, automatic writing, endurance walking, and throwing himself into risks and into the speed of risk and wakeful danger. John Perceval fasted, sealed his mind in prayer, and tried to "speak in tongues." Others have found the key in rapid, nonstop talking. And others have found it in the great effort it takes to enter a "vow of silence." Some stare into candles or streetlights all night long. There is a metaphor for this kind of exertion in a short story called "The Rocking Horse Winner" by D. H. Lawrence. An unusual child "drives" himself by frantically riding his wooden rocking horse, in order to work himself up into a clairvoyant state in which he can predict the winner of horse races in the future. All of these are efforts at bringing something about, forcing the issue, delivering from one's mind a transformative experience.

SUBSTANCE

Usually, a substance is found that will fuel the momentum of the coming transformation. Preferably, it is an "excitant," an accelerator. Alcohol and marijuana are the most popular (and the cheapest) these days. But every other kind of "street drug" is also used, the hallucinogens obviously being the most powerful. Very high dosages of caffeine even work when nothing else is available. So does nicotine. Perhaps food can also be considered an accelerating substance, as it is during fasting or during bulimia with forced vomiting. Increasingly, one hears about patients using their prescribed medications ("antipsychotic" or "antidepressant" drugs) in toxic amounts to imbalance the system and create "altered states." I have recently seen a woman do this with Artane, a medication used to suppress the side effects (muscle spasms) of major tranquilizers. Other medications that have this potential are reported almost monthly in the psychiatric literature.

MINDLESSNESS

To be mind*ful* means to be precise, accurate, "in touch" with, and able to track the phenomena taking place inside and outside oneself, to be in direct contact. To be mindless is to forfeit that contact and sense of presence, by an inversion and perversion of mindfulness. Mindlessness comes in several varieties: "blanking out," becoming "numb," fixating on particular sensations to the exclusion of all others, being absorbed in a narrow band of concentration with the loss of a larger vista. In the *Ion,* Plato refers to a madman as "a bird fluttering and looking upward and careless of the world below." The unrequited and idealizing lover—the one desperate to become another, through another—fixes his mind on his beloved. He attempts to avoid the natural flow of perceptions and ideas that might distract his thoughts from her, as if by such one-pointed concentration he could be in communion with her, not lose her, or "bring her back." In the second state the mindless one may indulge in conjuring her back by symbolic words, acts, or gestures.

The destructive effects of mindlessness are seen clearly in a condition of little children, known as "autism." Who knows what the dire predicament of such children really is, although, occasionally, there is no doubt that it is the direct result of extreme conditions of environmental neglect or malice.[64] Typically, these children become "lost" in hallucinated states or in "blank," automatonlike states, from which they cannot be shaken or "awakened." They can be seen to be grotesquely at work at this, to actually "crank it up." They work at developing movements, usually involving rapidly rotating movements of a hand around the mouth, or a "tapping" with a seemingly inhuman speed. What infernal vibrations, rhythms, and waves do they invoke or provoke within themselves? But the result is clear:

> The autistic child, through his own efforts, achieves a state of nonattentiveness to stimuli which has all the appearances of a state of dysfunction of the system serving arousal . . . This he does, for example, by his monotonous, continuous self-stimulation which arises, in part, from his motor behavior. In a sense, any stimulus from the outside is then lost, either by being blotted out, or in the concentration on inner sensations alone.[65]

Imbalance

The entire "cocktail" (or even any combination of its ingredients), has a traumatizing effect on one's total physiology and chemistry. The dramatist August Strindberg said about the onset of his psychosis: "Then I feel, at first only faintly, something like an inrush of electric fluid. I look at my compass, but it shows no sign of wavering. It is not electricity, then. But the tension increases; my heart beats violently; I offer resistance, but as if by a flash of lightning my body is charged with a fluid which chokes me and depletes my blood."[66] The function of every internal system is altered. Chemicals, energies, impulses, and reflexes, normally held in a delicate balance, are disrupted. The early investigators of psychosis often said that it was an illness of "disharmony." But it is a unique disharmony. The poet Gérard de Nerval said of his own psychosis: "I do not know why I use the word 'illness,' for as far as my physical self was concerned, I never felt better. Sometimes I thought my strength and energy were doubled, I seemed to know everything, understand everything. My imagination gave me infinite delight. In recovering what men call reason, do I have to regret the loss of those joys?"[67]

There are a number of different ways in which this imbalance can be seen. In the speculations of both Perceval and Custance,

what is unbalanced are two kinds of "nervous systems"—a gross
or outer nervous system, and a subtle or inner nervous system.
This is not an unusual idea. Many people who have experienced
the ravages and exaltations of the second state have also wondered about the existence of such parallel systems. In a similar
but much more developed manner, medical practitioners of
Tibet, India, China, Japan, Korea, and elsewhere for many centuries have seen madness as a serious imbalance of the energies
of a "subtle" system. They each describe and work with energies, channels, and energy focal points that are not acknowledged to exist in modern neurology.[68]

On first taking a hallucinogenic drug, Michaux was inevitably
drawn to ideas about a chemical instigator of madness:

> Certain sentiments . . . manufacture certain nervous poisons
> capable of damaging the controls, like that of the diencephalon,
> the great regulator and master of sleep, and other controls be-
> sides, and, through the non-resistance of the controls, start a new
> acceleration of ideas, over and above the first, thus breaking
> through all restraint, all self-control.[69]

NEUROTRANSMITTERS

It is safe to say that knowledge about the hallucinogens has
changed the history of madness. Yet, the hypotheses are endless. In the Western medical tradition, one or another "toxin
theory" of psychosis has had supporters for at least two hundred
years. What was being looked for was sometimes called a "toxin
X." This theory states that the body begins to produce noxious
chemicals by some wild and aberrant synthesis. Consequently,
this theory has come to involve consideration of enzymes and
genes. The psychiatrist who introduced Aldous Huxley to mescaline came to believe that a supposedly "weak" hallucinogenic
chemical (which he called "adrenochrome"), ordinarily a minor
intermediary metabolite of the important neurotransmitter
adrenaline, somehow accumulates to toxic proportions. Now
there are many species of such toxin theories.

Can there be some "generic" shock-substance, flowing in the
veins of unfortunately "marked" people, which acts as a natural
neurotransmitter of the second state?

It remains a haunting fact that the most potent of the natural
hallucinogens are homologous to the neurotransmitters. That
is, the organic hallucinogens and the neurotransmitters are of

the same chemical family and of the same origin. With only minute changes of atoms on the basic, fixed structure, a neurotransmitter may become a hallucinogen. In this way the essential neurotransmitter serotonin can become the hallucinogen psilocybin. Much of the recent manufacture of underground "designer drugs" is based on chemical rearrangements of the neurotransmitter structures. Oddly enough, it seems, our mandatory and precious neurotransmitters, in some variation or other, are also "out there" in the earth in mushrooms, cacti, and vines.

In current research, the greatest attention is being paid to the role of the neurotransmitters within us. It is they that seem to be principally affected by the class of medications that at times is helpful to people in psychosis, the phenothiazines. Many of these medications implicate a particular neurotransmitter, dopamine, as having a major role in the activation of psychosis. Dopamine itself is, along with mescaline, one of the alkaloids of the peyote cactus. But the role of dopamine, with its various molecular actions and reactions at the junction of nerve cells, has turned out to be far more complicated than originally suspected. Also, dopamine is only one of a dozen other neurotransmitters that can be shown to have tremendous power in effecting neural transmission, the wiring of the brain. The best estimates indicate that there are as many as two hundred such substances residing in the brain and elsewhere in the body. We are swimming in neurotransmitters.

However, dopamine has been given a special place through the astonishing research of Dr. Oliver Sacks.[70] His patients demonstrated that dopamine itself, without any metabolic change, is as powerful as any hallucinogen. He worked with people whose original disease (encephalitis lethargica, stemming from the infamous flu epidemic of 1918) had selectively destroyed the ability of their brain cells to produce or store the neurotransmitter dopamine. This is also the pathology of parkinsonism, with which these patients suffered to extreme degrees. People who for twenty, thirty, or more years had been frozen in time, arrested at the moment of their fall into "sleeping sickness" and occupied only by dreamlike states, who were seemingly inert to the world around them, could suddenly spring to life and come back "into time," when the neurotransmitter dopamine (via its precursor, L-dopa) was given to them.

Even though the story of these "awakenings" has been told

many times in the past decade, its great psychological significance has yet to be fully appreciated. These findings, Dr. Sacks
rightly claims, are not only of "profound therapeutic interest,
but of momentous physiological and epistemological interest."[71]

When L-dopa is first given, the accumulation of dopamine in
the brain acts like a "reverse hallucinogen," a transmitter capable of awakening one from a most extreme chasm-situation (in
this case a cataclysm) of mental and physical "arrest." These
patients describe transformations that are as dramatic as any
seen in the human experience. However, when L-dopa continues to be given it has an opposite effect: One may be overwhelmed in a hallucinogenic ordeal, with nightmare speed, "attacks of possession," and manic consciousness. Thus, under the
conditions of large dosages, or a developing supersensitivity, or
other conditions of cocktail-induced imbalance, dopamine has
all the qualities of a "drug." Depending on the conditions, dopamine is either a wakeful energizer or a "psychotomimetic."

Here are examples of how it happens. After several days of
L-dopa administration, one patient, Mrs. Y, who had for decades
lived almost immobilized in a crippling state of extreme parkinsonism and catatonia, "exploded . . . and before incredulous
eyes walked the length of the ward." She began to talk of "freedom," a liberation far greater for her than simply the release
from her bodily torture. About her newfound freedom she de-
lightedly and repeatedly exclaimed: "I'm a new person, I feel it,
I feel it inside, I'm a brand-new person. I feel so much, I can't
tell you what I feel. Everything's changed, it's going to be a new
life now." Another patient on L-dopa felt himself to be a messiah "called on" to do battle with demonic forces. Patients in
their mid-seventies began to talk of L-dopa as filling them with
health, energy, and "grace." They called it a "miracle drug," a
"blessed drug," and they went around proclaiming "the gospel
of life according to L-dopa," all of which must have sounded
disturbingly similar to the way the hallucinogen LSD was being
talked about.

However, within a month, Mrs. Y was noted to have become
overexcited quite easily, even by her own clapping:

> Her movements were extraordinarily quick and forceful, and her
> speech seemed two or three times quicker than normal speech;
> if she had previously resembled a slow-motion film, or a persist-

ent film-frame stuck in the projector, she now gave the impression of a speeded-up film . . . Her threshold of reaction was now almost zero, and all her actions were instantaneous, precipitate and excessively forceful.[72]

Once again, we find *speed* to be the energy that drives the system. Usually, it comes in *"waves"* of energy and strength, "each wave rising high and higher towards some limitless climax."[73] Many of these patients talked of "waves running through them, or of being tossed up and down like a boat in heavy seas. These undulant images seem entirely appropriate, if one departs from the notion of simple, sinusoidal waves, and instead visualizes torrential excitements which *surge hyperbolically,* getting steeper and steeper, as they get higher and higher, and thus have the potential of infinite height."[74] With this "continual proliferation of new excitations," Sacks believes the brain is *"lit up."*

It is not surprising that these patients who for so long had lived with bodily inhibition, spasm, and rigidity would experience the energy of speed to be bizarrely exaggerated in their bodies. As one of them said after being "switched on" by L-dopa, "Before I was galvanized, but now I am vivified." All their "tics" and other sudden automatic movements, including new ones, were maddeningly accelerated. Explosive movements, which were like "streaks of lightning," were caught on film, and playback revealed them to be hundreds of times faster than normal. The pure analogue of the micro-operations was being expressed through the body, via the "derailed" motor system.

At the same time, speed drives and propels the thinking process. Mrs. Y would episodically experience "a kinematic 'delirium' in which a variety of perceptions or hallucinations or hallucinatory patterns may succeed one another with vertiginous speed, several a second."[75] In other patients, there was also a similar rapidity of speech and a startling ability for mathematical calculation. Several patients passed from a "gentle amorousness to an enraged and thwarted erotomania." All their needs and desires were marked by a speed-intensifying continuum of ambition, greed, and voracity.

These patients became caricatures of manic pressure. They were now "overflowing" with the administered neurotransmitter dopamine, after having been so long deprived of it, and they entered the domain of manic and psychotic energy: "Our pa-

tients, then, ascend higher and higher into heights of exorbi-
tance, becoming more active, excited, impatient, increasingly
restless, choreic, akathisic, more driven by tics and urges and
itches, continually more hectic, fervid and ardent, flaming into
manias, passions and greeds, into climactic voracities, surges
and frenzies . . . until the crash comes at last."[76]

Most of them also experienced the "tearing down" phenomena, the personally shattering experiences of the hallucinogenic
second state. Of one, Dr. Sacks writes:

> Certain violent appetites and passions, and certain obsessive
> ideas and images—could not be dismissed by her as 'purely phys-
> ical' or completely 'alien' to her 'real self,' but, on the contrary,
> were felt to be in some sense releases or exposures or disclosures
> or confessions of very deep and ancient parts of herself, mon-
> strous creatures from her unconscious and from unimaginable
> physiological depths below the unconscious, prehistoric and per-
> haps pre-human landscapes whose features were at once utterly
> strange to her, yet mysteriously familiar, in the manner of certain
> dreams. And she could not look at these suddenly exposed parts
> of herself with detachment; they called to her with Siren voices,
> they enticed her, they thrilled her, they terrified her, they filled
> her with feelings of guilt and punishment, they possessed her
> with the consuming, ravishing power of nightmare.[77]

They also developed their own "demonologies." They talked
of "possession" by "presences" who would sometimes visit during the night, erotic or satanic spirits who transformed and
controlled them. Like Michaux (and also William James), who
spoke of a demonic self, composed of all the agglutinated nega-
tives of oneself that rise to the surface; and like Perceval's "perverse self," or Custance's demons composed of the "return of
the rejected opposites," Dr. Sacks talks of "opposed forms of
being [who] fight to possess us, to dispossess each other, and to
perpetuate themselves."

Regulating the dosage for people being maintained on
L-dopa (and thus the amount of dopamine in the brain) became,
without fail, a terrible problem. When it was stopped completely, or sometimes merely reduced, patients would revert to
a depressed state that was far more distressing and disabling
than the original "pre-L-dopa" state. It became impossible in
most cases to find the increasingly elusive precise dosage that
was neither too little nor too much: "they *needed* L-dopa, *but could
not tolerate it.*"[78]

This is exactly the situation of the tens of thousands of chronic mentally ill people currently being "maintained" for long periods of time on the "antipsychotic medications." The ultimate site of action of these medications is on the neurotransmitters. Typically, and increasingly, one hears of the dilemma of psychiatrists who are futilely attempting to regulate the knife-edge dosage of their patient's medications: *"He can't live with it and he can't live without it!"* That is, too great a dosage of the neurotransmitter blocker stupefies him; too small a dosage permits the cycle of excitation and agitation to begin. There usually comes a time when there is no middle ground, when the distance between too much and too little is only a fulcrum flipping one into excitement or depression. What happens with the "chronic" use of antipsychotic medication is the same as is seen in every patient maintained on L-dopa: "His tolerance for the drug becomes less and less, while his need for the drug becomes greater and greater: in short, that he gets caught in the irresoluble vicious cycle of 'addiction.' "[79]

What one is witnessing in these patients is the bimodal, paradoxical, or "double action" of the neurotransmitter dopamine. Dr. Sacks summarizes the experience of his patients, but he might just as well be speaking of the experience of the person who takes an overdose of a hallucinogen, or the person who enters psychosis by means of the "cocktail":

> For a brief time, then, the patient on L-dopa enjoys a perfection of being, an ease of movement and feeling and thought, a harmony of relation within and without. Then his happy state—his world—starts to crack, slip, break down, and crumble; he lapses from his happy state, and moves toward perversion and decay.[80]

This is probably the case for many other neurotransmitters as well. Since the mid-1950s, the same "double action" has been suspected of the neurotransmitter serotonin (structurally related to the hallucinogen psilocybin and LSD). Other neurotransmitters, related to the amphetamine family, also seem to work in a "paradoxical" way. There is also a host of synthetic drugs created by substitutions on the amphetamine nucleus that act paradoxically. Such a drug is Ketamine, a respected pediatric and veterinary drug that acts as an anesthetic at one dosage but is a potent hallucinogen at one-tenth that dosage.

However, the situation is far more complex than a single neurotransmitter being at fault. All the neurotransmitters work *in concert,* in a network of other neurotransmitters. Not one in particular is to be "blamed." When any one of them is in either excess or deficit, many of the others rearrange, and different patterns or "profiles" of neurotransmitters are created. The various neurotransmitter systems are in a precarious balance with each other; interference with one neurotransmitter system affects the functioning of others and imbalances the whole network. For a person entering psychosis, the "cocktail" is an alchemical event that imbalances the network and turns naturally existing neurochemical "awakeners," medicines, into "poisons."

Just how the neurotransmitters affect the mind itself is unknown. But everything indicates that they affect the *rhythms* of the brain and the rest of the body. Molecules of dopamine and other neurotransmitters in the brain do only one thing: They excite or inhibit nerve cells, and thus they control the "firing pattern" of nervous tissue. There are thousands of different patterns of such firings within the brain and elsewhere. Everywhere there are patterns and rhythms of activity. There are menstrual cycles, breathing rhythms, heartbeats, and cellular oscillations; even the microparticles (known as organelles) inside each cell have been found to be rotating and vibrating. Every particle of human life is involved in the "musical" activity of producing rhythmic waves of energy.

More obviously, the firing patterns within the brain can be driven by sensations coming from the "outside." Flashes of light or pulses of sound, touch, odors, or taste are well known for their ability to capture and "drive," or "entrain," rhythmic neural activity. For instance, repetitive drumming, sometimes known as "trance drumming"—performed in great variety in every corner of the world—is ritually used to implant new rhythms, by subduing and "taking over" personal rhythms. It does not take long in listening to classical Indian music to realize that such music—through intricate and interlocking beats, tones, and rhythms—actually operates on our neural codes and thereby works on our emotions. Literally hundreds of different vocal practices of chanting, singing, and recitation have been discovered to affect different regions of the body and to musically excite or calm the mind through harmonic manipulations and resonances.

Is it not possible that thoughts—obsessive and imperious thoughts, spinning and drumming thoughts, intensified and ponderous thoughts—could also pulse the neural pathways and thereby influence the physiological rhythms of the body?

There are, as well, many different "background" rhythms of spontaneous firing in every area of the brain. Even tissue cultures of cells isolated from the brain show spontaneous rhythmic firing. Such activity appears to be the inherent nature of the appropriately labeled "nervous" tissue. Brain-cell rhythms are usually observed to have "cycles" of activity. Some cycles, known as "circadian rhythms," are related to day and night, light and dark. These rhythms are also connected with the rhythm of the seasons. Some cycles occur hourly, or over minutes, seconds, or microseconds. Many of these cycles are suspected to be "driven" by the periodic "pulsing" of neurotransmitter substances, or neural "messenger" proteins, or by pulsing hormonal secretions in what seems to be infinitely complex feedback loops or self-regulating mechanisms. And all of these have some relation to the cycles and tempos of the organs in the body.

When a hallucinogen enters the body, or when the psychosis-inducing "cocktail" produces a neuro-chemical-electrical imbalance, it commandeers and plunders the intrinsic and "unconscious" rhythms of the body. The imbalance brings rhythms to the surface. It accentuates hidden rhythms; synchronizes and hyper-synchronizes archaic phylogenetic rhythms; "recruits"[81] and gathers weak and insensible vibrations into swelling waves and undulations, which then readily drive and pulse the tempo of "thinking." New and accelerated neural "pacemakers" become dominant, and it is now these to which thinking has to conform. The ordinary "stream of thought"—the "streaming" of ideas, mental images, thoughts, apparitions, daydreams—is disrupted by unprecedented rhythms. These new waves and their tempestuous frequencies are what overrun the normal frequencies and "open up" the nervous system to speeds of activity that, until then, had remained only latent. This speed reverberates within the nervous system and it becomes directly palpable as waves and undulations throughout the body and the mind.

For Michaux, the "temporary madman" (intoxicated by a hallucinogen) and the involuntary madman stunned by psychosis are both changed:

> But, whether they are for one hour or ten thousand hours, both
> of them are present in the throes of the same evil: in the same

inexplicable sea, an omnipresent agitated sea, from which they
cannot escape, with waves everywhere, a way of being themselves
a sea as much as in the seas or traversed by seas, a sea of things,
of time, of space, a new world with too many variables, in which
the idea is in the wave, in which observation and judgement are
in the wave, in which things and coordinates are in the wave, and
simultaneously in tiny and almost imperceptible, imprecise varia-
tion-undulations which abound, which superabound, which
harass the mind, prevent it from getting away from the 'waves'
phenomenon in which everything vacillates, oscillates, is fantastic
tumult, without frontiers, without delimitation, invading everything, but which remains secret and imponderable, jolts producing jolts, a tumult which makes everything tumultuous and stirs
up and provokes agitation, agitation for its own sake, and makes
the mind skid and slip in incessant false turns.[82]

Thus, enraptured and entrapped by waves, a second state of
mental functioning is accessed.

The Second State

In the second state, micro-operations are at liberty and without opposition. The increasing speed has both released and
unveiled them. In the normal state, they functioned under the
surface of the comparatively laborious progression of macro-
operational thinking. But under the conditions of imbalance and
acceleration, the ordinarily hidden fabric of the micro-operations begins to surface. They make their appearance one by one.
First comes the speed, then the repetitions, then multiplications,
and so on. Soon, these are all operating at the same time. The
result is complete dislocation, outside of time, in a foreign place,
where one is utterly alone, except, that is, for the uncanny presences caused by infernal animation.

Michaux called this another "zone" of consciousness. Basically, it is a neutral zone where *pure impermanence* is the only
governing law, indifferent and dispassionate toward the meteoric appearances and disappearances of thoughts and images.
This has previously been referred to as the "waking zone,"
where all mental activity can be seen with tremendous clarity
and precision. But this experience of the fundamental state of
intelligence is also "unstable" and does not usually last for very
long.

The neutral zone almost inevitably becomes colored by "fascination." Michaux said: "If madness is physical and biological, it is also fascination." Everyone knows of the possibility within oneself to become fascinated, not being able to "get it out of my mind" (call "it" a melody, a person, an image, a premonition, a fear, an impulse). It can occur in varying intensities. But in the second state one may experience the most extreme sense of "absorption" in an object; a feeling of being irresistibly drawn to, captured, and held by a real or imagined object, feeling powerless, or even bewitched. Concentration may become riveted. When the apparition of a naked woman appeared before John Perceval, beseeching him to follow her, it took all his strength and will power to violently tear his attention away from her. Michaux encountered "presences" from whom it was seemingly impossible to escape. When they "caught" his attention, "fixed" him in their gaze to the point that he became them, he no longer felt he had any volition of his own.

Patients transformed by L-dopa talk of a *crisis of fascination*. They often displayed an "uncontrollable watching," visually grabbing and grasping the object of gaze and "unable to relinquish it till it passed from [the] field of vision." One said, "It was uncanny. My eyes were spellbound. I felt like I was bewitched or something, like a rabbit with a snake." Another patient "would find that his entire attention had to be concentrated upon whatever object compelled his gaze: and this phenomenon was called 'fascination,' 'being spellbound,' or 'witch-craft.' " Ideas, images, or memories would repeat themselves in an "inner litany" that "could not be banished from mind during the crisis: they were reiterative, peremptory, overwhelming, and would exclude all other thoughts from her mind." Some were compelled to count. Some were absorbed in "nothingness." Sacks tells of one woman patient, in a state of "great inner stillness and of 'acquiescence'; her attention would dwell for hours on whatever object or thought entered its field; she would feel herself completely 'absorbed' and 'engrossed' by all of her postures, perceptions and thoughts" and would "spend hours and days and even weeks reliving peaceful scenes from her own childhood."[83]

As always, whatever happens in the mind is also intensely paralleled in motor behavior: "grasp-reflexes . . . became exaggerated, and caused forced grasping and groping of the hands, and a strong tendency for them to 'stick' to whatever they happened to touch."[84]

By "fascination" (as if becoming "fastened to") the neutral

zone is "split up" into multiple consciousnesses, into subzones, or subconsciousnesses. It can occur by fixation on a sight, sound, taste, smell, body feeling, or mind sensation. Each is capable of becoming an "entranced" consciousness—a "trance" zone. These trance zones are usually experienced in fluctuation from one to the other. The seemingly unitary consciousness of the "normal" state is torn apart at the seams within the second state, and each part can independently become fixed and entranced. Every one of these fixated states of consciousness can clearly be seen in the phenomenon of psychosis, where one might stare "into space" for hours, or listen intently for far-off commands, or feel locked into a body part, or be unable to escape from a body odor.

Absorption in the consciousness of thoughts and ideas can produce a unique form of rapture. Donald Crowhurst, crushed between the sea and the sky in his lonely machinations of calculation and deception, became intoxicated with "turning" thoughts and revolving ideas just as fixedly and hypnotically as any autistic child is "lost" in repetitive tappings and twirlings (called "twiddling"). "Lost" in this sense refers to a stupefied experience of mind-watching-mind, which watches mind-watching-mind, which watches . . .

But it is a fascination or absorption in particular ideas that leads to the zone of consciousness called manic consciousness. These ideas usually expand on virtues of one's SELF. It seems to be a most popular zone. The one in the second state is under the pressure of the micro-operations, with his world expanding, to the maximum, to the immense, to the infinite. He cannot "control" it, as Michaux said, "Immense is around him, is in him, is on him. Immense traverses him." His nervous system seems to be built on the principle of hyperbole, a "going to the limit." "But look," says Michaux,

> he is going to spoil everything . . . He is going to create a personal relation with that. (He can hardly be blamed. He is pretty much forced to.) He tries to find a suitable place for this excess and to live with it. How to find a suitable place for excess? An essential excess. Work suddenly appears to him petty (as do other people). He is in a reigning place. Sovereignty is in him . . . A little longer (how can he resist?), and finally, unable any longer to leave unfixed, impersonal, anonymous this prodigious monopolizing and supreme greatness, the secret which is choking him, being a

simple man who believes in simplifying and who believes he has
understood, he declares himself to be Napoleon.[85]

Or a saint, or a messiah, or the "greatest" of anything. He
feels he must call himself something! This invasion of sovereignty, which fills him with such excellence, could not long remain unemployed.

In a cascading expansion, without stopping or being able to
stop, he dilates to the maximum into every notion of himself,
"not one of which he can let pass without pouring himself into,
without stretching out in it perfectly." Every student of human
nature has commented upon a dormant and potential "omnipotence" within us, a space for Napoleon to fill. It isn't difficult to
find out how this space—now energized by manic consciousness—came to be. As for Michaux:

> His childhood, too, like that of so many others, gave free rein to
> his ideas of grandeur. What does the child want? To be every-
> thing, to possess everything, to attract everything, to taste
> everything, to overcome everything, to know everything, to run
> everything. To be loved by all, recognized by all. No less. Such
> is the child of man. Enough to produce dozens of deliria of
> grandeur and thousands of megalomanias. Humanity will always
> have a plentiful supply.[86]

Consider one poor woman who lives on the streets. She is
juggling assorted bags filled with remnants of possessions. She
calls them "objects of power." She is destitute, yet she parades
her self-sufficiency. Impudently, she asks for money to support
her "holy cause." She has an "urgent mission to fulfill" and an
"emergency message" that only she can deliver, a message that
"affects the WORLD," which swells in her, with which she is
bursting. Going to a shelter is beneath her, she says. The woman
has gone to an extremity of satisfaction and pride in having
joined a venerable tradition of wandering ascetics. She enjoys
and perhaps flaunts her "freedom of the streets." She berates
the authorities and will sacrifice even her life to expose their
abuse of power. In doing this, she declares herself a "maiden
warrior." It is simply inadequate and even misleading to speak
of her "grandiosity" or of her "folly of greatness." Instead, she
suffers from the folly of the enormous, an abounding energy,

dilating to the maximum, where everything is caught in surges of delirious expansion.

THE AUTISTIC ORDEAL

Michaux, the writer, painter, musician, and scientist of unique talent, has often been called a "genius." But there was always something "different" about him. He avoided notoriety as if it were a disease. In an age when artists are required to publicize themselves, he did just the opposite. Even as he was becoming well known in the Parisian art world, he gave very few interviews, restricted the publication of photographs of himself, and was often unreachable except by his closest friends. For many years he lived in a little room in a modest hotel. He rarely visited the cafés, avoided intellectual gatherings, and when he was finally and belatedly awarded one of France's highest literary honors (the Grand Prix National des Lettres, in 1965), he rejected it. Many thought he was simply eccentric. Others wondered about a deep-rooted pathology. But few people really knew him except for his almost-legendary tendency toward asceticism. In short, he lived like a recluse in the very heart of Paris.

Yet everyone who met Henri Michaux was struck by his dignified presence and uprightness, like a judge's. Younger poets who consulted with him spoke of his humility and courteousness. When the young Allen Ginsberg stopped in Paris on his way to India—thirty years after Michaux had done the same—he managed to meet with Michaux, who he later described as being "like all geniuses a man full of natural sympathy who could be trusted to approve enthusiasm, heart, common humor or any humane crankiness as long as it was unaffected . . . he was a benevolent presence on the planet."[87]

Michaux developed great compassion and was deeply dedicated to people who were in extreme mental suffering. He called them the "unfortunate ones" and "brothers, brothers without knowing it, no longer anybody's brothers." He seems to have easily identified with them. Mescaline had opened his mind to madness. This allowed him to "exchange" with the experience of those who must dwell in psychosis, to experience their ordeals. In almost every book he wrote after beginning his drug research, Michaux throws some light on the nature of psychosis. During the years of his hallucinogenic explorations he realized that he was becoming a translator for those in psychosis and at times he seemed to feel this to be his mission. Michaux says, "I will speak in their name." Perceval says, "I open my mouth for the dumb, who simply cannot speak for themselves." This compassionate action to offer one's own shattering experiences as knowledge to others is shared by every character in this book.

Michaux himself was not unfamiliar with psychological anguish. His childhood was filled with mental pain and he sometimes wrote sorrowfully about it: "from the abdomen of memory, from the depth of my being, from the depths of my childhood that never received its due and which three centuries of life could not satiate, so great were its needs."[88]

He entered the world in the small Belgian town of Namur, into a household that was simply and starkly inhospitable to him. He said that he was an "untouchable" to both his parents and that he experienced a coldness and emotional withdrawal all around him. In fact, his mother told him, "I wish rather you had never been born." He recoiled and withdrew: "From the age of six months, I was all refusal . . . I gritted my teeth in the face of life."[89] He said that he "rolled himself up into a ball," turned away from eye contact and deeply into himself, and dreamed deliriously of a "perfection" accessible only within himself. As best he could at the age of five, he strove for perfect self-sufficiency.

His personal and secret discipline as a child was to reject intimate contact with the world. He became the personification of what he called "refusal": "The thick lips of Buddha closed to bread and speech." He said, "The more I look back upon my childhood, the stronger is the feeling that I was a stranger in the home of my parents. My first words were to cry out that I was a foundling."[90] His parents did not know what to do with him. They consulted physicians who recommended that he be sent away from home, to a small country school where the ruggedness of life might stimulate him. There, in fact, his world was penetrated and he allowed himself to become domesticated: "Perfection gone, nutrition and comprehension came. At the age of seven he learned the alphabet and ate."[91]

In his pre-mescaline days Michaux often wrote stories about himself (as well as "everyman") through his imaginary characters. Two of them talk poignantly about refusal:

> Until he reached the threshold of adolescence he was a hermetic,
> self-sufficient little ball, a dense and troubled universe, closed to
> everything: to parents, to affection, to objects, their reflection, to
> their existence—unless they were turned violently against him.
> For 'they' hated him; 'they' said he would never be a man . . .[92]

The end result of that way of being is described by another
character:

> I am so weak (I used to be extremely so), that if I was able to
> coincide in mind with anybody at all, I would immediately be
> subjugated and swallowed up by him and entirely dependent on
> him; but I am keeping a sharp lookout, for I am dead set on being
> always very exclusively myself. Because of this discipline I now
> have a better and better chance of never coinciding with any mind
> at all and of being able to move about freely in the world.[93]

Years later, this pain of human confrontation is in full display
under mescaline:

> The effulgence of gazing eyes (of people in good health) hurts
> me like the pulverizations of a shower. I should like to unburden
> myself of their gaze, and yet it is not particularly inquisitive,
> reproachful or evil. What disturbs me is that I no longer possess
> what is necessary to stand up to the pressure of a normal gaze,
> and from this I suddenly understand in a different way the neces-
> sity, when one is weak or ill, of having gentle and pliant nurses.[94]

All the qualities that Michaux assigns to his early years—a fear
of encounter, a dread of reliance on others, a kind of vow of
solitude, refusal, anonymity, and a stubborn self-sufficiency—
are the dominant phenomena of what is known as infantile or
childhood "autism." In conventional diagnostic psychiatry autism refers to a relatively rare disease process of children and it
is now heatedly debated as to whether this is caused by brain,
genetic, or psychological abnormality. The medical researchers,
geneticists, biochemists, behaviorists, and statisticians seem to
agree among themselves that the autistic disorder is a reflection
of a brain dysfunction already present at birth.

Currently, there is a great deal of misunderstanding in regard
to the origins and treatment of childhood autism. Autism has
become one of those diseases in which there is hot pursuit for
a genetic "marker," and the highest awards of science could be
given for such a discovery.

But there is something suspicious about this claim of genetic determination, one that is increasingly being made also about psychosis, panic disorders, many addictions and compulsions, depression, even loneliness. The great strides that have apparently been made in genetic technology might intimidate any researcher who holds a determining view other than a genetic one. Also intimidating is the expectable bitter reactions from the parents of autistic children who feel that any view other than the genetic one will once again be used to "blame" them. Because of the competition for limited research funding and scientific prestige, there are many political overtones to this debate on the nature of autism.

The "politics" of this situation become clear when one considers the work of ethologist and Nobel laureate Niko Tinbergen.[95] His is the most impressive and meticulous observation ever made of autistic children and demonstrates that recovery is possible through intimate human care. Despite this, his work has been completely dismissed by the experts, and references to this work in the large literature on autism are almost nonexistent.

What is really at stake, of course, is the treatment and care of autistic children. Those who hold the genetic view cannot help but feel that autistic children are basically incurable unless their genetic and biochemical code can be cracked, and that medication is the only hope for easing their pain. Those who do not hold the genetic or brain damage view feel that they have seen autistic children fully recover even to the point of brilliance, and that intimate human contact is what makes it happen. These researchers generally feel that relying on medications for the treatment of autistic children may obstruct the process of recovery.

When the term *autism* was first introduced to the world of psychology by Eugen Bleuler early in this century, it was used to describe the fundamental dynamic of adult "schizophrenic" existence and the primary mechanism to which all other symptoms are secondary results. However, Bleuler always believed that autistic mechanisms were a universal feature of human nature and that normal and ill people differed only in the degree to which they manifested; in illness, a normal human mechanism had simply reached a pathological degree.[96]

More recently, Tinbergen and his wife, Elisabeth, have made precisely detailed observations of both normal and autistic children. They too conclude that autism is a common human dilemma, a pathological exaggeration of inherent and ordinary human tendencies. Normal children may have episodes of "temporary autism" when they are ill or abused or are involved in a paralyzing "motivational conflict" of whether to approach or escape. More subtly, at the very start of each new encounter with a new person or an unfamiliar situation, the ordinary child fleetingly displays at low intensity the same tendency to withdraw as does an autistic child. But with the ordinary child this response is soon "replaced by a less and less inhibited social or exploratory approach."[97] With autistic children, the withdrawal remains dominant and they live in an almost-continuous state of aversion, of keeping their distance: "It looks as if this distance-keeping is indeed their main concern in life; a thing to which they give constant priority."[98] These observations by the Tinbergens point to "a continuum, all the way from normal, through merely 'shy' or 'timid' or 'apprehensive' children, through very mildly and less mildly autistic children, to severe autists."[99]

The autistic child can take the tendency of withdrawal or refusal to its excess, to the point of a "cut-off" (the childhood, or elementary, form of "switch-out"):

> The child often fails to respond to stimuli that normally would make him approach but which his anxiety prevents him from actually acting on. Closing the eyes [gaze aversion] or (equally common) putting the hands over the ears is a mechanical means of achieving this 'cut-off,' but these children also protect themselves by a central nervous cut-off, by simply refusing to see or hear (without showing overt withdrawal) and perhaps even by actually not seeing or hearing.[100]

From what Michaux tells us of his childhood, he had an intimate appreciation for and understanding of autistic withdrawal and he became extremely sensitive to this state of mind in himself, and also in others. His studies with mescaline greatly increased this sensitivity and they add yet another dimension and meaning to the autistic process. Even in one of his last works, a study of the drawings of very young children, Michaux believed he could see the "marks," or the footprints, of their struggle with autism. From the beginning of life, Michaux implied, we have at our disposal the ability "to refuse," to withdraw our body, our senses, our emotions, or our awareness. Many children are secretly aware of this as a sense of "power." And many children, for one reason or another, cultivate their power of refusal to unusual degrees. The ones who become typically autistic are virtuosos of refusal. The autistic child develops an immense repertoire of means to avoid human contact. This begins with his gaze, the only protection he feels against the possible enslavement by another. Even in the little language he will allow himself to use, the autistically derailed child will refuse to use the pronoun "I," refuse to be pinned down and captured in an "I." Michaux believed he could find the embryonic forms of autistic withdrawal in the drawings of even the youngest normal children:

> Refusal. No to participation, to eating, to speaking, to walking, even to games . . . More strongly than one thinks, the child knows the temptation of stopping himself, of no longer letting himself be dragged along the developmental route down which he is being led, efforts which don't finish, does he continue? where does he stop?[101]

Like Bleuler and Tinbergen, Michaux saw autism not as a specific clinical disease, but rather as a "trait," which may be activated and make its appearance in many, if not most, children to one degree of intensity or another. In this view it is possible to think of a continuous spectrum of autism, from the "soft core" to the "hard core"; perhaps everyone shows the marks or scars of having been through a battle with autism. From the work of Bleuler, the Tinbergens, and Michaux, if geneticists ever do isolate the gene that makes one vulnerable to autism, they will probably find it in all of us.[102]

The crises that autistic children experience (terror, violence, and extreme fixation in another world) show all the signs and marks of their terrible struggle with the deranging micro-operations of the second state. Autistic children, too, have their own unique predicament, intention, exertion, substances, and mindlessness. They have recurrent periods of imbalance, when with a child's mind they attempt to cope or come to some equilibrium with the second state and manic consciousness.

Mescaline makes the autistic trait glaringly apparent. Enamored by an inner fascination with the excesses of the second state and magnetized by its micro-operations, one's autistic trait is exaggerated. It may appear to be an extreme introversion, but actually it is verging on an autistic "cut-off." Ordinarily, we are protected from such excess, but "if memories were not both fantastically rapid and almost unperceived, we would spend all our lives in them."[103] In the second state, eventually withdrawal and silence descend on one from the "excess of everything that one presently sees and feels, that one could never express. Autism through honesty."[104]

Michaux appears to have struggled with the residuals of a childhood scarred by an autistic disposition until well into his adult life. His recovery was gradual and painful. Eventually, writing and painting became vehicles through which he believed he could heal himself. "Readers trouble me," he said, "I write, if you like, for the unknown reader . . . I write to wander over myself . . . to travel through myself. To paint, to compose, to write, to travel through myself—that is the adventure of being alive." Yet there were doubts: "I hesitated about continuing to write. What I wanted was to be cured, as completely as possible, and to learn what is, in the last analysis, incurable." But it would not be until he began his work with mescaline that Michaux would discover what was truly "incurable." In this way he struggled against the universal roots of autism, which he found in himself.

At the age of twenty Michaux abandoned his medical studies and left his home in Belgium to work for two years as a seaman shipping coal in the North and South Atlantic. In 1928 he was trekking in the mountains and jungles of Ecuador. By the next year he was traveling in Turkey, Italy, and North Africa. A few years later, after both his parents died (within ten days of each other), he began to travel in earnest. For a year he traveled in India, staying in Calcutta and southern India, and then to Nepal; after that, to Ceylon, China, and Japan.

It was India that changed his life. In India he studied true spiritual disciplines, not simply the creative ones he was forging for himself, but ancient ways. He traveled alone. In northern India he studied hatha-yoga and breath control (pranayama) with a teacher he referred to as "my yogi guru." He wrote about this man who perhaps had some of the qualities of Michaux himself: "This extraordinary man, whose superb chest swallowed up quarts of air, which he then distributed into his soul, who seemed rather young in spite of his eighty years, had nothing of the saint about him either. He was above human misery, inaccessible rather than indifferent, with a kindness that was almost invisible, and also perhaps a slightly pained look like those persons who are suffering from gigantism, or who possess more talent than personality."[105]

In southern India, among the Tamils, Michaux learned from another who would lastingly affect his life, whose teachings would continue to permeate all his own writings and his psychology, perhaps more than he would ever realize. This person was Ramana Maharshi: a retreatant like himself, who at the age of sixteen entered lifelong seclusion and meditation and by middle age was renowned as a Hindu saint. At this time the seeds of the practice of meditation decisively entered Michaux's life. Even at the age of seventy-three, Michaux would say of India: "far away by now, comes back, absorbs me for moments, for long moments. The lands where 'Profound Peace' had its sovereign value have not left me. Profound invasion. Delayed invasion. Resurfacing."[106]

On returning from Asia he settled in Paris where he began to work with what he called his personal "weakness" in a new way. His writings took on a further mystical dimension: He wrote accounts of magical lands, cultures that were like personalities, and of people who were the embodiments of civilizations. His travels had aroused a global view of life: "Man needs a far-sighted aim, extending beyond his lifetime. A training rather than a hindrance for the coming planetary civilization."[107]

He married in his early forties. His whole world "opened up"; a new dimension of existence was revealed, a lightness and playfulness that he had increasingly come to believe was congenitally unavailable to him. He was unreservedly happy with his young wife. But during the food shortage of occupied France during the Second World War, she became ill with tuberculosis. Later, they traveled together in Egypt while she was convalescing. Then, after seven years of marriage, she died from the burns caused by a fire. A complication of the burns had led to a minute but lethal blood clot. Michaux had lost his only real companion. After the tragedy, he once again withdrew and "wrote less and less and painted more." What he did write were clearly songs of mourning. Several years later, at the age of fifty-six, mescaline entered his life.

In some ways, he was an unlikely person to have taken hallucinogenic drugs. He was temperate in his habits, which verged on asceticism. He said that he was "more the water-drinking type. Never alcohol. No excitants, and for years no coffee, tobacco, or tea. From time to time wine, a little. All my life, in the matter of food or drink, moderate. I can take or abstain. Particularly, abstain."[108]

Soon after Michaux began his explorations with mescaline and other hallucinogens, his experience of life and his own outlook on the world began to change once again. The change continued long after he ceased his drug "trials" and persisted and matured over the next thirty years of his life. Very few of Henri Michaux's readers realized (then, as now) the extent to which he had entered what can be called a journey of recovery from autism. In order to make this journey, Michaux became something of a "healer"; that is, in the original sense of the word, one whose intention and energy was to "give voice" to suffering people. He turned his whole life to the task of unveiling the nature of mind, which meant exposing both the madness and wisdom within "disoriented" mind, mind dislocated from its usual place. Historically, those who worked with and for mad people were called alienists. Henri Michaux became an alienist, and few have appreciated the alienated mind as well as he.

From within drug consciousness Michaux stood "on the bridge" that overlooked the operations of both madness and rationality. His particular intelligence was in his ability to accurately mirror and discriminate events and apparitions even when deeply shaken by the drug. From his painstaking self-observations he gives us the opportunity to exchange or identify with both the ordeals and brilliance of people in psychosis.

How did the drug experiences contribute to Michaux's recovery from an overly strong autistic trait? It happened in stages. What he learned, he said, he learned like a beginner, little by little, and by the end it surpassed anything he thought he would learn. He took varying dosages of mescaline under a variety of different conditions that he set for himself: sometimes in the mountains, or while reading, or in a research laboratory, or just lying in bed, even when physically ill.

At first, there was what he called a "great opening." In the days following his third experiment with mescaline he found that he was more talkative, less reserved, and less protective of his treasured anonymity: "For the first time in my life [I] preferred telling a secret to keeping it. Even worse. I could hardly wait to divulge secrets which I had promised myself never to reveal.

Releasing them was like a sort of ejaculation . . . I approached people wide open, enjoying laying myself open, of seeing them open."[109]

The autistic imprint and residual with which Michaux had lived until then was one in which he had come to take some satisfaction and pride: not giving of himself fully, of "keeping a certain margin of security," or what he called a "refusal to make the gift." It was not that his "social opening" was simply an aftereffect of the drug. It was the result of events that took place during the drug experience, when he practiced the means that allow "opening" to occur. In the throes of the drug Michaux discovered just how desperately he would cling to his familiar position of observer, tracker, and impartial recorder. From his earliest years, this had been his customary "position" in life. But it was being broken down, he was being dislodged, "thrown out of my dugout." When he tried to take notes, they were clearly the words of a madman. The more he tried to hold his identity of scientist-observer, the more the drug seemed to tear him apart, mock him. Michaux, in his identity as the impeccable drug traveler, the chronicler, was exposed in his deeply entrenched position of safety. It was a sophisticated "cover story" of aloofness and nonengagement, for what he called his "refusal." He realized that clinging to this niche was the source of his agony not only under the influence of the drug but also in the rest of his life. How painful it was for this humble man to face this hidden reservoir of arrogance.

By his fifth experiment with mescaline Michaux understood what was being required of him: "to let go, to let go of myself." Only some kind of "surrender," he felt, would allow him to go beyond his stubborn stronghold. The drugs, he found, gave him multiple invitations, and even instructions of a sort, to learn how to let go. (What Michaux was learning and trying to put into practice during his drug experiences has been previously described in the section "Mastering Mental Speed.")

He learned how thoughts, images, and emotions can pass with the rapidity of a bird in flight across the window of awareness. And he learned how to "let go" of them as they arose and began to repeat, then multiply and proliferate. He learned not to attach to either side of a micro-opposition. He learned how the power of infernal animation might trick him into false convictions. He learned to abandon ever-proliferating new identities. He learned the mechanisms of "fascination" and how to relinquish his grip; how not to yield to the onslaught of temptations; how not to believe in each new insight and enlightenment. He came to trust in the existence of a waking zone in his depths. In all, he learned that he had to cultivate his strength of nondistraction and that this alone could prevent his being blown about like a leaf in the winds of mind during the second state. This was Michaux's education in the fundamentals of "letting go."

> The screen of current realities, there was no longer anything upon it.
> The screen of history, there was no longer anything upon it.
> The screen of territorial survey, of calculations, of goals, there was no longer anything upon it.
> Liberated from all hatred, from all animosity from all relationship.
> Above decisions and indecisions beyond appearances
> here where there are neither two nor several
> but litany, litany of Truth
> of That of which no sign may be given
> beyond antipathy, beyond denial, beyond refusal
> BEYOND ALL PREFERENCE
> in the enchantment of absolute purity
> here where impurity can be neither conceived, nor felt, nor have any sense
> I heard the admirable, grandiose poem,
> the poem interminable
> the poem of the ideally beautiful verses
> without rhyme, without music, without words
> which unceasingly scans the Universe.[110]

Even long after he ceased his hallucinogenic explorations, Michaux's poetry bore the mark of his experiences with the drugs—both the tribulations and the ecstasies. In spite of experiences of "illumination," or "illimitation," he did not cling to them; in fact, he remained somewhat suspicious of them: "All the same, how strange it is, taking these short cuts! Infinity undeserved."[111] And by the time Michaux was sixty-two years old, he said, "I am less interested in the visions that people have with the drugs, now I am more interested in how they manifest their experiences after-ward, what they do with it later."[112]

After several years of experimentation with hallucinogenic drugs, Michaux abandoned them. He had "tracked" himself down to his core and he also realized how dangerous and "unmanageable" the drugs could be. He attended to his own slogan: "Rare indeed are the madmen equal to madness." Yet, he could not help but wonder whether small doses of psilocybin under the right conditions might not be of great benefit to severely autistic people, the "shut-ins," or those in the "psychosis of arrest." If such attempts at treatment have ever been made, their results have gone unreported.

The hallucinogenic drugs have already swept through a generation. By 1975 an estimated 7.5 million people had "experimented" with these drugs, and by now it is many times more than that.[113] Of course, for Michaux "the drugs" meant only a very special class of intoxicants: either the organic "hallucinogens" (as they are called, because of the energy and power that they release in the nervous system and the mind) or their essential chemical extracts, some of which have been synthesized in the laboratory (mescaline, psilocybin, lysergic acid). Now, after being illegal for almost thirty years, the open enthusiasm is over. Still, journalists and scientists of all kinds are attempting to document the cultural and individual psychological effects of the earlier excitement. The history of the usage of hallucinogenic drugs has been told many times, from anthropological, sociological, pharmacological, psychological, even political, points of view.

It would seem that the waves of interest in these drugs should have affected our culture's understanding of madness. But the effect has been paradoxical. Of those that took hallucinogenic drugs, many became curious about the nature of mind, and many others actually became frightened about their minds. Some were led to "spiritual" interests and became involved with meditation and other practices. Some people felt wounded by the drugs, experiencing an unknown and dreaded depth of paranoia in themselves. Millions of people have tasted their own madness and have glimpsed the possible horrors of their own egomania in countless "bad trips." Yet, many of the same people have felt they glimpsed a vast and indestructible sanity within themselves. After taking these drugs, some people experienced a curious sense of depression and impoverishment: a painful comparison and contrast between one's conventional, everyday state of mind and the nakedness and intensity of the drug experience. They were left with a vague apprehension that something was missing in ordinary life, a nostalgia for the drug and, eventually, a distant longing. There were some who came to a new appreciation and empathy for people enmeshed in psychotic states, and many of these have turned out to be especially skillful in working with the chronic mentally ill.

Today, psychiatrists and psychologists hardly ever refer to these particular drugs. The ancient hallucinogens have become associated with an international trade of humankind's great addictors—the "opiates," heroine, cocaine, and so on—that necessarily involve traffic in armaments and the struggle for control of many Third World countries. Each year there are new reports of clandestine drug experiments by certain governments, of secret experiments in which people have died, of chemical-warfare plans, of military stockpiling, drug wars, and cover-ups.[114] The hallucinogens have become associated in people's minds with international crime, squalor, misery, and an insidious pandering to addictive societies. The world of all mind-altering drugs is a dangerous world. It has always been a dangerous world. Even in Pre-Columbian Meso-America, when usage of hallucinogens was ritualized among the Aztec people, the drugs were restricted, their usage was controlled, and illegitimate usage was punishable by torture. With the coming of the conquistadors the drugs were seen as demonic and their use was prohibited and driven underground.[115] More recently, in the same regions, the covert use of the drugs by healers, curendaros, and sorcerers has been fraught with jealousies and bitter rivalries,[116] yet, these are the same drugs that are referred to as "medicine" among the native healing societies, in recognition of their "magic" and their power to heal, as well as their power to destroy if used improperly. Everything depends on their proper usage, and precious few native healers remain who know how to use the drugs for healing.

Even now, or especially now, it is risky to talk about the meaning of hallucinogens, except in the most trivial of ways. It was the risk that Michaux took upon himself. By saying that there is something vitally important to learn from the drugs, one may be charged with defending them, or promoting their popular usage and, ultimately, their trade! This kind of stigma has contributed to Michaux's unpopularity and relative obscurity, and to the threat of censure that he faced through the last thirty years of his life.

Compared to the methods of Henri Michaux, the current usage of these drugs is often promiscuous and haphazard, motivated by a particular restlessness (a "call to fragmentation," said

Michaux) as well as by psychological and spiritual greed. The historical records predict that just such degraded usage would be the end result of the ancient tradition of hallucinogenic healing when it became exposed to a materialistic culture.[117]

Psychosis is, as well, a risky and dangerous world and, just like the drugs, if investigated intimately it may have consequences that are deeply personal, and political, and can affect one's health. Henri Michaux dared to explore these drugs and to learn from them—as in ancient days when they were used to educate and instruct—and he knew that they were gradually changing the course of his life. He reported his findings faithfully and periodically in a series of documentations that are unparalleled in the history of the drugs.

At the age of eighty-four, a year before he died, Michaux made his last report on the hallucinogens. He was alone at home and found a packet of a hallucinogen left for him years ago by a young woman whose name he couldn't remember. What could have possessed him to do it? Almost a quarter of a century after having abandoned the drugs, he swallowed it! And then it was upon him again, "mysteriously thrown into gear," the waves, the dislocation, the ravages, the fear of insanity, the need for surrender, and also the "great gift" of another world: "A magnetized world, where even if nothing more of it remains one still feels the dense absence."[118]

PART TWO

THE MEANS
for RECOVERY

CHAPTER 5

Discovering Islands of Clarity

In Part One the development of madness was illustrated through four "parables" of psychosis—each one going into further microscopic detail. Now we return to the possibility of recovery from madness and also look at it microscopically, but now going from higher to lower power: from the microexamination of islands of clarity, in this chapter, to the macroanalysis of the therapeutic home in chapters 6 and 7. In the foregoing chapters I have tried to point out the universal moments of recovery that always exist in the midst of even the worst psychotic experience, for when we microscopically examine this experience, we also find the elements of recovery. These elements are at the very foundations of our minds; they are elemental to our intelligence.

For anyone to fully recover from psychosis, one must not only recognize and see through this awesome micromechanics of losing mind but must also become a student of the psychology of recovery. And, in its own way, the journey to recovery is just as dramatic and hectic as the descent into madness itself. Just as madness forces a confrontation with oneself, so does recovery. Moreover, recovery is not a temporary process, a fire through which to be burnished and then forever healed; it is an ongoing achievement in which one may have to face essential realities about oneself over and over again.

But anyone recovering needs to learn how to return to normal life on earth and needs especially to know the obstacles one faces. In this and succeeding chapters I hope to offer observations that might ultimately provide people in recovery with the means to learn these things, the means to heal themselves. These observations are generally based on the profiles of Part One and on other cases we shall meet in the following pages. Each has something to teach us about obstacles and healing, since each lived through many obstructions to recovery. We should make no mistake about this point: In the end, no matter how much help is provided, full recovery from psychosis requires valiant personal action and a lifelong commitment to health. Everyone recovering from psychosis needs to learn how it ";works." If not, as John Perceval warned, "their delusions wear out, their impulses waste themselves, but they relapse because they do not discover the secret of their disorder, they do not exercise the same scrutinizing spirit, or they are not taught by the same experiences which were given to me."

COMING OUT

From the view of an observer, the experience of recovery is not unlike a coming out, a tentative process in which the patient begins to peek out from his enclosed world. The way in which this process of recovery is "put together" is similar to the way the night heron builds its nest, as described by ethologist Konrad Lorenz: "Between the slightest intention movements, which only an expert sees, and the full behavior pattern that fulfills its biological function, there exists *every conceivable transition.*"[1] We could look at experiences of recovery from psychosis with the same precision since they also show every conceivable transition and successive approximation.

Lorenz continues: "A night heron sitting in the branches in early spring shows the expert the awakening of reactions pertaining to the year's propagation cycle by getting obviously and rather suddenly excited out of the deepest calm, bending forward, grasping a nearby twig with its beak, going through the building-in motions a single time, and relapsing the next moment, 'satisfied,' into its former repose." Moments of recovery often occur in much the same way. They may be tentative, quickly withdrawn, hesitant, practicing motions, as though by trial and error.

"If we watch even more keenly, we may perhaps spot the first traces of nest-building even earlier the following year; a fleeting fixation of a twig, together with a suggestion of the bent-over position that is often adopted in the nest later. From such rudiments, the full sequence of activities that leads to the building of a nest develops in the course of days and weeks, in a smoothly flowing transition." Similarly, moments of recovery begin to merge into a full sequence, and spread into many areas of one's life.

There is a moment in the midst of madness when things suddenly begin to make sense again. One feels that one has come back into oneself. One has become the "operator," as Henri Michaux called it. It is an island of clarity where one is suddenly freed from the fixed mind of delusion. Some people describe this as a feeling, almost a physical sensation, of "clicking in." Frequently this moment carries with it an uncanny confidence that the worst is over and that one will become well again. Sometimes the moment is fleeting, sometimes it endures. But however brief, moments of recovery from psychosis are universal experiences—yet everyone who suffers with psychosis experiences them and reacts to them in different ways.

Spontaneous flashes of clarity occur all the time during psychosis. They are generally experienced as moments of freshness of mind, or relaxation from intensified mind. These flashes represent a fundamental intelligence of the "intrinsic health" that exists beneath the psychotic delusions. All the characters depicted in Part One experienced many moments of recovery as spontaneous, natural events that interrupted the psychotic phenomena. These moments of "wakefulness" (alert awareness or connection with "reality") may manifest as doubts, sudden insights, awakenings, or clicking in. They are fragile moments, and they need to be acknowledged and respected. This simple act will greatly facilitate anyone's recovery from psychosis.

Even when one is well on the way to recovery, what Michaux called the "dislocating wound" of psychosis, the wound that leaves one estranged from conventional psychological moorings, may continue to exert its influence. The residuals from all that one has been through manifest themselves in a peculiar hypersensitivity as soon as one tries to reorient to the outside world. And once "outside," as Michaux said, "how quickly everything becomes complicated, irritating, and one cannot always control oneself."

In the immediate "coming out" stage, one's world seems incredibly fragile; one may feel broken, ragged, or simply worn out. The appalling quality of this first stage of recovery was described by John Perceval. He wrote that the mad person enters the world with a "child's sensitivity and an imbecile ability to control wild thoughts." A "child's sensitivity" refers to feelings of nakedness and vulnerability to hurt or insult. It also refers to an innocence or lack of comprehension about what on earth has just happened. The "imbecile ability to control wild thoughts" refers to how dreadfully damaged one feels in not being able to resist the enticements of "fascinations." This extremely excitable state has its origin in the *second state* of mental functioning; the micro-operations of the second state are still at liberty, although not presently dominant. Even as one comes to one's senses, physical and mental imbalances persist for several months at the least. Regardless of whether the psychosis that one is recovering from is of a long or short duration, it is important to have rest of a special kind. As I will explain, this involves resting the body, relationships, and one's mind.

At the beginning of recovery one feels an edginess, like a pull in two directions at once—into the world of human drama and into a dream world. At times both are equally accessible, and it is not always clear which way is forward and which way backward. This situation can last a surprisingly long time. Even after months of appearing free from delusions or "interferences," someone may still experience interruptions of consciousness that hold one in fascination and obsession. A word or words can set this off—particularly harsh, judgmental words.

This hyperexcitability is far-reaching. Just as the patient on L-dopa described in the previous chapter would get caught up in madly clapping her hands and could not be stopped, so a person recovering from psychosis can get caught up in ideas and emotions. Even moderate emotions may be felt as waves of energy rippling through the body. The speed of the second state is always accessible, easily aroused, and comes in surges. This is why many people who are recovering from psychosis appear to be so tentative. They fear they will become carried away too easily and react too quickly, especially to anger and the urge to withdraw.

It is obvious that under these conditions of vulnerability tranquil and stable surroundings are paramount to a healing environment. Perceval strongly advised that one be in a peaceful environment and with gentle company when attempting the demanding journey of recovery from psychosis. Unfortunately, this is not the usual situation faced by someone coming out of psychosis.

THE WISDOM OF HEALING ENVIRONMENTS

Joining Heaven and Earth

The impulse to create a healing environment to care for an ill person appears to be universal. It arises naturally because we possess a deep, sometimes intuitive, understanding that one's mind, body, and environment are enmeshed and interdependent.

Once after I had given a lecture on "environmental treatment," a young man described to me how he had attempted to help a childhood friend who had been hospitalized for an acute psychosis. He visited his friend in the hospital and found that he was getting worse; his friend continually resisted medications and tried to escape. The young man managed to take his friend out of the hospital, and together they went to live in the woods. They were both experienced woodsmen; they set up a campsite of tents and a fire pit. For a month they fished and cooked and took hikes and talked long into the night. The young man said that the experience was extremely difficult; his friend's mental turmoil was exhausting to him, and he often doubted his own sanity and ability to continue. But their mutual love of the woods and the mind-stabilizing effects of natural living prevailed. His friend recovered enough so that he was able to return to his family and gradually resume his life.

In another instance, I discovered that the friends I was visiting—a couple with two young children who lived on a small farm in Nova Scotia—had taken in a distant relative, who for over a year had been almost catatonic in a Toronto hospital. The relative was quiet and obviously struggling against a tendency to withdraw, but also very intelligent and hardworking. He managed to live in a tent behind the house and helpfully tended the goats and cared for the children.

The healing potential of such environments is well known in the back country of traditional societies. A seemingly primordial urge to heal through an extended family has led to the development of many healing clans, medicine families, and healing circles among the indigenous peoples of the world. From the Alaskan Inuit to the African !Kung, from the Mung of the Vietnamese mountains to the Sioux of the American Great Plains—the basic healing environment consists of a circle of people who encouraged healing through the *"joining of heaven and earth."* In the principle of "heaven" we find awareness and attention to the spiritual dimensions of life, and the "earth" principle in the sacredness of all the elements and the preciousness of the human body. Heaven and earth can be joined by the human activities of ritual, attention to detail, and compassionate relationship. This is referred to as the "man" principle, which brings heaven and earth together. Wherever these activities occur, a place of healing is created.

What might be thought of as the quintessential healing environment is represented in the traditions of the Lakota Sioux. Most descriptions of Native American healing ceremonies focus on the power of the ceremony to cure by achieving a dramatic removal, or exorcism, of illness. However, my own experience of the healing ceremony has led me to another view: The ceremony portrays a drama of healing in a universal way, through which the ill person is first instructed in the decorum of confronting illness. The crux of the ceremony lies in the joining of heaven and earth through a variety of rituals. Examples of these rituals are given by Black Elk in his outline of the seven basic Lakota ceremonies.[2]

The people being healed may experience the ceremony as a singular event in their lives and something to be reflected upon for many years afterward. The ceremony may allow for someone to experience an opening or expansion beyond a preoccupation with illness. In such moments that are like the ventilation of fresh air, mental and physical energies can become *balanced.* But beyond that dramatic experience, the ceremony imparts timeless instructions—through chants and rituals—about how to join heaven and earth in one's everyday life. The ceremony is an expression and celebration of a pathway to recovery, which can be followed throughout one's life. It is meant to strengthen and empower the ill person to take the necessary steps to recover from illness. It also empowers the other participants to help in the healing process.

Explicit instructions about how to heal oneself are given. Sometimes these need to be interpreted and elaborated later by the medicine man or one of his attendants. The instructions are always about how to live in balance, and they concern three areas: diet, behavior, and working with one's mind. Diet refers not only to what one eats, but to when one eats, and to recommended herbs and medicines. Behavior encompasses one's decorum in the world: relationships with other people and to one's own body and livelihood. The instructions for working with one's mind are more complex. They are an injunction to follow the disciplines of a "warrior": to maintain a sense of wakefulness within the dream of life; to directly experience fear and the continual presence of death; and to arouse a faith in the existence of inherent sanity, the goodness of all beings, and the sacredness of man's ability to join heaven and earth. In the Lakota Sioux tradition, this experience of the sacredness of the world is called *wakan.* In the Buddhist tradition, it is called *bodhicitta,* or awakened heart.

In our postnuclear age, when the deterioration of values is a universal lament, these ideas may seem quite romantic. But these ideas and experiences are too elemental to be merely romantic; they are part of our human heritage, and they have great power. They allow us to translate "healing" and "balance" into contemporary treatment situations in a way that no other psychological or social theory can.

The Tradition of the Alternative Hospital

One of the modern-day applications of these traditional ideas is the "alternative hospital." No one really knows how many such hospitals there are (or have been), especially because they are usually short-lived. Perhaps the most famous and infamous of all was Kingsly Hall (located in London), which was directed by the late Dr. R. D. Laing and lasted for about five years. Obviously, these "alternatives" are not conventional hospitals, but their work is inspired by the original intention and spirit of hospital care.

The concept of the hospital as a specialized place in which to treat many ill people has a long and formidable history. The idea first arose in the third century B.C., when the wrathful Emperor Asoka—ruler of the entire subcontinent of India—was converted to Buddhism. After his conversion, Asoka devoted his life and the great treasury of his kingdom to humanitarian projects (much to the consternation of his heirs). He established the first centers for treating people and animals and for cultivating botanical medicines, which even then were vanishing. In an outpouring of compassion and generosity, Asoka also developed hostels and hospices for the care of wanderers and poor people.

The notion of creating hospitals passed from India to the Greeks. The famous hospital founded by Hippocrates on the island of Kos is on a mountain overlooking the Aegean Sea. The mountain paths, lush pine forests, and white temple buildings all express the intention to join heaven and earth.

Another venerable healing center in the Western world arose in the township of Geel, Belgium, in the fourteenth century. Geel is a magical name in the history of hospitals. The legend is that in the late sixth century a king beheaded his daughter and her companion near the settlement of Geel: "It is reported that these cruel deeds so greatly frightened several lunatics who witnessed them that they became cured, is if by enchantment."[3] Over generations, Geel became a pilgrimage site and a haven for mad people. At first it was organized by the Catholic church but then was directed by the local government. The patients were entrusted to householders (*nourriciers*) and there was a smooth interchange between foster families and a central infirmary. It has undergone many phases of development and expansion in its millennial history. At one time almost four thousand mad people lived there, many of whom were escapees from what was called asylum "barracking." It must have been very difficult to supervise such a community; there were many abuses. But there were many virtues that were talked about at the time: "They were concerned with the concept of liberty, literally in the 'free air,' the absence of restraint, and the possibility of living a happier, healthier, and more useful home life than in the traditional asylum."[4] There were also opportunities for employment, for patients to be able to pick up and continue their former occupations and live "a more familiar life-style than that permitted in the asylum which was part palace, part barrack, and part prison."5

Geel was the first organized "alternative" of homelike foster care in the world, and never since has it been done on such a large scale. It should be noted that, for the compassionate people of Geel, this practice of homelike care has continued to be their vocation to the present day.6

As the hospitals of Western Europe were secularized—that is, as they became dissociated from the principles of heaven and earth—they became well known as dangerous places. Hospitals became warehouses for the "unwanted": poor people, disabled people, prisoners, and mad people alike. Early accounts describe them as places in which to die, and the term "hospital fever" was coined to refer to the deterioration of health caused by the accumulated noxious exhalations of many physically and mentally diseased people.

But might not one ill person, living in an environment with many healthy, caring people, benefit from the overwhelming sanity and health of his or her environment? Perhaps this was the belief of George Fox and his Society of Friends, who spearheaded what was called the "moral treatment of the insane." Fox and his supporters held that the caretakers of the insane should not only be medical doctors but also spiritually advanced people, capable of relating directly to the spiritual and religious confusion that Fox believed was at the very heart of madness.

This movement, too, was beset by all the reflexlike tendencies toward an "asylum mentality" and an asylum environment. But though the movement was short-lived, it planted seeds for the future. When the "lunatic doctors" (of Perceval's time) visited both the community at Geel and the York Retreat (where Fox's moral treatment was being carried out), they came back with mixed reports. Some said that they had observed the most advanced and humane care of mad people, others reported that each community was as degraded as a conventional asylum. Yet, some visiting doctors later became supporters of the English and Scottish "cottage systems," which were small communities of foster homes for people recovering from psychosis.7 The domestic family model of Geel was their prototype. All these "alternatives" lasted only a few years because of fierce opposition from the leading asylum psychiatrists, one of whom called them "utopian and absurd." These systems also passed into oblivion, but, needless to say, John Perceval was a vociferous advocate of the domestic cottage system of treatment, especially since he was fortunate enough to live in and make his final recovery in one such alternative center, Seven Oaks.

Another alternative hospital was established at the old monastery at Rhineau, Switzerland. In the late 1800s, Dr. Eugene Bleuler, one of the founders of modern psychiatry, converted the monastery grounds and buildings situated along the Rhine into a community for treating the chronic mentally ill. It was a radical social experiment, where staff and patients worked together on farms and recovered patients could bring their families to live.

Such "alternative" care, in spite of much official criticism, continues to survive as a viable tradition. Just as the care at Geel continues to survive (although now reportedly in great danger because of local industrialization), so do the many seeds that Geel planted by its model and inspiration. But even more so, this tradition is guaranteed survival because it is a spontaneous and continually creative response to the needs of people recovering from psychosis.

When I informed Eugen Bleuler's son, Manfred, of our attempts at creating the Windhorse healing communities, he said that he and his father had always "dreamed" of creating such treatment teams at the Burghölzli Hospital in Zürich, but many hundreds of admissions a year made it impossible.

RECOVERING IN A HOSPITAL

Creating the proper environment for recovery from psychosis requires some degree of planning and foresight. Before I had set up the treatment situation I am about to describe, I had very little experience with designing a therapeutic home environment. I probably would never have attempted such a thing were it not for an unusual and auspicious combination of events.

A woman I will call Andrea, who lived in a small farming community about two hundred miles from my home in Colorado, phoned me to ask if I would treat her sister. The sister, Karen, was twenty-nine years old and in an acute psychotic crisis. Karen had been in psychosis several times during the preceding twelve years and had been hospitalized, usually for several months and once for three years. The two sisters were very close; twice when Karen was in crisis, Andrea had managed to care for her at home. Together they saw the crisis through without hospitalization. But this time, because Andrea had young children, she could not devote the energy and time she knew would be needed for her sister's care.

I hesitated to become involved with this treatment proposal because I knew from past experiences just how consuming such a case could be. I agreed to consult for a period of ten days and helped to arrange for Karen to be admitted to the acute ward of a small, private hospital in Boulder. My intention was to evaluate her there and then to come to a conclusion about where she might best be treated. Throughout our negotiations, I had the uneasy feeling that Andrea was really expecting me to do more than that.

As soon as I began meeting with Karen, I realized that she was not the burned-out, chronically ill person her dismal hospital records had led me to expect. She was as vitally alive as anyone I had ever known. She was a strong, well-built woman who, when I first saw her, was in a frantic argument with her "other world" in the middle of the hallway of the hospital ward. But then, with what seemed to take great effort, she stopped in order to relate to me. That impressed me. I could not help but think of this action as coming out of some kind of primitive courage.

Karen seemed to be in the midst of a psychotic transformation and probably was involved in the phases I have previously called *insight and power* and *beyond the law* (see the seven stages of psychological transformation, chapter 3, page 111). She immediately included me in the cosmic story line she had devised to account for what was happening to her. It was a complicated plot in which she was being elevated to a supernatural place in the order of things by the power of love. From the beginning, she called me "Dr. Love" in front of everyone, and I could never tell if she knew that it always embarrassed me.

Being alone with someone who seems to be filled with electricity and living in the realms of the "great speeds" was familiar to me. Nevertheless, I felt on the edge of panic when in Karen's presence. I felt pathetically and dangerously slow in all my internal and external reactions. At moments, I felt I might become dizzy and incomprehensible or I might sink into some retarded state. Then my impatience would lash out, and I would catch myself with a gasp or a deep sigh. Each time I had this experience I was confronted with the same fears; it was as if all the images I carried within me of my own insanity were being played back to me. In working with Karen I knew that I might not remain in one piece. My experience in the realm of healing had shown me that there is little possibility of one's patient recovering from psychosis without a simultaneous recovery on the part of the healer. The healer will be dragged out before himself. If the patient is truly to progress, he must fully express his feelings about the healer, and once again confront him with his hidden multiplicity of selves: professional, arrogant, humble, frightened, despondent, sane, and insane.

I wound up working with Karen in the hospital for the next four and a half months. I met with her several times a week and with the hospital staff as often as I was able to bring them together. The hospital staff was clearly uncomfortable with the intensive individual psychotherapy that I was accustomed to practicing, and at times the staff was quite suspicious of me. I had very little control over Karen's environment, and I felt subject as much as she did to the hospital requirements and conditions—such as frequent changes in room and roommates, behavior controls, inadequate diet, and the general inflexibility that characterizes most modern hospitals.

Karen struggled most of the time against what she felt was "demonic" possession, yet at other times she was engaged in feelings of tremendous bodily bliss. Before my eyes she was beset by surging speed, repetitions, multiplications, proliferations, oscillations, infernal animations, delusional convictions, and so on. She lived within a rampage of the micro-operations. I did my best to help her acknowledge these phenomena—to demystify them—as they were continually unveiled and let loose.

During our meetings together, Karen was filled with delusion. My only choice was to become as familiar with her world of magic and chaos as I was hoping she would become with my mundane world of eating, walking, talking, bathing, and sleeping. But that took a long time. Her lack of sleep became frightening and potentially life-threatening. After two weeks during which she got almost no sleep at all and experienced escalating maniacal excitement, I felt desperate to find a sedative that would work. I shared my dilemma with a senior physician who was visiting at the time, and he suggested that I give her intramuscular Valium and, most importantly, stay with her while it took effect. I followed his suggestion that night, and Karen slept well for the first time. She had little problem sleeping after that.

Much of the time, Karen was a "behavior problem" on the

ward, and when she became threatening to the staff or to other patients she was put into the seclusion room, as was the custom at the hospital. Seclusion was the hospital's idea of "rest," or of behavior control that would "isolate offensive behavior." It was felt that somehow she would learn something by being isolated. But it didn't work.

I dreaded having to meet with her in that seclusion room. But I knew that I had to spend time in there with her to see what it was like. Nowhere was she more insane than in that room. I was painfully reminded of everything John Perceval said of his own experience of seclusion and of being strapped down. When in seclusion, he wrote, he lost the last shred of control over his mind and he was swept over by oceans of tormenting delusions. He called it "the scene of my horrors." It looked to me like Karen was living through the same thing, but she went further. She virtually threw herself into insanity. She no longer tried to live in "two places at once"; she seemed to give herself over completely to the other side. At no time did I feel more hopeless about Karen than in the bleakness of that seclusion room. During my visits with her there, my own mind raced with thoughts of death or sank into an unearthly calm and detachment. My own autism reared its head.

In spite of everything, there was hardly one hour among all the hours I spent with Karen in or out of the seclusion room in which she did not exhibit moments of recovery. They could come at any time. As far as I could tell, they were associated mostly with those times when I relaxed with my own state of mind—whatever that happened to be—when I was more accepting and gentle with her. These were usually very tender moments, filled with an inexpressible sadness. And sometimes they were moments of great hilarity; we laughed so much that people outside the room wondered what kind of "therapy" was taking place. However, each time we came to a point that proved to be too much for her, when her emotions would surge into delirious expansion and enthusiasm. I came to think of these moments as experiences of "recovery running wild." Karen would again become caught up in a rush of hallucinations.

It was not simply that Karen had moments of lucidity and rationality. She experienced some profound moments and sometimes prolonged periods in which she recognized with penetrating insight into her illness exactly what she needed to do to get well. At these moments she felt deep compassion for herself, the other patients in the hospital, her parents, and for all the great suffering in our world today—a suffering that she would feel most agonizingly at these times. But this, too, was subject to "expansion"; the original moment of recovery was lost in a wave of micro-operations, overrun by a bombardment of unceasing thoughts, images without intermission.

Sometimes the genuine sadness and remorse she felt intensified and expanded into self-hatred and depression and was enacted in her psychotic world through voices and hallucinations that accused her not only of minute infractions but also of crimes that she could never imagine committing. At other times, her sense of sadness and tenderness expanded into "sovereignty" or the "space of Napoleon" (to use Michaux's words), and she found it impossible to resist bringing the message of love to the world.

At first, it was difficult for me not to be disheartened by the arising and sudden collapse of these moments. But then I realized that there was a continuity to these moments; they had a life of their own. They were islands of clarity in the midst of an ocean of psychosis and they were connected beneath the waves. In any case they were good, no matter how long they lasted, and very gradually they began to accumulate and coalesce.

I gave Karen medication with the aim of allowing her to gain some control over her excitement, but I was always uneasy that it might also obstruct her clarity. I was under increasing pressure from the hospital to use more medication when her excitement was too great for the staff to tolerate. It is an accepted practice to give more medication (or to add new medications) at such times. But as I increased the dosage of her "major tranquilizer" Karen actually got worse, as if some sort of paradoxical reaction was taking place. During this time, my meetings with Karen became tortuous. Once when I left one of them to write a brief note at the nursing station, all I could write was "Totally fragmented!" Soon after that I realized that Karen was actively counteracting the medication in a peculiar way.

From the start she had hated the medication and always resisted taking it. But now, she no longer complained about it at all and took it without hesitation. I began to feel that she was actually transforming the antipsychotic drug into an excitant and that her psychosis thrived on it. I had previously suspected that such a thing was possible, but now I was sure of it. There seems to be a way in which the effect of a sedative, tranquilizer, anticonvulsant, or antipsychotic drug can be fought off, flipped, and used as fuel to gain more speed and energy. When I reduced Karen's medication and held it steady, her escalation stopped.

When Karen began to have more frequent "clear days," I again switched the logic of the medication. Instead of giving her smaller doses, as befitted her improved clinical state, I steadily increased them. Each time she had a prolonged period of clarity, I increased the dosage slightly; when she was more chaotic, I decreased the dosage. In this way her medication dosage increased gradually.

Once as I watched Karen eating a meal with several other patients at a long table in the middle of the hospital ward, I was dismayed by what looked more like animals at a trough than people eating a meal. I was reminded of a scene in Goya's painting of madmen and John Perceval's description of mealtime among "lunatics." After that I occasionally arranged for Karen to eat dinner in her room with a nurse whom she liked. Together they had a meal on a card table with a tablecloth and flowers, and their interactions were almost completely lucid and mutually enjoyable. Karen accepted easily and appreciated this arrangement of her environment and the introduction of homeyness into her life.

Meanwhile, it was becoming obvious to everyone concerned with her care that soon Karen would have to leave the hospital and continue her recovery in another setting. But where and how were big questions for me and her family. Andrea believed that if we all worked together we could put something together in Boulder. First we would assemble a "team," then find a roommate, and finally combine it all in a household. Naturally, all the personal and professional risks of undertaking this unusual venture dawned on me, and many colleagues and friends cautioned me about the legality and liability of taking on this responsibility. But nothing else made more sense.

In spite of my many doubts, I found that two important experiences had given me the confidence to go forward with this new project. I felt that I was actually learning something about treatment environments and how they can promote sanity or cause chaos. A year before I met Karen, I brought my mother to live in Boulder. While living alone on the East Coast, she had aged and deteriorated rapidly. She had been overmedicated with insulin for diabetes, and she was becoming hopelessly senile. In Boulder, I arranged a home-care situation for her.[8] She lived in

her own apartment with a roommate, and she had several hours
of attendance and good company each day. Through my
mother's situation I saw the powerful effect that a healing home
environment can have on the process of recovery.

Five years earlier I had visited the Lakota Indian medicine
men of the Black Elk lineage at the Rosebud Reservation in
South Dakota. I had witnessed the traditional wisdom of these
men in forming healing communities or medicine circles. I
learned how such healing communities can arise spontaneously
and function with great simplicity and dignity. And I recognized
an essential element of these small gatherings: Although they
are ostensibly dedicated to the recovery of one individual, in
reality they are committed to the health and well-being of the
entire community and every individual in it. This memory of the
true meaning of healing community cut through all my hesita-
tions and provided guidance as I went about creating a home-
care situation for Karen.

A home-care team came together more quickly than I had
anticipated. Simultaneous with my work with Karen in the hospital, I directed a small supervision group of eight graduates of the
Naropa Institute master's program in psychotherapy. Everyone
in the group was working with highly disturbed people in a
variety of treatment settings, and we had been meeting weekly
for two years to share our experiences. The group had become
very close and had many common bonds. All the members of the
original group and most of those who later joined the home-care
team had trained themselves for some years in the principles of
heaven and earth. We were students of Buddhism, practiced the
discipline of mindfulness-awareness sitting meditation, and attempted to bring the psychology and practicality of the meditation process into all aspects of our lives. One of the key influences on the group was the study and practice of what are known
as the Shambhala teachings.[9] These are ancient teachings, based
on Buddhism, that focus on creating healthy societal structures.
The Shambhala teachings are similar to Confucian teachings in
that the creation of a naturally balanced household is itself considered a spiritual journey.[10]

To this group, I presented the idea of discharging Karen from
the hospital and establishing her in a "therapeutic home," and
to my great surprise, every member of the group wanted to be
part of the therapeutic team.

Karen's reaction to this development was mixed. Mostly, she

was frightened of having to relate to so many new people and asked, "What will we all do together?" This turned out to be exactly the same question that the newly formed team asked: "What is our 'work' with Karen? What are we supposed to do?" I had no answers for these questions; somehow I trusted that we would figure all that out once we had begun. One evening, after a supervision group meeting, we all drove to the hospital to meet with Karen, who prepared for the occasion by trying to look sophisticated. We met in a large room and formed a circle. Karen had reactions to each member of the group and was blunt in her expression of feelings. The meeting was filled with awkwardness, friendship, and good humor. We agreed that from then on one team member would go to the hospital to meet with Karen for a three-hour period each day. It is unusual for a hospital to accept the introduction of a different style of treatment alongside their own, but the hospital administration graciously agreed to this arrangement. Immediately after the group meeting with Karen I experienced a great relief on finding that I was no longer alone in my work with her.

In the meantime, Andrea contacted a friend of hers, Marcy, who she felt was just the right person to be a roommate in the therapeutic home; Marcy was tolerant, kind, and capable of managing a household, and she very much wanted to leave her current home in Los Angeles and make a change in her life. Marcy arrived in Boulder along with her young daughter and sister, and she began to meet with Karen at the hospital. Together they looked for a house to rent and soon found a small, detached house on a tree-lined street. Two weeks later, I discharged Karen from the hospital and as we drove to her new home we were mostly quiet; we seemed to be equally uncertain as to how this adventure would turn out.

THE WINDHORSE PROJECT

Suddenly I was responsible for another household: Not only was I caring for my own home and supervising my mother's care, I now felt responsible for Karen and Marcy as well as Marcy's child and sister. This situation forced me to examine my ideas about proper patient care. It gradually dawned on me that the only way to manage all of this was by using the metaphor of the healing ceremonies at Rosebud; I had to expand my view of treatment to include entire household environments rather than just the patients within them.

We named our group "Windhorse." In the Shambhala tradition Windhorse refers to a mythic horse, famous throughout central Asia, who rides in the sky and is the symbol of man's energy and discipline to uplift himself. Windhorse (Tibetan: *lung.ta*) is literally an energy in the body and mind, which can be aroused in the service of healing an illness or overcoming depression. A small Windhorse flag usually flies in front of the homes in the villages of Tibet, Nepal, and northern India and symbolizes the joining of heaven and earth within the household.

While the therapeutic home was being established, the team no longer had questions about what their therapeutic work was to be. All attention shifted toward establishing a homesite: stocking the kitchen, finding and borrowing furniture, unpacking, cleaning, shopping for food, and decorating. It was hard and exciting work; it had the flavor of an old-fashioned barn raising, a new beginning.

The fact that even a strong, athletic woman like Karen became easily exhausted was completely understandable. That she required such a great deal of sleep—often twelve hours a day—was a surprise. Karen herself was quick to distinguish when the time she spent in bed was necessary and when it gradually became a cocoon, a shelter from the world. Often she experienced a fear ("like ice water in the veins") upon awakening from sleep and had to stay in bed under the covers. Fears of every variety became the topic of our meetings together. In psychosis, she displayed a primitive fearlessness; in recovery, she was overrun by fear.

Our healing circle took further form when the entire team—Karen and I, the eight team-therapists, and the roommates (usually, just Marcy)—started to meet together weekly. These were planning meetings but they also quickly became very personal. Whenever family members visited, we met with them in the context of this group. The team celebrated together on birthdays and holidays. There was no formula for what we did together, although each meeting of the team did include a review of how the house members and team members were fairing. Clearly, Karen was suffering from a massive desynchronization of body and mind as a result of her "imbalance," and when we were with her we also tended to experience similar glimpses of desynchronization. Together at meetings, we were able to talk about how to take proper care of ourselves and how we might transmit this knowledge to Karen.

And it was not just Karen and her household that benefited from these discussions. Each team member's own household began to show the signs of a healing environment. We found that we were able to practice in our own homes and relationships what we were learning as a team. At the same time, we became extremely aware of our sudden eruptions of asylum mentality; we had to continually monitor our own insidious tendency to form an asylum around Karen. For example, our secret pride in making this rescue operation happen carried the danger of shutting ourselves in, turning more inward to our group to the exclusion of the outside world.

Our work with Karen in the therapeutic home lasted for four months. She was reintroduced to her life and she did well. Though the team effort gradually wound down, for years afterwards Karen continued her friendships with several team members. She continued to live with Marcy for another year, during which I worked with her on an individual basis.

Even before we disbanded Karen's therapeutic household, we had decided to create another healing environment if the opportunity arose. At about that time a young man was referred to us who was on the verge of being discharged from the state hospital to the streets. We set up a therapeutic home for him; and while that was going on, we arranged still another one. By the time we created the third household we had made a conscious decision to commit ourselves to further develop our therapeutic model. At one time we had five such households functioning simultaneously and a combined staff of over thirty people. The organization was formally named Maitri Psychological Services, Inc., (*maitri* means friendship and warmth) and was known informally as the Windhorse project. During the six-year life of this organization, we treated a dozen people in this way. From our point of view, our work was successful: We had given all our patients a wonderful opportunity to change the course of a chronic illness, and—in spite of many difficult times—most of them did just that. We were confident that everyone who took part in our healing community—clients, their families, and the staff—had greatly benefited from it, at least during the time we worked together. Our follow-up studies indicated that most of our patients continued on a process of recovery by integrating Windhorse principles into their lives.

Gradually, a specialized discipline for team therapists had come about to help people in recovery develop a stability of mind and an ability to rest the mind through a great variety of means and in every aspect of living. We began to think of this as *principles of basic attendance.* As we steadfastly maintained our overall focus on the health and sanity of each household environment, eventually the principles of a *therapeutic home* evolved. These are the topics of the next two chapters.

During the next six years we learned a great deal about the care and treatment of people in psychosis. Everyone felt that the camaraderie among the group members was truly remarkable and that it had affected our lives deeply. Needless to say, the work was also difficult and time-consuming. At least one household was having something of a crisis at any given time, and when two households were in crisis simultaneously, my personal life came to a standstill.

We had created, without intending to, a small hospital, and with all the problems that go with it. As time passed, we experienced the enormity of administrative detail common to every modern hospital, regardless of its size: corporate regulations, payrolls, medical-legal liabilities, insurance coverage for all occasions, restrictions imposed by third-party payment, marketing, and so on. And we found that during this period of being forced to become a "business," it was only through constant vigilance that we could maintain the integrity of our treatment program.

Eventually, a time came when the three therapeutic homes that were in operation were approaching closure at about the same pace. At that point, instead of choosing to go further into the hospital business, I made the difficult decision not to accept new patients—to finish our work with the remaining patients and then to disband the healing community. My personal plan was to take some time to study and integrate this unique experience and to communicate what I had learned by way of writing this book.

RECOVERY FROM MEDICATIONS

By the time Karen left the hospital, she was on a large dose of antipsychotic medication (Stelazine, 80 mg a day). One week after she entered her Windhorse home, I began the steady and incremental reduction of the medication, until at the end of three months she took none. This was a somewhat quick withdrawal, but I felt that Karen had the courage and the right state of mind to do it. Above all, she hated the medications for what they did to her body and mind. The withdrawal required not only a great deal of effort on her part, but also a sense of risk for her team. In a similar way, all the patients we worked with in the Windhorse project were more or less withdrawn from their medications. This is one of the goals of the Windhorse style of treatment.

Currently, there is great debate as to whether it is advisable to remove the medications that some believe to be the "life-support system" of those who have been on a long-term program of medications. Some feel that it is even morally and professionally reprehensible to do so. It is both a critical and complex issue involving treatment philosophy, the law, social policy, and a huge psychopharmaceutical industry. This combination of social factors has produced enormous debate and confusion about the medications. The proper usage of the chemicals has become *the* public health issue in psychiatry today.

The view against medication withdrawal is counterbalanced by many former patients who have been forced to take the medications for extended periods, and who warn of the dangers. For people who are on "maintenance" medications, the natural history of the drugs becomes bound up with psychosis itself. Chronic usage of the medications leads to a readjustment of one's brain physiology and microanatomy. The drugs become part of one's brain-mind system and produce an unstable state. As was seen in the case of L-dopa, patients frequently cannot live with them or without them. The urge to be "medication free" becomes one of the most powerful motivating factors in one's life. Then, the struggle against the effects of medications, and finally against taking the medications, can become as great as the struggle against psychosis itself.

In spite of over thirty years of widespread use of these drugs, there has been virtually no thorough examination of their psychological effects on normal "control" subjects or volunteers. Apparently, there is much more fear and reluctance to experience the effects of antipsychotic medications than there is to experience the psychosislike effects of hallucinogens. But anecdotal evidence abounds: These medications cause incomprehensible and painful body sensations and a generalized intellectual deterioration in anyone who takes them. (This can be easily demonstrated. It has been said that anyone can experience this effect when the drug is merely taken for four consecutive days, while others say that even a single dose can give you a glimpse of these effects.)

By this time, it is well known that medications are not a "cure" for psychosis, that they do not specifically affect voices, visions, or delusions. Primarily, they have been given to control behavior. But at times, they do lower the "amplitude" of outrageous sensory phenomena, or they lower the excitement and panic caused when the senses are in disarray. All this is important when the medications are given with great care; that is, when they are *given in as small a dose as possible, and when they are incrementally withdrawn as soon as their therapeutic effect is achieved.* They may give a patient an opportunity to live with some relatively quiet moments, when the sensory phenomena are not so imperious, and when one can turn away from the hallucinatory demands to live in "two places at once." There may be some precious spare time to relax, to begin to approximate reality, and to gain some semblance of dignity by not appearing to others as continuously distracted and forgetful.

But, for those who rely only on the medications, the "other world" remains just under the surface. And, they find that very gradually, the quality of life in the other world becomes progressively poorer. A young man, who I had not seen for two years, took me aside at a mutual friend's birthday party to tell me how the medications had transformed his life. Indeed, he looked transformed, he looked about twenty years older. We quickly found our sense of connection and friendship, in spite of my dismay. Since I had last seen him he had begun a "maintenance program" of medications, and there and then he wanted to share with me a gift of his final deliberation about the medication effect. He said that the medications had not stopped his run away delusions and interactions with an exotic and organized other world; but they had transformed them into a tawdry and degraded version of their former selves. For years, his life had

revolved around a stormy relationship with a beautiful and powerful woman who lived in the cosmic dimension of his other
world. The subtle effect of the drug, he said, was that she gradually changed into a demanding derelict. Now the only remnant
of her former power to change the universe in a moment was her
paltry ability to torture him. I thought to myself, is this what it
will take—her loss of power—for him to break this master-slave
bondage? But after that happened to her, he said, his own life
also began to deteriorate; he was "getting along," he added, but
he had little enthusiasm for his life because he felt destined to
live the same impoverished existence to which she had been
reduced.

This is one genre of medication-induced recovery, one that I
have come to recognize many times since it was pointed out to
me. There are many variations. A young college student consulted me about her "depression" and her inability to do her
schoolwork. One year earlier she had taken LSD and had a
terrifying reaction to it. At first it was ecstatic: She experienced
herself as a messiah who had been "sent" to help all human
beings. She was briefly hospitalized, treated with antipsychotic
medications, and sent back to her family to "recuperate." She
was told she would have to remain on medications for a long
time, and that if she reduced the dosage her "latent psychosis"—which the professionals felt had been activated by the
LSD—might reappear. Because of this threat, she and her family
decided to "play it safe"—the medications were never withdrawn and she resigned herself to a lifetime of medication dependency. As time went on, she became increasingly depressed
about the loss of her former life. Since early childhood she had
studied music with great interest, had painted, been vivacious,
and had many friends. Now, she dreaded awakening in the
morning to face a day of vacuity, boredom, lack of curiosity, and
a sense of "laziness." As soon as she and I began to reduce her
medications, she had dreams of being in a Garden of Eden,
where people were kind to each other and where she glimpsed
her lost joyfulness. Within two months after complete withdrawal of medication she started to regain her former energy
and exuberance.

From many experiences of this kind, and from the success in
withdrawing Karen and others, I have come to believe that medications can and *should* be reduced when the correct preparations
are made and some guidelines are understood. Such guidelines,

for one reason or another, are not available in the "scientific literature." I find the most informed procedure for drug withdrawal to be in a little-known manual called *Dr. Caligari's Psychiatric Drugs,* published by the patient advocacy movement.[11] It advises the "10 percent formula": a reduction of 10 percent of the original dosage each week, as long as the patient's response is positive, although smaller reductions may be needed as one approaches the end. It is always best not to do the withdrawal alone. In the Windhorse project a whole team of people were attuned to the withdrawal schedule and helped the patient in what needed to be done. In this way there was a very sensitive monitoring of the body and mind effects of the withdrawal schedule.

In most traditional medicine the most fundamental and favored type of treatment is the modification of behavioral and dietary patterns, as it is the most *gentle* manner of therapy and the first to be relied upon for the treatment of anything.[12] The further instructions for diet are more difficult to establish. In general, the daily diet of people who have been on maintenance medications for many years is atrocious, always verging on being toxic. This is usually a reflection of their lack of attention and care of themselves, to the point that any change of their diet is usually resisted as a massive intrusion. But the work of recovery in general, and withdrawing from medications in particular, involves a process of *cleansing.* This requires quite a shift of attitude. A modified "macrobiotic" cleansing diet is the best that I have seen for this purpose, and obviously, the difficulties of adhering to such a diet are greatly reduced when the whole "household" is on it. There are also two herbal medicines that I have often found useful, valerian and bancha root teas, freshly brewed and taken several times a day. Valerian is noted for its calming effect on the nervous system (and incidentally, the only remedy that John Perceval found useful to him); and bancha tea is known as the great "balancer" in the macrobiotic system.

In coming off the drugs there are some minimum requirements in regard to the instructions for behavior. The right amount of exercise has proven to be important. For example, long hikes are good, not only for helping the body eliminate the drugs, but also to overcome listlessness, stiffness, and uncomfortable body sensations. But, as Dr. Caligari cautions: "Moderation is a key principle: as you increase your activities, do so gradually."

The actual experience of "coming off" is, of course, very individual and is completely dependent on one's own attitude, state of health (for example, the amount of drug accumulation in body tissues), and the maturity of the people that one is with. Let us use the example of withdrawing someone from long-term usage of Prolixin (about fifty times more potent than Thorazine). There are bodily reactions to this experience of withdrawal that are surprisingly similar to reactions to withdrawal from opium dependency.[13] The reactions to Prolixin removal may peak during the first week and then gradually diminish: "flu-like symptoms, such as nausea and vomiting (at times severe), sweating, runny nose, insomnia, diarrhea, restlessness, headaches, and aches and pains. With the exception of severe vomiting, all these can be suffered through without special attention."[14]

The experience of "restlessness," however, does merit special attention. Fidgeting, leg-swinging, pacing, and agitation are not only signs of being uncomfortable in one's own body, they are also expressions of surges of energy appearing in the mind. For people who have been taking the medications for a year or more, sometimes even the slightest reductions can unleash a mental speed that they are unaccustomed to handling. And with this comes an extreme sensitivity to the environment, especially to how one is being treated by others. It is a time when one may no longer feel docile, submissive, or simply submerged in his "own world."

In this sense, withdrawal from medications and recovery from psychosis are similar: They both expose certain sensibilities. To one degree or another, the recovering one becomes very critical of the treatment he is receiving. And that expands: He is bitter about a long series of treatment failures and disparages many people in the links of the "system" (crisis services, police stations, acute wards, back wards, halfway houses). He speaks corrosively about the faults that he uncovers, even those from his childhood, which now he remembers. John Perceval believed that this state of "outrage" was a mandatory stage of recovery. Of course, the outrage may also be his undoing. But he feels up against a ruthless paradox: His anger on the one hand may inflame the speed, which leads to a major "imbalance," yet he feels that anger is his only vehicle to make his voice heard and to avoid the injustices and errors that he sees in his treatment. This is not simply the result of a mechanical event whereby natural chemicals are released from suppression and exert their psychosis-inducing excitations, the so-called withdrawal psychosis. It is also the time of a generalized awakening to his environment, and to the conditions under which he has suffered.

To him, he feels that if he suppresses this new found freedom of caustic expression he will be reduced to some dumbfounded state of being, where he cannot progress at all and where he will once again fall under the dominion of his other world. He may also remember that, in the past, when he clamped his excitement and critical intelligence, he succumbed to a profound depression, the so-called postpsychotic depression. In any case, depression seems unavoidable when during islands of clarity he awakens—to disillusionment; to a sense of humiliation and guilt; to fear of what comes next, what to do next; to a feeling of impoverishment, lacking the strength and skills to go further; to a nostalgia for the power and superiority of "manic consciousness"; and to the disloyalty of his shift of allegiance away from the despotic protagonists of his other world.

Patients and doctors seem to generally agree that abrupt withdrawal from long-term medications is ignorant and dangerous; the shock to a nervous system that has been habituated to them is too great, and the whiplash can be overwhelming. Even the graduated withdrawal of medications can be a difficult process. On the other hand, there is a great deal to be learned by the person who gradually withdraws. In small increments, one can experience energies of mind being freed from restraint. Under these conditions one can learn to watch one's mind in a new way and observe subtle changes in one's concentration and emotional intensity. Such attention to the details of the real changes that occur during withdrawal from medication has proven to be very important in one's overall recovery from psychosis; it strengthens one's ability to discriminate mental events and can give insight into how one functions.

When a doctor and a patient agree to the withdrawal of antipsychotic medications they should have a common understanding of what they are doing. This common understanding can be summed up in the following "memo" which was given to all staff and patients of a Windhorse-style treatment community.

Medication Reduction Guidelines

There seem to be two broad categories of medication reductions:

–Reduction due to acute toxicity (e.g., liver damage, abnormal movements) or subclinical toxicity (e.g., nausea or drowsiness). Basically, someone is taking more medication than he needs and the excess is making him sick. As quickly as is possible and safe, dosage should be reduced to the minimum needed for stability. There is no immediate goal of further reduction to substantially smaller dosages, though this might follow later.
–Slow, graduated reduction for therapeutic purposes. Someone is stable on his present dose and the team agrees that it is time to reduce gradually. This is a slow and open-ended situation. For example, dosage might be gradually reduced to 50 percent of original dose, held stable for awhile, increased briefly when necessary, and eventually reduced to zero. In order to reduce side effects and enhance stability, no medication should be reduced more quickly than 10 percent of the original dosage per week.

To further support the medication reduction process, life-style changes and disciplines such as those listed below should be encouraged. How one's overall life will have to change, in addition to simply swallowing fewer pills, will be a major focus of team meetings and basic attendance shifts. The following general guidelines, while somewhat ideal, can be tailored to individual cases.

BODY

1. *Changes in diet.* Less consumption of foods that increase toxicity (red meat, sugar, alcohol, coffee) and more use of foods that have a cleansing effect (bancha tea, whole foods such as brown rice and fresh vegetables).

2. *More physical exercise.* Physical activity helps the body process and eliminate toxins, improves overall health, and provides a channel for energy freed up by reducing medications.

3. *Taking all medications.* Ironically, one has to take meds in order to reduce meds. Sporadically "cheeking" or refusing meds undermines the whole medication reduction process. Only by knowing exactly how much of a particular drug is entering someone's body can we gradually reduce the intake.

4. *Uplifted environment.* Cleaning one's room, doing chores, wearing clean clothes, and keeping one's body clean are especially important when reducing medications.

SPEECH

Medication reduction requires open communication between client and team members, and among the community in general. For example, if team members think a client is escalating and might need a slight increase in dose for awhile, and the client cannot hear that concern, this could undermine the reduction process. On the other hand, reducing meds may heighten clients' clarity of mind, so that they notice aspects of staff behavior they had overlooked before. So if a client complains of feeling mistreated by a team member, it is crucial that everyone listen and be receptive to each other's views. In addition, it is important that the entire community understand how medication reduction works and who is reducing what. We can actually share a feeling of celebration as a community in this process.

MIND

There are a million details we can learn to pay attention to: how you feel in the morning, when you feel irritable, how your mind gets speedy and how it slows down, when the world inside demands attention and when the world of sights and sounds seems more important. By tracking these states of mind, as well as bodily sensations and emotions, we can learn how we are affected by medications, diet, exercise, and so on.[15]

The prescription and withdrawal of medications can both be made simpler by understanding *why* the medications are being given. Whatever else a medication should do, it should address the major suffering of a person at that time. When one is recovering from psychosis, there is no event more constantly disquieting than the struggle of living in "two places at once." A recovering person may be going along quite well, only to run up against a great fear that "unbalances" him and triggers the demanding presence of that other world, the one that he thought he had left behind like an old nightmare.

A journalist from a British magazine has told the following provocative story of her illness and recovery from a split world. After working many sleepless nights on an article about "spirit possession," and on her way home one evening, she experienced a seizure of self-revulsion and an "urge to transform": "I longed to be quit of it all. I longed to get quit of my physical body altogether, by sheer effort of will. I longed with an intensity that made my head begin to feel quite queer and dizzy."[16] That night, she awoke from sleep and experienced herself split into three different dimensions, from the solid body to the "etheric," and the "spiritual" body. For the next couple of days she was in a massive sensory disarray, during which all her thoughts materialized into vivid reality. Within days The Delusion formed: a "fiend" had gotten inside her body, had seduced her, and now she was forced to bear a fiend-child.

Thousands of voices later, her other world took on greater shape and complexity and involved many characters. For long periods she lived only in that world. It was interspersed with episodes of blood curdling screams and shrieks and all the torments of living in the realm of "hell." But, all that time, she says, "I was fully aware that I had gone mad . . . fully aware, from that indescribable shattering of my brain-substance by those screaming voices, that I had gone out of my mind."[17] And then she lost that awareness and passed into a delirious unconsciousness. Awareness of her situation came and went.

She was brought to the hospital and there she lived through vivid experiences of her death and revival, being pulverized to dust and reformed, over and over again. Separate zones of consciousness either fully dominated to the point of trance, or might disappear altogether. Once, for days she lost all bodily consciousness whatsoever, yet at the same time, her auditory consciousness was absorbed in a continuous hallucination of a single musical composition.

She was entangled in the voices. They attacked her, commanded her, beguiled her, and promised her damnation or beatitude. She struggled continually by reasoning and arguing against them, until finally she would give in and do what they told her, no matter how ridiculous. All of this was happening in the other world, which she called the *"thought world."* During this, her body felt lifeless and she appeared to be dead. Then, after about two weeks: "One evening I suddenly awoke to normal consciousness—I mean consciousness of my real, bodily surroundings—and found myself out of bed, with two nurses standing one on each side of me, supporting me. I remembered all that had been occurring, and I felt so weak and ill I could scarcely sit up."[18]

That shock of awareness, followed by an immediate reaction of horror and revulsion, led to a quick relapse. The voices returned, as enticing and tormenting as ever, even more so. Other short-lived islands of awareness would then occur, only to become also quickly covered over. Soon, these "lucid" intervals came more often: "I began to gain more consciousness (at intervals only, most fragmentarily) in the following days." She became convinced that the medications (probably bromides), which she was forced to take, caused her to lose her awareness. She said that each time she was given the medication, her "heart stopped" and she would become lost in the frantic activity of the "thought world."

The islands gathered and seemed to peak with her singular experience of a physical and mental "clicking in." When this happened, she had no choice but to speculate about this experience, which she labeled *the* "moment of recovery." Later, she developed her own theory—a "metaneurology," as Custance would have called it—and it was based on exquisite bodily experiences. She theorized about a particular kind of "imbalance" that she felt was worthy of "scientific" scrutiny. Briefly, it is this: A "dislocation of the physical brain-apparatus takes place in acute mania, and no mad person can 'recover his sanity' until that dislocation has become re-set."[19] From her point of view, losing one's mind is a terrible mind-body desynchronization. The consciousness of self becomes separated from the physical body. And the physical body is separated from the "etheric" body (still another expression of being in two places at once). She says that this can happen by degrees: "The trouble in madness is that a separation has taken place between two 'sheaths' (the physical and the etheric) which should never be separated during the lifetime of the physical body; and which cannot be separated, partially, without causing serious physical injury, or completely, without causing the death of the physical body."[20]

From all such accounts, a general rule of recovery could safely be stated: Anything that promotes body and mind synchronization will further the appearance of islands of clarity, and anything that induces or accentuates body and mind separation can become a fatal obstacle to recovery.

Can there possibly be a medication that would address this situation? Wouldn't the search for such a medicine be more fruitful than the current narrow pursuit of chemicals that always disorganize the neurotransmitter network? Supposedly, it once existed. It has been called "Sanjivani": a drug used since ancient times in India because of its tendency to "draw back" the mind into the body again and knit it more closely together—thus insuring the normal unity that they should have. This medicine is said to have the effect or property of "bringing back" the consciousness, after it has been "driven out" by an anesthetic or otherwise.[21]

What is Sanjivani? What is in it? No one seems to know if Sanjivani still exists or ever existed. No Indian or Tibetan herbalist I have asked has heard of it. In Hindu mythology it was said to have been an herb that grew in the foothills of the Himalayas and only on the south side of certain mountains. Even the Hindu deity Hanuman could not find it. He had been instructed by Lord Krishna to gather the medicine and bring it back. Hanuman found the mountain but could not identify the herbal plant, so he brought back the whole mountain instead. If it is a mythical medication, it certainly seems to be the ideal medicine to heal the body-mind problem of psychosis.

SHIFT OF ALLEGIANCE

Synchronization of body and mind is a key notion of the Windhorse treatment. For the most part, it is achieved by means of the domestic disciplines inherent in any ordinary living situation. This is not very exotic compared to the profound principles of joining heaven and earth, of balancing mind and environment, which were discussed above. The actual "work" with patients from the Windhorse point of view is surprisingly domestic, very concrete, very earthy. Connection with the "earth" qualities of this world, or any "other world," can actually be made while preparing food, cooking, cleaning, gardening, house maintenance, and so on. The inner aspect of all such activity is that one is relating directly to all the senses, even when they are in disarray.

When one is in a struggle between "this" world and the "other" (the "thought world") anything that activates the senses gives one something "real" or concrete to work with. An interesting and *useful* point about domestic disciplines is that they are so simple and ordinary that they are subject to very little "interference" from the other world. Their simplicity and lack of intellectual content leaves little room for them to be corrupted by delusion.

The essence of this kind of domestic synchronization can be stated in a nutshell: "Train in cleaning up after yourself." This was actually a motif, or a slogan, within the treatment households. It refers not only literally to one's decorum, for instance in a communal kitchen, but it is also a metaphor for how one might conduct relationships, and how to relate to one's own mind.

It is, of course, a truism that mind and environment are in a continuous and subtle, even unconscious, interaction. When we enter a new environment there is an impact—the colors, the lighting, the space, the furnishings, the textures, the smells, the whole setup. Possibly, it is startling. Certainly, it is arousing in some way and has a definite, but not always known, effect on our state of mind. Different rooms affect us differently. When we enter a bright, airy room, we know that it immediately affects us differently than when we enter a dark, claustrophobic cell. We know that when we enter an old-age home, a madhouse, a ghetto, a motel, a concert hall, or a cathedral, we have different "reactions," scenarios, or stories. But even before that, there is a change in the texture of our state of mind. We do not know exactly what that connection is, or how that interlock occurs. Yet it deserves some study, because simply examining the moment of mind-environment interaction tends to heighten one's awareness of environment altogether. In the case of Windhorse, this issue was of great importance since it was our exacting intention to be able to design environments of people and structures in which islands of clarity could flourish. This was our basic mission.

So, the Windhorse staff trained in the subtleties of environmental awareness in a unique way, known as the practice of "maitri space awareness." It is typically practiced in the context of a small community of people who are making the same study, and in conjunction with mindfulness sitting meditation. The practice takes place in five specially designed rooms, each of a different architecture, color, lighting, and emotional quality. A specific posture is maintained within each of these environments. Each room highlights one of the five general patterns of energy, called "Buddha families," which are associated with colors, natural elements, landscapes, seasons, personality types, areas of the body, and phases of psychological development.[22] The "Vajra Room" is a deep royal blue penetrated by crystalline blue light from slitlike windows. The "Ratna Room" is a majestic yellow bathed in warm, golden light from large, round windows. The "Padma Room" is a fiery red illuminated by glowing red light from large, rectangular windows. The "Karma Room" is a forest green with green light radiating from its apex. The "Buddha Room" is a flat white awash with a muted, indirect white light.

Experiencing one's body and mind and environmental interactions in these rooms intensifies the different patterns of energy inherent to everyone. Both the "neurotic" and "sane" aspects of each energy can be directly experienced and discriminated. The effect of this practice is that one becomes more appreciative of the different energies of spaces and of people.

At the most subtle level, this practice examines the relationship between the element of space and one's own mind. We generally do not think of space as an element. Even in most traditional medical systems there is earth, water, fire, and air or wind. Here, there is a fifth element, space. It is associated with the "Buddha Room." You take a posture on your knees and elbows, with your hands supporting your head under the chin, like a lazy washerwoman, and do your best to hold it for forty-five minutes. Your gaze is diffuse but centered down on the white wall about a foot in front of you. In this room the various qualities of "indifference" arise—from a feeling of casualness to acute boredom—replete with their mental dramas. In the midst of these dramas, the mental practice here, as with all the rooms, is to simply come back to awareness of the environment—awareness of the color, the texture, the space around you and your special posture in it. This takes advantage of and highlights a natural phenomenon whereby the environment and space spontaneously "take us out of ourselves," and draw us out of reverie into the here and now, or "nowness." Here is the real meaning of "coming to one's senses." Becoming aware of space has a certain "power" to it. This awareness is a fundamental aspect of our "intelligence"—you could call it the wisdom of space—and it is the source of what has been called "islands of clarity" during the experience of recovery.

Rarely in Western medicine are instructions given to a person recovering from psychosis about how to care for their mind. This is understandable since present-day psychology and psychiatry pays so much attention to the content of mind, and so little to mental "process." Most modern psychological treatments are typically designed to work from the inside out: They explore the emotional conflicts, personal history, and other things that prevent the patient from working with the details of his or her body, environment, and relationships. But in the view of treatment that I am presenting, one works with the patient's external world first, going from the outside in. As in the discipline of meditation, the first step is to arrange an environment of wakefulness. Then you "take your seat" comfortably in that environment, adjust your posture so that it is upright and dignified, and after that, you relate to the movement of your breath and the stream of mental contents. First you develop the precision in working with the details of the outer world, then relating to your state of mind naturally follows from that.[23]

In the previous chapter I gave "emergency" instructions for people in the acute stages of mental derangement. Now I would like to introduce a few guidelines for people in the stages of recovery about caring for their minds.

Caring for one's mind in general involves the ability to continually bring back the attention of a wandering mind and to focus concentration. According to William James, it is an ability that is hard to come by: "The faculty of voluntarily bringing back a wandering attention, over and over again, is the very root of judgement, character, and will. No one is *compos sui* if he have it not. An education which should improve this faculty would be the education *par excellence.* But it is easier to define this ideal than to give practical direction for bringing it about."[24] In the Windhorse style of treatment, it is one of the specialties of the team therapists to be able to instruct patients in how to do just this, and to transmit this knowledge within the context of domestic disciplines.

How to do this comes from a basic understanding of the psychology of attention. The Windhorse staff, comprising different teams of people, practiced mindfulness meditation, usually alone but sometimes together. And because we are psychologists and therapists, we also studied the "psychology" of meditation—a "micropsychology"—which develops from the laboratory of the meditation experience.[25] Certain aspects of this meditation are particularly important to us, such as the experience of coordinating the body, breath, words, and mind activity. Simply put, body-mind synchronization is being mindful of body, mind, and one's activity all at the same time. This kind of "tuning" and being present is a key point in the mindfulness-awareness meditation practice. Out of this formal "root" discipline comes an understanding of how such attunement could extend into all other daily activities, which is "meditation in action."

The formal practice of meditation is also referred to as "resting the mind." This sense of rest means quieting down the mind. It means not trying to "do something" with one's mind, letting things be as they are. It means allowing the natural flow of thinking to appear and disappear, without lingering on any mental imagery or subvocal gossip. When practiced correctly, this kind of resting also inevitably leads to a relaxation of the body. That is why it has traditionally been called the practice of "peacefulness," or "peacefully abiding."

The Windhorse team therapists longed to be able to offer their patients the means to relax their minds and bodies. Those who suffer from the invasion of mental speed and surges of expansion appear to have preciously few opportunities for such mental and physical respite. And everywhere one looks among those with long-standing psychosis, one finds a phenomenal array of self-taught methods and gimmicks that are desperate attempts to calm the mind. Usually, these are meant to get rid of intrusive thoughts and feelings. Although such attempts at "self-control" may sometimes be ingenious, they usually fail; they wear out, and one has to try harder at it, until the mental trick becomes a caricature, or a futile, stereotypical action.[26] Instead of uncovering an interlude of peace and quiet, it becomes a struggle against one's own mind. The famous case study by Sigmund Freud called the "Rat Man" vividly describes how his obsession- and compulsion-ridden patient tried to produce a cessation of terrible ideas by reciting the Lord's Prayer quickly. When that began to fail he renewed his ability to quiet himself by saying it *backward.* John Perceval reported that he had tried the same method.

With each patient in the Windhorse project the staff eventually came up against the same dilemma: We wanted to teach more of what we knew about resting the mind, and yet we recognized that it could also be dangerous. If done incorrectly or at the wrong time, or with an agressive intention, or if it is misunderstood or thought of as a means of "transformation," a practice of mindfulness could be perverted into one of mindlessness. This dilemma led to many impressive and highly technical clinical discussions among the staff about the meaning and use of mindfulness meditation for "highly disturbed" people. It is an area that is just beginning to be discussed by those therapists who are trying to join their personal practice of meditation with their interpersonal practice of psychotherapy.[27]

But our own experience began to teach us that there could be no easy formula about the offering of meditation techniques to our patients—it is a highly individual matter and it raises many questions. How could we protect ourselves and our patients from using meditation as just another "pill" or another "therapy"? How could meditation be used in the context of treatment when in fact the personal journey of meditation is much vaster than any kind of therapy? How might we be able to modify the technique to make it less problematic and at the same time not dilute it? And then there was the most subtle question of all: Might not the teaching of meditation and meditationlike techniques to our patients be another disguised version of "asylum mentality," where out of frustration and self-righteousness one begins to prescribe a view of life?

Only when patients showed a sustained interest in working on themselves through meditation practice did we arrange for them to receive meditation instructions. This was always taught by people who were outside the Windhorse community. In this way, not only did the meditation discipline remain separate from the treatment work, but it also expanded the community of people with whom they became involved. There was every variation in response to this: Some began the practice quickly; others were unable to practice because of their turmoil; and some began the practice only after they had left treatment, sometimes long afterward.

A general conclusion was drawn from our experience of people recovering within the Windhorse project: At the point when someone reaches a fairly stable state of recovery, he needs to begin to *take responsibility for taming his mind.* Some kind of "mind training" is required, because only that can allow one to break the weak links in the psychotic chain reaction. Once again, we are at the level of a micropsychology that fundamentally can only be affected by the patient himself.

The legendary French psychiatrist and hypnotist of nineteenth-century Paris, Jean-Martin Charcot, said: "There is a particular *moment between health and sickness* when everything depends on the patient."[28] This observation is made more poignant when we consider that Charcot had championed the organic, degenerative hereditary theory of psychosis and hysteria. Even he believed that recovery ultimately depends on the patient's own effort. One recovered patient refers to that effort as a "state of constant vigilance," because, in retrospect, one is always surprised that islands of clarity have been happening all along, and much earlier than one had recognized at the time.[29]

This effort also involves an awareness and monitoring of the psychotic chain reaction, which, following the studies of Henri Michaux, can now simply be stated as attachment (the power of "fascination" within the second state) and a tendency to trance (the lingering effects of "imbalance"), which becomes an intensification of ego (the stages leading to "manic consciousness"). It is the tendency to attach to and identify with thoughts and emotions that is at the root of the psychotic chain reaction, and it is the one most directly cut through by the practice of mindfulness meditation, and perhaps in other traditional mind trainings as well.

One person in recovery from psychosis said that "psychotic illness is depletion, and wellness happens only through living well."[30] From this point of view it is important that at a certain time in recovery from psychosis one engages in some discipline(s) that allows one to slow down the speed of mind and weaken powerful internal habits of attachment and subsequent trance. Again, recovery becomes a continuous effort and not a "cure" that can be achieved once and for all.

What can one do on one's own? The equipment is there to do something. It requires a shift of allegiance to "living well," to cultivating one's own health and sanity. This involves a commitment to action to develop "presence of mind" and is the ultimate antidote to being in two places at once.

Ways to develop this mental presence have been taught by such classical mind-body disciplines as t'ai chi ch'uan, Zen archery, aikido, hatha-yoga, ikebana (Japanese flower arranging), calligraphy, and others. All of these have helped people to slow down their mental speed and become more observant of their minds. If one studies the micropsychology of attachment, then many other ordinary disciplines (e.g., drawing, dancing, music, etc.) can also become vehicles for cultivating nonattachment. In the Windhorse project, from the very beginning of a person's treatment, and even in the most acute stages, we nurtured an attitude of nonattachment via "domestic disciplines." This gradually strengthened a person's ability to deal with "distracting thoughts," "thought interferences," and so on. Members of a Windhorse-style treatment team should become familiar with many different methods of synchronizing mind and body.

Going even further, this same attitude should be applied even to moments of clarity: They, also, should be abandoned. The tendency to become fascinated by, and to desperately cling to, experiences of clarity and well-being is the major instigator of what has been called "wild recovery" (à la John Custance).

There are in fact simple "exercises" that are useful in developing nonattachment at a very literal level. Here is one I have used that comes from hatha-yoga, a simple "spinal twist," to be performed after the back is a little warmed up: With eyes open, stand upright, feet comfortably wide apart, arms outstretched to the sides; on an exhalation, gently twist to one side and turn the head to look in that direction; inhale on returning to the center and exhale while twisting to the other side. It is important to blink repeatedly while doing this, focusing momentarily on each point of visual contact—as your gaze moves across the texture of the wall, the picture, the window, the horizon, and then the wall. This can also be done by sitting on the floor or in a chair and simply rotating one's head. It could be done for only a few minutes, several times a day. This exercise involved the practice of continually "moving through" and letting go of visual attachments and the mental content they evoke.

Breathing exercises to cultivate mindfulness and nonattachment have been known in many different traditions. John Perceval reported that his spontaneous practice of breath control regulated his mind and greatly contributed to his recovery. The Zen teacher Thich Nhat Hanh calls it "Taking hold of one's breath": "You should know how to breathe to maintain mindfulness, as breathing is a natural and extremely effective tool which can prevent dispersion. Breath is a bridge which connects life to consciousness, which unites your body to your thoughts. Whenever your mind becomes scattered, use your breath as the means to take hold of your mind again."[31] He advises the practice of "counting the breath" in a way similar to the pranayama teachings of Yoga: with eyes closed, count to oneself (about one per second) and become familiar with the length of the naturally moving in-breath and out-breath; be mindful and feel the texture and body sensations of the breathing; gradually extend the length of each breath so that you are evenly and quietly breathing in and out to a count of six or eight; thoughts will come and go—"big" thoughts, "little" thoughts, it makes no difference—let them be and simply return to the sensations of breathing. This is called practicing nonattachment by means of the breath. It could be done several times a day, while sitting up or lying down—ten to twenty full breaths being sufficient.

Gentleness is the key to any of these practices; being gentle with one's body, with one's breath, and with one's mind. The effort or energy expended while doing such practices is not an aggressive one. The necessary attitude of doing them, and any other practices, is not one of trying to attain something, to become a better person, to do anything perfectly, or to become more powerful. These are only the insidious attitudes of an "urge to transformation," epitomized by Donald Crowhurst.

But the other world is usually not gentle. Most of the time, one's life in the "thought world" is filled with aggression directed toward oneself. Take, for example, the "taunting voices." They can be unbearable, and there is no medication known that can stop them for long. How does one "turn away" from this?

Even when one is in a bad dream or a nightmare, it is sometimes possible to simply "wrench" oneself from it, but it feels like a great force has to be exerted to do this. Also, in those rare times when one awakens from a dream but the force of the dream continues, it seems to take a monumental effort to keep from fading back into the dream. Or, sometimes we experience a daytime reverie that is so strong that it requires a "tearing away" to awaken from it. From these experiences we might come to believe that turning away from the other world *also* requires some kind of violence.

But in a nightmare, aggression is usually met by further aggression. When you try to rage against the oppression, it retaliates with equal force. And in the second state, by whatever means it is entered, when you try to banish a thought or emotion it returns like a persecutor. I have heard some therapists say that when you are under a continual siege of tormenting or beseeching voices from the other world, you could try shouting at them to "Fuck off!" This might work for a while—giving one a glimpse of confidence that one has some power over the other world—but then the voices return and it becomes something of a game. Perceval observed that when he attacked his voices head-on he "became more lunatic than ever," and his later attitude became the gentler "I will not meddle."

Aggression toward the other world is basically aggression toward one's own mind; it cannot help but have negative effects. If there is to be a genuine turning away from the other world it can only be done with an attitude of light-handedness and gentleness. The Tibetan medical tradition takes this notion much further: When someone feels he is suffering under the influence of "beings" in the other world he is advised to be compassionate toward them because they only attack him out of their own misery.

Over time, a Windhorse style of treatment can give one the opportunity to reverse or transmute each ingredient of the psychosis-inducing "cocktail": Mindlessness, by body-mind synchronization; substance, by diet and proper medicine; Exertion, by attention to resting the mind; Intention, by a shift of allegiance toward one's own health and sanity; and Predicament, by the simplicity and dignity of a homelike environment. But because people who are recovering from psychosis find the gentleness needed to accomplish this so hard to come by, being treated kindly and warmly by members of their own team provides a crucial experience. Being related to with acceptance and kindness is the necessary step in developing a similar kind of consideration toward one's own body and mind. We call this kind of treatment and care "Basic Attendance."

CHAPTER **6**

Learning Basic Attendance

THE WORKING TEAM

Basic attendance is the discipline of caring for people that gradually evolved over the course of the Windhorse project. It is basic in that it is basic to treatment of any kind: basic psychotherapy, basic nursing, basic attention to what a patient—or anyone—needs in order to recover his health. Basic attendance appears to be deceptively simple from the outside. However, there are many degrees of sophistication to the discipline of basic attendance because it deals with the intricate function of synchronizing mind with body and environment. It is the concerted effort of a whole group of people who practice basic attendance—with the patient and with each other—that constitutes the work of a healing team.

The turmoil of psychotic mind is excessively burdened by close proximity to other confused minds. Inside the asylum or the hospital, it happens occasionally (though rarely) that healing friendships develop among patients. But, for the most part, the camaraderie that exists among inmates tends to be based on defiance of authority and in shared complaint against institutional life. Yet, it is repeatedly noted by those who recover that highly disturbed people, when grouped together, run the risk of becoming more confused; when they are in the company of healthy people, they are likely to become more sane. That is the purpose of a "treatment team." This idea might seem like a truism, but it is hardly put into practice by the majority of people who do intensive care.

The gentleness toward oneself that is so greatly needed by anyone in the process of recovery is difficult to find in light of all the aggression within the state of psychotic suffering. Our experience in the Windhorse project has been that when a person is treated kindly and warmly by members of his own team a necessary experience is provided, one that may not have happened much since the patient became ill. It is the most direct way for a patient to develop a similar consideration for his own body and mind. Among the members of a healing team, this kind of gentle care is cultivated by the practice of basic attendance.

I have asked a great variety of people: "If *you* were ill, who would you want to have on your team?" Sometimes, people initially have difficulty in picturing themselves in enough mental distress as to need a team; such a catastrophic mental event may seem unimaginable in spite of the fact that it is so prevalent in our society. Nevertheless, anyone would certainly want to be in the company of relatively healthy people who would not add to one's confusion. One might want them to be patient and have a sense of humor. They might be people who could simply be quietly by one's side when communication is not possible. Above all, they should not attack one out of their own frustration when, under the influence of the great speeds, one makes mistakes and is continually losing the thread of what one thought one knew. Never, say the ancient hallucinogenic healers, never scold someone who is struggling to maintain control of his mind.

Perhaps one would want an equal mixture of men and women on one's team. Of course, we cannot dictate what their personalities should be, but we might like them to be interesting and certainly to be interested in us. We don't need them to be self-sacrificing and overly dedicated—thereby expecting too much of us—but they should be able to take the time to be with us and be completely present. And they should "know" something; they should have some understanding of the struggles taking place in our mind, and of natural cycles of work and relaxation, and how to bring out the best in us. It isn't necessary that they know *exactly* what is going on inside of us, but they should appreciate our obstacles, the walls we run into, and our heightened level of fears of all kinds. All of these are qualities that inspire friendship and trust.

There is probably no way that we could gather such a group of people around us by ourselves, especially since in our pain we may actually have been alienating people. But we could start with *one* person. He or she might then be able to magnetize a team of people with whom we could work. That person is called the *team leader,* who finds and puts together a working team and introduces them to us. These team members are not meant to be "professionals" who are exercising some theory of what is wrong with us and what needs to be set right, or who try to talk us into becoming sane. They simply know how to attend to our life, and they are as interested in being part of the working team as they are in our "case."

At the Windhorse project, magnetizing a team is comparatively easy. There are a large number of students and graduates of the Naropa Institute psychology program who are interested in and capable of this kind of work. But there must be many qualified students in other schools as well who would learn much and whose lives would be enriched by being a member of such a therapeutic team. Being on a team requires only about ten hours a week, and this means that some people could be team members on a part-time or volunteer basis. The availability of potential team members depends to a large extent on one's local community resources. But whether one is forming a team in a large city or a rural town, some amount of creativity (and luck) is always needed. A team may include members of one's family, friends, volunteers, nurses, psychology and psychiatric students and interns, students of dance therapy (or any kind of therapy), mature high-school students, retired and elderly people, and, of course, people who have recovered from psychosis and are inspired by an alternative means for care. Also, this idea of team treatment, difficult though it is, has proven to attract many different kinds of people; every psychiatrist I have met prefers this form of treatment for his or her own family. Putting together and coordinating such a team of about eight people is part of the job description of the person who assumes the position of a team leader.

If you are the patient on such a beginning treatment team,

there are some typical experiences that immediately begin to shift your perspective. As a team gathers, you find that you are involved with a small society of people who are together only because you need a special kind of care and help in the ordinary activities of life. In team or small community meetings you will work together to create a schedule so that each team therapist will meet with you for a three-hour block of time (a "shift"), twice a week. You might be having anywhere from one to three such shifts a day, depending on your needs. Even though you might never have had this kind of attention before, you may at first consider this schedule something of a burden. There can be some discomfort at being pulled away from your absorption in the other world, and with the possibility of two shifts a day your schedule is becoming full. The team members understand that at times you may look forward to a shift or you may resent it as an intrusion in your life. But an even more subtle burden is that you do not know what to do for three hours with a team therapist who you hardly know. You may feel that it is up to you to "entertain" the shift person who seems equally awkward about what you will do together. This is actually the way a basic attendance shift usually begins.

In fact, this is not as much of a problem as it might seem; it is merely two people meeting together on an open ground of uncertainty and it becomes the opportunity to do new things, or just to do what is needed or what you have been putting off doing because of loneliness or an inability to "get started."

In order to become familiar with these burdens, the team members train themselves in a special "exercise" of doing practice shifts with other members of the team. I know of no other single exercise that is more conducive to team-building. This is an important practice for training in basic attendance and it should be done *routinely* by any group who is attempting a Windhorse style of treatment: Each team member arranges to do a mock shift with another team member and then they *both* report to the entire team on their experiences of the same shift. It is surprising how much information can be shared about the nature of "shift work" through these exercises. Almost all the difficulties and satisfactions of attending to someone on a shift, and of being attended to, are exposed in this mutual supervision.

There is another change of perspective that occurs regularly during basic attendance. During a shift a potentially confusing

phenomenon may occur: For moments, the role distinction between patient and therapist spontaneously alternates, and you
cannot tell if you are attending to the other person or he is
attending to you. If this experience does not threaten you, then
it becomes an opportunity to relax.

Before Karen left the hospital to go to her Windhorse home
I decided to experiment for myself at doing one of the three-
hour shifts, which were soon to become such a major part of her
treatment. I usually went to see her at the hospital for our daily
meeting but on this particular evening, instead of meeting with
her in her room, I took her out of the hospital for three hours.
She had not been out of the hospital much in the past months,
and when the hospital staff did have the time to take her off the
grounds she gave them a difficult time by trying to run away or
refusing to come back. I thought it would be interesting to have
her see my office, where she would soon be meeting with me
regularly after her discharge from the hospital. But we were
both hungry and so we first went to a tavern close to the office
where I often had eaten between seeing patients.

Karen was delighted, actually overjoyed. However, she immediately became overexcited. She strode quickly to the bar, sat on
a bar stool, pulled her skirt to her hips, and without hesitation
began to boisterously flirt with the two men on either side of
her. She was telling them about her erotic adventures with delusional lovers. I tried to talk her into sitting at a table, but she
would have none of it and the two men resented my intrusion.
They began to feel that they were protecting her from me. "This
is all a mistake," I kept telling myself, as she began to drink one
of the beers that they offered her. I just couldn't blurt out, "You
see, I am a doctor, in here with this sick woman who has just
come from a hospital . . ." Instead, I ordered two hamburgers
and coffee to take out and waited around like an unwelcome
chaperone until the food was ready.

When the food arrived I had to almost drag her out of there.
We then took the food to my office, to have a "picnic," I told
her, cajoled her. She was beginning to calm down but once
inside the office her excitement increased. She insisted on looking at everything, touching everything, opening every drawer,
going through the closet, trying out every chair. Then she sat on
the floor, tore open the bag containing the food and began
ravenously to eat her hamburger, while spilling coffee over her
dress. She suddenly looked up at me and said, "Oh my God, I

eat like an animal! This is disgusting." And she began to sob, and then she wailed. I sat on the floor facing her. I said to her several times, "Take it easy on yourself. Let's just have our dinner and talk, or not talk if you like."

She had frightened herself with a vision of her own voracity and wildness. "I'll never be able to do this," she said, "I'll never get out of the hospital." I told her that what she was doing was all right, that she should give herself more time, and that she might try to relax her body. She asked me what she should do and I told her to gently straighten her posture, breathe more freely, and eat slowly. I did the same. We sat in the middle of the office floor and we ate. We talked about all the shifts she would soon be scheduled to have, and how difficult it might be for her and also for the person doing the shift. But, I told her, she might also find shifts useful; for instance, one of the people on her team could help her learn how to play the guitar, something she yearned to do. "Do you know any songs?" she said. We then quietly sang a song that we both knew. "This really was a picnic," she said. When we were finished she helped me clean up the office and I drove her back to the hospital. We walked in the clear night air for a while and then entered the hospital building. It was quite a shock for both of us to be back on the acute treatment ward after a night on the town.

In the years since that time, the Windhorse project and its several offshoots have offered many thousands of hours of basic attendance shifts. These have occurred with a large variety of different patients and during every phase of "losing mind" and of recovery. While the shift experiences revealed very detailed observations of individuals, they also confirmed the crucial vision of Windhorse-style treatment: The shift therapists are attending to the entire household as much as they are to the patient. This is a key point for those who practice basic attendance. The shift therapists are not focused on the patient alone, they also maintain a larger awareness of a person's entire environment. They attend to the patient's living space and to the people who live there, and even to the patient's friends and family.

One time, I severely injured my back while lifting large rocks to construct a garden wall. For several days I was flat on my back, unable to move and in much pain. For another four weeks I was unable to work or get around by myself and I would easily became anxious and depressed about retreating from my work

with many ill people. But soon after the injury the Windhorse
community of therapists came to help. A team leader gathered
a group of people who could do shifts with me each day. Naturally, it intrigued me to be the recipient of the kind of care that
for years I had been setting in motion for other people. Each
team member had his own particular style of basic attendance.
They gently eased me out of a television-watching habit, which
I was beginning to form while having to lie on my back. Some
read to me very beautifully when I was unable to read by myself
because of the interference of painkillers and tranquilizers. I
watched how they skillfully divided their time between just being
with me and also attending to cleaning, food shopping, cooking,
and regulating the environment. When it was clearly time for me
to become more active in spite of my reluctance and fear to
move around very much, they took me for rides in the car,
engaged me to stand up and help unpack the groceries, and later
escorted me on long walks.

The process of recovery in general, and from psychosis in
particular, depends on creating an atmosphere of simplicity,
warmth, and dignity. When the team therapists together perform the actions needed to establish that kind of environment
and tone, recovery begins to happen; *islands of clarity* begin to
gather and flourish, and one can take his ease and rouse the
confidence to recover.

And what constitutes the activity of the team? Quite simply,
the concerted effort of basic attendance. In conventional psychiatric language, when the words "treatment team" are used they
sometimes refer to a "multidisciplinary" group—that is, a psychiatrist, a social worker, a psychiatric nurse, and maybe a recre-
ational therapist—who sometimes consult together about their
individual work with a patient. Or, it describes a loose collection
of therapists who treat people with the same type of illness, or
in the same stage of life. However, the kind of team we are
discussing is much different than that. The treatment team that
practices basic attendance—with the patients *and* with each
other—cuts across professional specializations. In a sense, basic
attendance is not just psychotherapy, social work, or nursing. It
is all of these. Each team member is multidisciplinary in his own
right, each has his own skills.

Team therapists have their own special expertise in promoting body-mind unity. One team member may be a student of
dance and naturally becomes interested in how the patient

moves and relates to space, how a person in an extreme state of mind begins to literally choreograph his life movements in a particular space. Another team therapist might know how to sew and knit and be creative with fabric. She can unlock the hidden clue to the magic of knitting, which a patient may have always wanted to learn. And she knows at just what point knitting becomes a mindless absorption activity rather than a practice of mindfulness.

Each team member has his own quality of energy, style, humor, intelligence, and also blind spots. Thus, we can speak of a particular "chemistry" of a team by bringing together a variety of people who can offer the patient a full palate of life-styles, talents, and even eccentricities. Once, when we were choosing a team for a late-adolescent boy, we included two team members who were also young and noted for their playfulness. This patient had a long history of dyslexia and so we also included as a team member someone who was a poetry student and had a love for reading and writing. On the team of a young woman whose illness separated her from her children, we included team members who had young children with whom she could relate. In general, it is always useful and endearing when people in recovery have the opportunity to relate to young children.

The relationships that are formed during the work of basic attendance are predictable, unpretentious, and free from a psychologizing that might make a patient, or anyone else, feel damaged or dependent. It is from this kind of relationship that a genuine friendship and a mutual caring between the patient and therapist naturally evolves. The patient has an opportunity to experience and discover an inquisitiveness and concern for other people, which liberates him from a painful self-absorption in illness. The result of this experience brings a sense of ease and freshness.

Ideally, an entire team consists of, along with the patient, a team leader, a principal therapist, several team therapists (shift therapists), and two housemates. Together they form something of an extended family. Each team member has a specific function, but the bottom-line activities of all of them are the clinical skills of basic attendance.

While each member of the team attends to the patient, the *team leader* does shifts with the patient and also attends to the entire team. This is a lot of work and it requires great precision and attention to details. From the beginning, he or she gathers the team members and housemates, facilitates the household interactions, conducts the team meetings, supervises individual team therapists, is the major liaison with the patient's family, and oversees the scheduling of shifts. Other team members also help in this work but, clearly, most of the burden of responsibility for the functioning of a team falls upon the team leader.

Usually, a team includes a *principal therapist,* who practices a more traditional form of psychotherapy with the patient. When I am the principal psychotherapist—as I was on most of the teams of the Windhorse project—I do this in the style that is called intensive individual psychotherapy. This is what I have been trained to do, but it is also what I have found to be useful.[1] The basic premise of this kind of psychotherapy could be said to be that recovery from psychosis is possible, and that it is much more likely to come about through the catalyst of human intimacy. There is no medicine that can ever substitute for it.

But I have often asked myself if the role of an individual therapist is really necessary for a working team. Is there a way you could do without it; is it merely a luxury? Has this role of individual psychotherapy been established only by the historical accident of my training? Does this position of principal psychotherapist exist only because it is politically, medically, and legally expedient?

Individual psychotherapy can play its own unique part in the context of a team situation. It is different from that which takes place only in an office, or anywhere else where the therapist is the single point of meaningful therapeutic contact. Here, instead, the principal therapist relies heavily on the work of all the team therapists, the housemates, and the team community as a whole. The individual therapist is only one part in the treatment network.

At first, the individual therapist does basic attendance with the patient and may do that periodically during their time together. Gradually, they settle into one place where they can talk and have some privacy. In fact, you could say that this kind of individual therapy is a specialized form of basic attendance. But because it is not action oriented (as is a shift), it can focus on other things, like the patient's relationships to the people on his team, how a psychotic predicament recycles, and how the patient might begin to take care of his mind.

Anyone who becomes a principal therapist will bring with him his own training and creativity. The basic point is that whatever form of individual psychotherapy one may be attempting to follow, if it is thoroughly steeped in the principles of basic attendance it will naturally become synchronous with the activities of the team. There is also a sense in which the individual psychotherapist attends the team leader, and together they lead and facilitate the team community.

The *team therapists* develop their own relationships with the patient and with each other (professionals and nonprofessionals, students, and former patients have been trained for shift work). It is from their experiences of working with patients that the disciplines of basic attendance have evolved.

The *housemates* have a unique role in this kind of community in that they are not trying to be therapists of any kind, and they do *not* do shifts with the patient. Being a housemate is its own specialized form of basic attendance. Because of the demands of keeping a household together, sometimes in the midst of great chaos, it is best to have two housemates living with one patient (although, under the right conditions, it is possible to have only one housemate). More than any other team member, a housemate needs to relax his therapeutic ambition for the patient. Then, he can be more honest and "down home" with a person, who becomes not so much a patient to them as simply someone with whom they live.

The actual structure of a therapeutic team can be visualized by the diagram on page 257. On the outer shaded band are circles representing a team of eight team therapists (including the team leader and the principal therapist). They all have ongoing relationships with each other and constitute a "circle of friends." Their work of basic attendance is directed toward the central square (representing the treatment household), within which are one patient and two housemates. But this microcommunity is even larger, because all the team therapists, as well as the housemates, draw upon and utilize their own life circumstances and affiliations in their work with the patient. This is represented by the squares at the outer perimeter, which stand for each team member's immediate home, family, children, friends, school, workplace, and so on. Thus, the life of a team is a very enriching experience for a patient as well as for the team members. The team begins to constitute a social fabric that is analogous to that of a tribe or a clan. Occasionally, I would bring one of the Windhorse patients with me when I went to visit my elderly mother in the household that we had set up for her

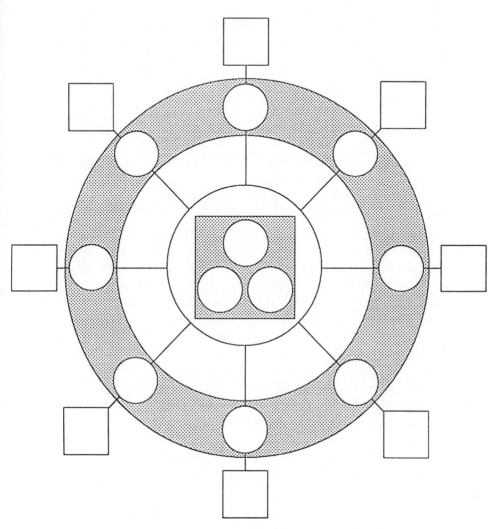

STRUCTURE OF A THERAPEUTIC TEAM

treatment. It was quite astonishing and amusing for the patient, not only to spend an evening with my senile mother (who began to think of the patient as a member of her team), but to see how I related to her and to her team.

THE WORK

Why is a shift three hours long? Simply because it is enough time for two people to really do something together. It is enough time to clean the kitchen and also take a hike in the mountains; to do some shopping and have a leisurely lunch together; and when there is crisis, there is time to settle into the situation, to reinvoke mutual concern, to inform other team members. We experimented with different lengths of time for a shift. In one hour, one has barely enough time to get acquainted or "catch up," and in any case all one can do is talk; in two hours one might have just enough time to actually do something, like go to a movie, but there is no real beginning or end, no leisure, no time to talk. Anything more than three hours becomes burdensome, and people need some relief from each other, time to be alone and experience the aftereffects of a shift. So, three hours seems to be a genuine and full interval; a full "season" of a day, a morning, an afternoon, or an evening.

At best, each team therapist has two such three-hour shifts a week with the patient. This is the kind of time and continuity needed for a real relationship to take root.

Here is an example of shift work that was presented to a basic attendance supervision group. The group was composed of myself and team members from a variety of teams. The therapist who is presenting paraphrases his "process notes" from a particular shift.

Presentation

Shift in July, at 2:00 P.M. (five months into household treatment):

Paul [the patient] is in bed, more than that, he refuses to get up. I remind him that it has been this way for the past several shifts and that last time he said we would try to get up today—he doesn't answer. This is the way it's been for two weeks. He falls back to sleep heavily, restlessly. I sat down and stayed there for about fifteen minutes. He is sleeping in his clothes and his room is a mess even though we cleaned it up three days ago. His poetry is on his desk, he has obviously been working on it. It's funny that his poetry is so grandiose in the midst of all this—this must be the way Rimbaud lived at his worst. He has his mother's picture up—that's new!

I don't know if I should push this more and try to wake him up again. I went to the kitchen and talked with John [his roommate] for a while, who had just gotten back from school. We agreed that Paul is doing alright, that he wakes up eventually and is active, and that I should be more patient. Even when he sleeps during a shift he knows that I am around here somewhere. Maybe I should schedule my shifts even later in the afternoon when he's more likely to be up. (I was grateful for the on-site supervision.)

I went to the garden and gave it some badly needed watering. John came out and weeded and we talked a lot. We were laughing loudly, and I guess Paul heard us. He came out to be with us—mostly to sit and watch us work. He was very groggy and irritated and had a hard time being with us. Then the three of us talked out there. Paul said that he has trouble getting up because of the medications. He said that he is nauseated when he gets up, and I'm beginning to agree with him that he might be having some low-level toxicity from the medication (even though his blood-level report is normal). I said that we should talk about reducing it further at the team-meeting on Friday. Also, he said, the voices attack him a lot and it wears him out.

He said he has nothing left to get up for anyway, that his life isn't going anywhere. Somehow, John and I conspired to get him to work along with us in the garden. While working we talked about his poetry and I asked him if he would like me to help him edit his writing, as we used to do on shifts. He said he'd like us to get started again—next time. He was almost romantic when he said that he wanted to write great poetry more than anything else in the world. I told him about the little writing I was doing and how difficult it is for me. He teased me, saying that I should make a schedule to write. I told him that I wasn't that inspired yet, but maybe he should do a schedule and I'd help him do it. We agreed, that for the kind of writing he aspired to do you'd probably need a schedule.

The whole notion of schedule soon bothered him. It extended

to everything—he said he should eat only three meals a day (he's feeling very uncomfortable about gaining weight); and exercise too, he should schedule that. He went on with other things he should do, and this escalated to the point that he was visibly depressed and agitated. He was overcome with his burden and his self-reproaches, and at that point I said: what was happening just now (in his speech, with me) is exactly what happens in his mind. This is the way the voices treat him. They start as if by trying to rouse him, then they order him around, and then they harass him. He added, that at times they are vicious. He is embattled, I said, no wonder he is tired all the time. It wasn't only the medications that were at fault. He starts with a healthy enough inspiration and then he attacks himself with it, just like the voices do. Who is following who?

In any case, there is a point of take-off, when either his inspiration and ambition, *or* his voices, suddenly switch gears, and escalate into excess. It's a tricky point, he could watch for that, I told him.

We went back inside into the kitchen because he was supposed to help with dinner preparation today. We spent the last part of our shift there and then as I left, he went up to his room until dinner.

The Discussion

This presentation evoked several themes in the following wide-ranging group discussion. We all felt that this had been a sensitively conducted shift and we encouraged the presenter to continue his work in the same way.

We discussed Paul's need to feel "productive" in spite of fourteen years of intermittent hospitalization and without the development of any useful skills. We agreed that his quest for productivity was crucial to his recovery. But was he in danger of distorting the issue, was he wishing to be productive just to get it over with, to establish a once-and-for-all productive "identity"? How does one feel productive, anyway: money? recognition? accomplishing one's aims? He is already more productive in the household. Paul wants all of these, but when is it enough? When is it ever enough for him? Is it possible that the team could become caught up in his speed to achieve this productivity quickly? There are a number of steps to becoming productive. In the past, Paul had definitely gotten caught up in a "production mania," and maybe the issue of productivity is at the heart of all mania. (We all wondered what the Marxists might have to say about this.) We felt it was good that another team therapist was also helping Paul develop his one-man lawn-mowing business (which might also work on his excercise dilemma).

His need to be productive, we felt, was not only inhibited by galloping expectations of himself, but also from a genuine and frustrated need to do something right, and to really help other people. His poetry of self-celebration would not be enough.

The parallel between Paul's interpersonal world and his private thought-world (or extrapersonal world) intrigued us. The way he talked about himself—and to himself—seems to have been modeled on the way the voices treated him, or vice versa. Perhaps they were interdependent. Who knows what archetypal family scene it reenacted. I told the group that in doing intensive psychotherapy I had often seen that the way one treats one's own mind, as a "thing," is often the way one's body (and one's life) had been treated by one's parents, particularly one's mother. But wherever it started, it becomes a runaway phenomenon and has its own habitual life, independent from its sources.

For Paul, an intelligent inspiration "expanded" to hyperbole. It became an aggressively tainted energy that turned on him, into command, and denigration, and made him feel incompetent and hopeless. But somehow in his poetry his voices pardoned him and lifted him up to great heights. Then he expanded on *that*. We thought it was interesting how the therapist instructed Paul to notice the surge-point of expansion, and we wondered if Paul was capable of that, or if it might further frustrate him. Someone said that he might not be able to do it but at least it could plant a seed for his becoming more precisely watchful of his mind.

There was a short discussion of the whole concept of "schedule," on which we rely so much for patients to learn something about working with their minds. Schedule is related to rhythms, cycles, number ("yantra" in Hindu philosophy), counting, the pacing of things, and also the movement of seasons.

More down to earth, we felt that Paul should drink more water—that would help with his desire to control his diet and also have some effect on diluting and flushing excessive medication.

The supervision group was very curious about the simple phenomenon of Paul being drawn into the garden where a lively interaction was happening between his team therapist and his housemate, and about how active the shift became afterward. Many of us had noticed the same thing with other patients. We concluded that it must be a common tendency for all of us to be awakened and brought along because we enjoy eavesdropping.

Essential Meetings

People meeting together in a variety of ways is the container in which basic attendance can take place. These meetings themselves are also another form of basic attendance in their function of being of service to the household and to all the team members. Thus, the meetings are also part of "the work," in that they make up the fabric of a Windhorse-style treatment community. In their different forms they allow for different qualities of patient and therapist interaction. Taken together, the whole purpose of these meetings is to build a wholesome community.

To maintain a *single* treatment team and its household, several meetings are essential. What follows is a list of these meetings in terms of a recipe, or a formula of meetings. If one were going to reproduce a Windhorse-style team—or any of its possible variations—these meetings must be considered.

1. The Household Meeting:
Present: The patient, the two housemates (or whoever the patient lives with), and the team leader.
Time: One hour.
Frequency: Weekly.
Place: The household. For example, a breakfast meeting.
Activity: The purpose of this meeting is to promote the harmonious functioning of the household. It deals with necessary household chores, relationships between house members, the household budget, plans for hosting (e.g., visiting family or friends), etc. The team leader conducts or facilitates this meeting.

2. The Team Meeting:
Present: The patient and all other team members (the team leader, principal therapist, team therapists, housemates).

Time: One and a half hours.

Frequency: Weekly. In times of crisis, this group may need to have extra meetings.

Place: An appointed meeting place (e.g., a central office, or at the household itself).

Activity: This is the primary meeting for the team community to be together. It focuses on the relationships between all members of the team, scheduling of all shift activities, developing a treatment plan, the health of the team members, and planning events. The team leader also conducts this meeting.

3. The Team Leader's Meeting:

Present: The team leader and the principal psychotherapist. When several households are in operation at the same time, all the team leaders of various teams meet together with the principal psychotherapists.

Time: One to two hours, depending on group size.

Frequency: Weekly.

Place: An appointed meeting place or at one of the team leader's homes.

Activity: This meeting is to support and supervise each other's work. It is meant to develop the skills of team leadership as well as those of individual psychotherapy.

4. The Supervision Meeting:

Present: Any combination of team therapists.

Time: One and a half hours

Frequency: Weekly or biweekly.

Place: A team therapist's home.

Activity: Here, team therapists describe and examine their shift work, as described above.

If *several* therapeutic homes are in operation, then additional meetings have been found to be important: a community meeting of all team therapists and patients; a staff meeting of just the team therapists; and a housemates meeting, where those who actually live with patients can share and discuss their unique activities. All of these larger meetings are obviously much warmer when they are held at the homes of team members and when there is an opportunity to socialize together.

BASIC ATTENDANCE: THE CLINICAL SKILLS

Work on a shift needs to be done both in the house and out of the house. In this, the team therapist has great flexibility and mobility in working with a patient. It is like the activity of a light cavalry: It can go anywhere, change direction easily, and respond quickly to emergencies. Basic attendance can occur in any environment: in the kitchen, in the mountains, at the school-yard, at an old-age home with the patient doing volunteer work, or even at the laundromat.

Conventional therapists might balk at this kind of work. Many think it is little more than a form of baby-sitting. They think it is too simple and too chummy for any "real work" to occur; it is not professional enough for them, or it does not utilize their skills of meeting one-to-one in a small office (or group therapy, for that matter, in a larger office) where everything is clearly defined and one doesn't have to become too exposed or involved. They feel that a basic attendance shift lacks the strict boundary of a "professional" attitude, which strives to keep a clear distinction between who is the patient and who is the therapist. Even student therapists, interns, and residents may feel that they are not learning the "real thing" when doing basic attendance.

Such therapists feel that basic attendance is "nothing special" and that "anyone could do it." "Anyone" means even those without professional credentials. And in this, they are correct. In fact, many people with the proper training could do it. That is its great virtue. But the proper training is not taught in medical schools, psychology doctorate programs, or in psychiatric hospitals. Perhaps there is some hint of basic attendance in the education of nurses because, at least in principle, they are inspired and trained in some notion of "service," and they are not afraid to "get their hands dirty" in their work with people. In my experience, students of basic attendance who also have been nurses seem to catch on to the principles of basic attendance more quickly than others.

Does this mean that basic attendance is some kind of glorified nursing? The answer is yes insofar as it involves genuine "nursing of the mind." So imbued is our culture with the notion of psychological treatment as being a white-collar, professional job where the psychotherapist does not have to reveal how he or she walks; eats; handles money; celebrates; does physical labor; relates to friends, children, and animals; and so on—or does anything but talk about the past, present, and future—that we think that anything else is "merely nursing," or case management, something inferior to offering psychological "insight" or the supposed science of prescribing medications.

The work of basic attendance requires more than just what one knows, it requires that one use everything of who one *is* and how one relates to the world. A deeper set of clinical skills needs to be cultivated to do basic attendance properly. It is not merely a disciplined "hanging out" (though at times that is just what is called for—and actually may not be so easy to do). Simply said, basic attendance is "getting down" to what is immediately relevant to being with someone during the process of recovery—whatever may be required, from taking walks to something approximating more traditional psychotherapy.

Of the many thousands of inspired attempts to encircle a person recovering from psychosis with an extended healing family—an impulse that is a natural outgrowth of human caring and wisdom—almost all have lacked an understanding of the mind of recovery and the healing disciplines necessary to stabilize it. I know of many instances where a family, out of frustration with the hospital system, simply employed a nurse or a college student to live with and care for a patient. These situations turn out to be completely inadequate to meet the demands of a true therapeutic home; even Geel was known to have tragedies with some poorly supervised foster care families.

For a household to be truly therapeutic it must understand that working with the mind of recovery ultimately means recognizing, appreciating, and directly relating to what have been called "islands of clarity." From the point of view of basic attendance, these are windows of opportunity. They are moments of spaciousness and relaxation, when things can be understood and life can be enjoyed. They may be sudden or gradual. If one is not attuned to their occurrence, they may easily be missed; and when they are missed, frustrated, or inhibited, things become worse.

Here is one example of thwarting the development of islands of clarity that is not unusual in today's hospital system. The father of a boy who was in a state hospital on the East Coast called me (I was familiar with the whole family) to tell me that his son's condition was rapidly deteriorating. Just before this he had been relatively clear for a period of three weeks. He had been on a patchwork of several medications, and they were withdrawn because they increased his confusion. And then, after a bout of high fever and antibiotic medicine, his confusion seemed to "spontaneously clear." During this clarity his delusional other world lost its power. He said it felt like "stepping back into myself." He was no longer deeply absorbed; he was open to people and he wanted to become more active. He was a trained athlete and longed for exercise and the out-of-doors, but because he had been a "runaway" and a "suicidal" risk, he was confined to the ward. He was kept on a strict "behavior modification" type of program where every "privilege"—such as fresh air—had to be earned by certain contracted cooperative behaviors. He pleaded to be let out of the hospital—to his home, a halfway house, anywhere. The hospital staff didn't give an inch and the boy was not allowed outside. He became sad, remorseful, and fearful about his future, and then his psychosis erupted again, seemingly more virulent than before.

Now, the boy is always trying to run away and escape from the hospital whenever the door to his "secure treatment" ward is opened. When he is forcibly restrained from doing this, sometimes he becomes assaultive. He is increasingly being held in "close observation" by the staff, but mostly he is confined to his own room, or to a seclusion room, or in "four-point restraints" for many days at a time. The hospital staff now believes that he should be transferred to the next chain in the system, a well-known "end-of-the-line" state hospital.

The father felt sad that everyone had missed the three-week opportunity—a window of access—when his son could have been given more liberty, friendship, and education. We talked about how not to miss the next one and what might be done to encourage the boy. We discussed the possibility of privately augmenting his care by someone doing basic attendance shifts with him right within the hospital. That would even help out the overworked hospital staff. We talked of getting an outside consultant—someone who could survey the situation, listen to the boy's needs, speak for him to the hospital staff, represent him. We talked about what a situation of home care might be like if the parents took him out of the hospital, and even of setting up a new Windhorse treatment household in Boulder.

What is needed by anyone recovering from psychosis is to have their moments of awakening appreciated for the opportunities they really are. However, it is more usual that these moments are met with either disbelief or suspicion, or they may be ignored altogether. The disciplines of basic attendance have been designed to overcome the obstacles to recognizing moments of recovery, to foster their appearance, and to relate to them thoroughly when they do occur. They are *basic* because they deal with the most basic and fundamental of situations: synchronizing body, environment, and mind by gathering attention and sharpening perceptions, within the ordinary activities of life. They are the principle of *attendance* because the therapist's intention and training is to be of service while tending to the needs of someone during the fragile and tentative drama of recovery. Service in this sense, at different times, has all the connotations of being a waiter, an accompanist, an associate, a chaperone, an escort, an usher, a guide, a coordinator, and sometimes a friend. The essential point is that in doing basic attendance with this attitude, one can learn how to work with one's own state of mind, and because of that, genuine mutuality becomes possible. Just about everyone who has practiced the disciplines of basic attendance has found that they have become better, deeper, more helpful in their friendships with others— they have become *better* friends. This is not surprising, since the skills of basic attendance are simply those of common human decency.

When learning basic attendance, no matter how much experience one has had in working with people, it is best to have a "beginner's mind," or the attitude of a student-therapist. This is not a feigned naivete; rather, it is an openness to learn from the person one is attending, and a willingness to discover the wellsprings of sanity.

The skills of basic attendance can be discussed in several phases, which build upon each other.

Being Present

If you are alone with someone and wish to promote their health, your full presence is required. Presence, in this sense, is a mixture of calmness, alertness, and vitality. To arouse that presence, you find that you have to work with your own state of mind in a special way. This does not mean that you are straining to be attentive all the time, or that your mind doesn't wander at all. In fact, when you are alone with someone who is agitatedly absorbed in "trance," your own mind may wander very much more than usual, and with intense, raw emotions, as if the mental speed of the patient were somehow infectious.

Picture, for example, as someone you are working with, a man who stays alone in his room, spending much of the time looking down at the ground in a fixed stare. He occasionally flinches as if about to be hit, mutters something to an unseen presence, and looks at you as if you were a stranger. He is intent on something, as if in torture trying to figure something out; and anything you say, however slight, he sees as a threatening intrusion, from which he takes refuge by going more deeply into his "thought world." He knows you are present but he is not sure if you are who you say you are, or that you even know who you are. He stays in his room much of the time and will not leave the house, for whatever reason: fear, agoraphobia, disinterest—who knows?

Let us say he is the patient with whom you will practice basic attendance. When you spend more time with such a person, you cannot help but wonder what is going on with him, what you could do to help, how you should be, or whether you should even be there. In any case, he is obviously suffering and you are part of it.

So, being present does not necessarily mean that you have a placid mind, but that when there *is* wandering, you notice that, and then come back to the environmental situation. It is like "coming back" in one of the colored space-awareness rooms: You return to your body and its gravity; to the texture and quality of the space around you; and to the mental activity that is in continuous interaction with that environment. The key point is to have that flexibility, to notice when you are "off somewhere," and to keep coming back, as a kind of dance. When you do that, you are developing a nonattachment to your own thought processes and you are practicing "meditation in action." This is one aspect of what is called "relaxing the mind."

Being attentive and relaxed at the same time also means being unobtrusive. Simply put, you must take your time. It allows for the other person to also be present. You might be just listening, but at the same time you can contact your own sense of presence and your own concern for the other person. He is in pain but you are not trying to take his pain away, necessarily. You are simply adding your presence to his painful presence. And if you are attuned to the whole environment, there will be no crowding of him, and your presence will not be imposing. Instead, there is a sense of lying low, or of meekness; in the *I Ching (Book of Changes)* it is given as the image of "crouching," or of supporting another's existence from the ground level.

Letting In

Repeatedly, while being present with the pain of the man who stays alone in his room, a reflexlike barrier of thoughts would develop in the mind of any therapist, or anyone else who was with him: "I am different from him; it is he who is unhealthy, not me; he feels his own pain and I feel mine; it is he who is indulging in extreme autism and I am the witness." But this barrier is unstable, it naturally breaks down—one becomes identified with the other's pain. And then out of some kind of fear, one tries to justify and fortify one's differences again by a further elaboration of thoughts. In Michaux's terms, this amounts to an excessive "reorientation," where one defines oneself within the environment, actually *against* the environment. The end result of this discursiveness is an increasing speed and impatience, which eventually manifest in the therapeutic aggression of asylum mentality.

The problem is that those barriers of who-is-ill and who-is-not-ill closes one off to a true experience of empathy. It can come to feel like one's "heart" is blocked to the patient, that in the presence of him you feel slightly cold, or unfeeling of your body, or somehow impenetrable. And then you come to find out that this is exactly what the patient was feeling just when he seemed to be most inert and "out of contact." Something beyond empathy is happening here, it is more of a spontaneous "exchange" of states of mind.

There is nothing magical or pathological about this kind of opening to another person. It is part of our natural equipment to have experiences where we are unified with the environment, where we do not carve ourselves out from it as separate and different. But sometimes this experience is tainted by a fear of losing one's individuality, or job description, or what can be called one's "therapeutic ego."

Some effort needs to be taken to fully engage one's own empathy and to nurture the seeds of one's own compassion. Although we already have the natural equipment for a greater depth of compassion, we do not always exercise it, especially when faced with someone who is stuck in his thought-world. Thus, when Windhorse therapists practice the clinical care known as basic attendance, they train in the formal practice called "exchanging oneself for another." Many healers have taught methods to dissolve the barriers to empathy so as to more deeply feel a patient's pain.[2] Many spiritual and psychological traditions consider this to be the birthplace of compassion.

The practice of compassion that is taught in the Buddhist healing tradition is known as "sending and taking" (Tibetan: tong.len). Here, after doing the formal sitting practice of mindfulness-awareness meditation, one adopts an attitude of warmth or health toward others who are in pain or need—including oneself—and this feeling is "sent out" along with one's outbreath. On breathing in, one "takes" in the sense of darkness, aloneness, heat, and claustrophobia of someone who is suffering, or of many people. While breathing out, one gives out from one's body and mind a sense of basic health, with a feeling of coolness, lightness, and companionship. This is a complex practice, done for minimum periods of twenty minutes by people who have achieved some discipline in mindfulness-awareness meditation. Though this actual practice is best done with the instruction of teachers who are adept in it, the complete instructions and commentary are available in English.[3] It is considered to be the crown jewel practice of the Buddhist Mahayana teachings for the purpose of awakening compassion within oneself.[4]

One doesn't actually do the practice of sending and taking in the presence of a patient, but gradually what develops from an ongoing practice of sending and taking is an all-pervasive attitude of sympathy and resonance for the patient. The patient's pain can be glimpsed and the reflexlike barrier can be dissolved. Perhaps his feeling of aggression can be recognized to be coming from his fear of you. Or you come to feel that the greatest worry with which he torments himself is what Søren Kierkegaard recognized to be *the* worry of all mental derangement: "One does not know whether one's suffering is an illness of the mind or a sin."[5]

This exchange, experienced in one's own being, may also be knowingly or unknowingly shared by other people in the patient's environment. If one is a member of a team, then it becomes very obvious that other team therapists are exchanging with the patient also. Especially at team meetings, where everyone is present, different team members will exchange with different aspects of the patient, including aspects of the patient's sanity and intelligence. Thus, they are able to represent him or help him speak. In the team situation, the exchange becomes more complete and multidimensional.

Genuine exchange is a wakeful experience and is not to be confused with "going crazy" with the patient, or any kind of "channeling," or entering into a mutual collusion of health. Therapeutic exchange is a conscious process and happens because one has gradually developed the full intention of "giving up" and "letting in." It occurs within the full awareness of what you are doing. And when it happens, you cannot hang on to it. Exchange does not develop into a fascination or a mental indulgence, because the true practice of exchange is also based on letting go (as on the out-breath) and extending one's clarity. With this kind of gentle contact a soft spot in the patient and oneself can become available.

Bringing Home

When you are beginning to have significant contact with the patient, even though no major communication might be taking place, you can still do things together "around the house." This could be called the mundane aspect of basic attendance. Together, you might straighten up the patient's disheveled room, or might do it alone until the patient is able to join you.

In this stage of basic attendance you further join with the patient around the earthboundedness of home activities. This is not any kind of artificial work. Maintaining a household, a homesite, or a campsite is not some sort of therapeutic "make-work," it is merely what needs to be done. It embodies the basic Windhorse slogan, a household ecological bottom line: *"Clean up after yourself."*

You and the patient do these activities together at first (which may be for weeks or months). When you work alongside the patient in this way, you do not do it with the attitude that you

are a supervisor, a teacher, or that you are filling in for a child
or a mentally defective person. But if the patient's household
chore is to vacuum the rug, it is a chore that may be part of your
shift, a chore meant for the two of you. Each of you does what
he can: If the patient can do only a little, you may do the rest
of it; if the patient is doing a lot of the vacuuming, then you
might attend him at it, and work in concert with him by emptying
the vacuum bag and cleaning alongside of him. Perhaps you will
have a cup of tea together when the chore is completed. And you
might talk together, or just sit in silence.

"Bringing home" is the basic attendance term for synchronizing body and mind. It stems from understanding that synchronization can happen just now, in any activity, in this present moment. Because of this, real life actions are the basis for any
therapy that would attempt to unify one's mind and life. It is an
anchor within the emotional tide of the thought-world. For the
patient, it involves an engagement of all the senses to help
ground his thinking and provides natural "brakes" to the system
of mental speed in which the patient is caught. For the therapist,
it means being aware of and attentive to keeping one's body and
mind together: One's words and actions are in harmony. There
is a sense of "one-pieceness" about the work of basic attendance. Your job and your life and your work are all the same, of
one piece; nothing special, but your work and the way you live
are interwoven. A Buddhist metaphor for this type of work is
that "You do your work with people as if you were cooking for
yourself."[6] This also turns out to be the best antidote for what
therapists like to call "burnout."

Letting Be

The important point here is to give up all hopes for results—
for a cure, for a healing relationship, for feeling good when the
patient begins to radiate recovery, for thinking of oneself as a
gifted therapist, for gratefulness from the patient or his family.
Or the converse—this is a hopeless case, nothing will happen,
this therapy is useless, I am a failure. All of these may come and
go, even within one three-hour shift. None of this is important
to the conduct of basic attendance. They are all thoughts and
emotions that are part of one's work with people. They can be
included in one's work, not in the sense that they are necessarily

a meaningful commentary on one's work, but that they are part of a larger situation. One's work with a patient contains steps forward and steps backward. It is not as simple as treatment going well or poorly. There is no "good" therapy session or "bad" one. It is more like the seasons, which are constantly changing, or like a marriage, which refuses to stand still.

Letting be means that you are practicing a sense of accommodation, without trying to change the course of things into what you think they should be. Because of the largeness of this attitude, it is also a state of quiet mind where anything can be accepted. It is a nonjudgmental openness to whatever is happening in the patient's mind, and in your own. This is sometimes referred to as a state of "equanimity." When basic attendance is practiced in this way a quality of transmission that contains some ease and relaxation takes place between you and the patient.

Bringing Along

Perhaps a month or two has gone by in your work with the patient who stays alone in his room. Moments of camaraderie occur and there is a glimpse of wanting to do more things together. Because of years of illness and the consequent impoverishment of his life, the patient is torn between the shut-in quality of his thought-world and the enticements of the outside world. Invite him out.

You don't need to create special events for him; simply bring him along into some of the richness of your own life. Your shift time together is not only for the patient, it is also for you; shift time can be spent doing things that you like to do, or need to get done. If you have wanted to see an exhibit at a museum or go to a sports event, invite him to go with you. If you need to pick up your child at school during your shift with the patient, or you need to go shopping, or return books to the library, you can go together. If you are planning a picnic with friends or going to another team member's birthday party, it is possible that the patient may also be welcome.

Is this getting too close for comfort? Does this kind of time spent with a patient violate some unwritten rule about the separation between work and life, between being professional and unprofessional? And for whose best interests is such a rule designed? When you are bringing someone along, it is not meant to be for anyone's interest particularly, it is more playful than that. Are you embarrassed about being in the company of someone who is obviously disabled? Well, that too is part of basic attendance. During the time you were working with the patient in his room because he could not leave it, you were virtually a guest in his home. But when he is able to expand out further, you might offer him the experience of being a guest in your home.

Recognizing

Not only are islands of clarity easily recognized in the work of basic attendance (they cannot be avoided), but the patient's entire history of sanity comes into view. The patient has a *history of sanity* as well as a history of illness.[7] It is made up of landmark events in his life that describe a developmental yearning for health. On the one hand they are historical moments, but also they can presently be cultivated through the activities of basic attendance. Here are seven types of landmarks, which anyone who does basic attendance can become attuned to since they may lead either to health or further illness.

The patient has periods of *revulsion* when he feels estranged from life and is nauseated about the way he is living. He awakens to his condition and is sick and tired of unceasing daydreaming and the vicious cycle of habitual thinking patterns. He has a heightened awareness of his own mindless absorption and this may depress him. Yet an intelligent discrimination has taken place between what is sane and insane and this can provide the motive force for change to occur. Team members need to support a patient who in these moments of clarity must also experience the "morning after." However, if the revulsion is not recognized as an intelligent response to his condition it can degenerate into a suicidal self-loathing. In the same way, all the islands of clarity in the history of sanity may easily be perverted into confusion and despair when they are not recognized as opportunities for further health.

The patient longs to *transcend* his stifling and constant self-centeredness. He wants to go further. On this basis in the past he has made many attempts to transform himself, as if by rebirth, into something more desirable, more powerful. Even now, he may be having a materialistic view of recovery as something that might change him once and for all.

He has an urge for *discipline,* to gain some control over his mind and body. He has had experiences in the past that teach him that this is right to do. Perhaps once, for a year, he had a daily discipline of swimming; he took care of himself and was more alive to everything he did. But he hasn't known how to maintain this discipline and he forgets that it is even possible.

He has a longing for *compassionate action.* It may not look like it, but it troubles him greatly that in his self-absorption he has lost his concern for others. His compassionate feelings and even his ability to exchange himself for others has become frozen. His regret and frustration at losing this basically human capacity is a powerful sign of his intelligence, although if he fixates upon this he comes to feel less than human.

There have been times in his life when he was capable of great *precision.* Now, his wildly wandering mind has made that impossible and he feels terrible that his imprecision causes him to make so many mistakes. But by being helped to track and be mindful of his wandering mind itself, he can again sharpen his precision.

He has *courage.* He has faced loss and desolation in the past, and even now, daily, he is confronted with fear and punishment within the thought-world. If his courage and his sense of humor are not supported by others, he will lose his confidence and abandon himself to psychosis.

All of these become apparent during basic attendance, where one can appreciate intelligent and wakeful impulses during the throes of illness. The very act of recognizing and appreciating them is an important event in further cultivating islands of clarity.

Finding Energy

Even when he is most stuck in his other-worldness he has flashes of energy directed toward real objects in his life. John Perceval, sealed in delusion, could not resist being "called out" by an attractive woman. There is always some little connection with concrete reality that a person has that can be contacted on the simple level of their sense perceptions. Even the person who has been psychotically depressed and withdrawn for years cannot help but be drawn to the bird that lands on his windowsill.

Perhaps he smokes mindlessly, but when he is offered a cigarette of fine tobacco he slows down and savors the aroma. While
eating, he is generally distracted and careless, but when the meal
is carefully prepared and presented, he admires the colors of the
food and comments on how good it tastes. He has no interest
in clothes at all, but when he is given a freshly ironed shirt he
enjoys the soft cotton against his skin. He seems oblivious to his
environment, but when music is played (especially live music)—
he cannot help himself—he is drawn into its rhythm. There is
always something to work with—as long as it is concrete.

One can always find a passionate point of contact with the
senses. It is in such a circumstance that the patient experiences
some kind of gentleness and goodness in the world. A key point
of basic attendance is to provide a wholesome environmental
situation that might evoke his interest, his curiosity, and his
appreciation of energies, colors, and space. Even though your
regular channels of communication with him are cut off, you can
still work with the pinpoint of his sensory energy. You do not
try to "wake" anyone up (this has been a frequent mistake); you
simply relate to his spontaneous wakefulness, whenever it occurs. That is startling enough.

Leaning In

There is a point when you need to increase his level of individual responsibility. In this sense, "responsibility" means things
he might do to care for himself. Ultimately, he is solely responsible for the care of his own mind, and it is one of the delights for
anyone doing basic attendance work when the patient begins to
understand this. But, to begin with, he needs help in how to
do it.

Leaning in means contacting the notion of discipline, of work,
and of being productive and useful. He is not accustomed to
discipline or arduous labor; possibly, for years he has been stuck
in the lassitude of hospitals and chronic medication. He has
become unfamiliar with how to begin, how to take a break, or
when to stop. When you work alongside him you notice a peculiar energy cycle so common to someone recovering from psychosis. There is an initial hesitation to perform a new activity
(such as drawing together): an autisticlike refusal, an insistence
on sameness, a fear of being dragged into a trap, or just not

"going along." Then, even if he wants to do it, there is an inability to get started: a unique inertia (e.g., when overcoming medications), a lack of simple knowledge (e.g., of the materials), a sense of embarrassment, or a fear of being judged. And, once into the activity, he may experience a wild enthusiasm or an immediate sense of failure. But if you stay with him, finally there is an opportunity for completion.

All of this may be experienced within a single three-hour shift. The skill and artfulness of doing basic attendance, and of leaning into discipline, is in knowing when to push and when to let up.

What generally—and hopefully—evolves is that the patient gravitates toward a particular discipline of activity with each therapist, one they both enjoy and explore together. In my experience these activities have been as diverse as cooking, hiking, flower arranging, martial arts, calligraphy, music, pottery, learning a foreign language, and working with children or dying people. Sometimes the activity may be simply reading aloud to each other.

Discovering Friendship

Within the intimacy of basic attendance friendly feelings develop. This is inescapable. It is related to appreciating another person's quality of energy, to enjoying being with them, to having mutual concerns, and to doing things together. It takes time to make a friend, and there seem to be certain obligations that go along with it. But what is most important for basic attendance is that a trust develops in which you can tell the truth, and even if it is unpleasant it can still be heard. And when friendship does develop, there comes a time when the patient cares more for his relationship with you than he does for the demands of the other-world.

This sense of friendship that arises between you and the patient is probably the most controversial aspect of basic attendance. Does friendship imply that the other person is always available to you? How possessive does it have to be? Is it a hypocrisy of friendship that it is time-limited and scheduled, and that you are being paid for service? Does it obstruct the therapist from being therapeutic, or the patient from being as ill as he sometimes needs to be? Does it mean that you always have to be on "good behavior," which may inhibit the honest expression of irritation or anger and the setting of limits? Doesn't the friendship of basic attendance run the risk of provoking uncontrollable, passionate impulses?

All of these questions, and more, constitute what in the Windhorse project we came to know as the "therapist-friend dilemma." These days, most therapists have been warned to be very wary of anything like friendship with their patients because it carries the stigma of what has been medicolegally called "undue familiarity." And so we had no choice but to carefully study this notion of friendship within a treatment setting. We also invited the patients to join this discussion whenever it arose: on shifts, in team meetings, in community meetings, wherever. In fact, these discussions about the true nature of friendship turned out to be some of the most fruitful of all.

We discovered that there are many levels of meaning and maturity to the experience of friendship, and that there is much to be learned from an open dialogue about it. Soon, both the team therapists and the patients became hypersensitive to this issue and we found that everyone—from the youngest children to the elderly—was concerned with how to make friends, how to keep friends, how to live up to friendship. We realized that this was not only a problem for basic attendance but that it is also a ubiquitous concern in the conduct of human affairs.

It can happen on a shift that you feel a sense of friendship and you wonder: Am I really being a therapist or a friend? It is a moment of some bewilderment, as if you needed to choose one of two different roles to play or identities to assume. When you do basic attendance you find that all your ideas and preconceptions about friendship are called into question. There may even be a moment of uncertainty and paranoia. Both patients and therapists have described it as a memorable moment because it suddenly becomes the opportunity to pare down into the nature of their friendship, of what is essential and what is not.

Learning

For the therapist, there is much to be learned at a personal level from working in this way. All your hesitation, withholding, clinging to yourself or to your "position," are mirrored back to you. Because of this, doing basic attendance work becomes a means for one's personal path of becoming a more responsive human being. In this sense, you are working on yourself as much as you are working with the patient. And that can be very important to him. He can recognize that recovery is not one-sided: You cannot just sit back and watch him on his journey, but *you* are also making a journey, and for long periods of time you may be learning more from him than he learns from you.

In some organic way, patients who have been the recipients of basic attendance also seem to learn these skills. Near the end of treatment, patients often become inquisitive about doing basic attendance themselves. It is always very revealing when a patient experiments with these skills and practices basic attendance with one of the team members. This may naturally occur when a team member is ill.

Many people have understood the spirit of basic attendance without having trained in the variety of its clinical actions. Probably, this is so because these skills are really only an extension of how people might naturally come to care for each other. For example, Manfred Bleuler, after a lifetime of experience in caring for people recovering from psychosis, succinctly expressed this spirit of basic attendance when he said that there were only three essential therapeutic interventions that are of benefit: expand the community of people with whom they are involved; increase their level of individual responsibility; and help them to relax.[8] These, I believe, capture the simplicity and directness of the work of basic attendance.

CREATING A TEAM: AN EXERCISE

In the past few years there have been many variations on the Windhorse theme, including team activity in the patient's own home, partial teams augmenting outpatient treatment, and even a group home for several patients. It has become an interesting training exercise—which also has many practical implications—to creatively apply the principles of a working team and of basic attendance to *all* kinds of treatment situations.

Once, I consulted by telephone with a family who lives in a distant part of the state. Their teenage daughter had recently been hospitalized during an acute psychotic episode. She had broken up with her boyfriend, and over the next three weeks became withdrawn, insomniac, and then agitated. Her mind was increasingly wild and she experienced visions of godlike beings who at first made her feel happy but later humiliated her. In the hospital, she was heavily medicated. She was terrified of the hospital and wanted to leave and return to her family—her parents and several brothers and sisters—with whom she felt very close. But the hospital staff felt otherwise; they prescribed long-term treatment (at another hospital far from home) and electroshock therapy. The family was torn between feeling that she would do better at home and feeling their terrible anxiety in going against the doctor's orders.

Along with one of the Windhorse team leaders, I met for a whole day of consultation with the girl and her parents at my home. They had a difficult time convincing the hospital to let her out for even that day. In our meeting together it was clear to me that the family was very kind and deeply concerned about each other. What was unusual was that there was also a large extended family who lived in the same area and who wanted to help the girl. We then discussed at great length how different members of the family might be able to help out by spending time with her. We actually went through an exercise of thinking of her home as a therapeutic household, with several family members as her team. We discussed some of the principles of basic attendance and how they might apply to their particular situation. Finally, we agreed on a plan: They would take her home from the hospital and gradually reduce her medications under the guidance of a new therapist, one who would be sympathetic to a home-care style of treatment.

When they went back home, they eventually carried through with this plan. Her recovery was complicated only by the difficulty of coming off the medications, whose effects were changing, from at first making her feel numb and groggy to now making her feel anxious and restless. When the new therapist was reluctant to decrease the medication, the family, during a teamlike meeting, decided to reduce the medication on their own. When even the first reduction obviously made her feel better, the therapist went along with a gradual withdrawal. Within several months she returned to school and did well.

Another exercise in forming a team is one that I use in teaching-seminars for therapists who want to learn this style of treatment. First, one of the therapists describes to the group a patient they are working with. Then, by choosing people from the group or the audience, I help the therapist create a treatment team. Of course, this exercise would apply to nontherapists as well, or any people who find themselves in a position of providing care.

The initial presentation to the group is not in the usual style of presenting a "case." It is a direct presentation of the patient, without any of the usual editorial comments by therapists about what the diagnosis is, what went wrong, who is at fault, and how to solve a problem. Here is an example: The therapist wanted to present a young married woman who she had been seeing once a week for almost one year. Because this type of "case presentation" is novel for therapists, I instructed her on how to describe her patient to us. The presentation-description is made in three categories: body, mind, and speech.[9] In terms of body, a literal picture unfolds: the details of the patient's structure, posture, gait, hair, eyes, complexion, clothes, diet, physical disciplines, general health, home environment, and so on. In terms of mind: how she relates to her mind; her degree of obsession; her ability to see her mind in motion; her degree of identification with thought patterns; her ability to come back out of daydream; her ability to notice natural gaps in thinking; what she does to relax her mind; her relation to states of mindlessness; her habits of altering her mind, and so on. In terms of speech (the interactional dimension): how she communicates; the energy and qualities of speaking; the degree of precision of speech; how she relates to emotions and their expression; her concern for other people; the quality of her relationships; the feelings she evokes in the therapist, and the course of their relationship.

This is the same method of presentation that is used in the clinical supervision groups mentioned before. The effect of this way of presenting is to heighten the possibilities of exchange— with the therapist for the patient, and with the group for both the patient and the therapist.

The therapist concluded her presentation by saying that it had intensified her feelings of being at a dead end with the patient. The patient's severe binging and vomiting of food had been getting worse over the year and was about to seriously damage her health. She was now extremely thin and she was always lacking energy. She was also increasingly depressed and apprehensive that the brief psychosis she had endured years ago might return. All of this had the feeling of a mounting "predicament." The patient and therapist genuinely liked each other but their times together had become stiff and morbid. The patient could not bear the idea of hospitalization, but it was likely to happen if things didn't change.

In this exercise, we assumed that the patient agreed to having her treatment supported by a team of people. Our idea was to work with the patient within her own home where she lived with her husband. Since the patient was now unable to work, she had time to do two shifts a day. Our idea was to give the patient a three-month trial period of team treatment. The therapist herself did not have the time to also be the team leader, so I chose one from the audience, someone who had previously been trained to be a team leader. I acted as a consultant to the therapist and team leader. Then, we called for volunteers from the audience and eventually arrived at a team of six more people. In front of the audience, this newborn team sat together and openly discussed some ideas of basic attendance. I then asked each new team member what he or she might imagine doing with this patient while on three-hour shifts.

One woman, who ran a preschool, said that she might invite the patient to the school, where they would both be around the children. (From the presentation, it was known that the patient was very fearful that she would never be able to have children because of the hormonal side effects of her starvation. Yet, she loved to be with children; those were times when she could relax the most.)

Another woman, who knew a great deal about natural foods, said that she would work with the patient in preparing and cooking certain foods, ones which would not cause her to gain weight and yet might still be reparative for her body. (The chain of events was made clear in the presentation: The patient's increasing debilitation begins with her fear of gaining weight and is compounded by her secret and fierce pride at being thin.)

The team leader said that on his shifts with the patient he would take her on periodic hikes in the mountains near her home. I said that it was probably not obvious to everyone how taking a walk in the mountains could be a skill of basic attendance, and I asked him to elaborate on this from his experience. He said that if the patient was absorbed and disconnected from the environment, for example, he might point things out to her, like the tiny bloom on a cactus, or a vast view of the horizon. He would walk beside her at her pace, or have her lead the way on the trail. If she was in an overexcited state, he might stop more frequently, ask her to wait for him to catch up with her, or sit down quietly by a stream and watch it flow away (an old Tibetan medical prescription).

This kind of hiking would have the effect of introducing her again to her geography. He might bring her husband along. He might even go hiking with just her husband! He would see his job as also attending to her husband, that is, to his comfort and strength in the household, and to his continuing with his career. (The patient formerly had exercised daily, but now she felt too weak to do so, and she mostly stayed indoors. In any case, now her desire for exercise was only motivated by the idea of losing weight.)

Another team member, a student of computer technology, like the patient was, said she might engage the patient around this mutual interest. Another woman said she would like to teach the patient some of the beginning forms of t'ai chi ch'uan, and maybe also involve a close friend of the patient.

The therapist herself said that she might now have the freedom to be able to look into the patient's addiction to an altered state of mind—the "high" of weightlessness, altering gravity sensibility, becoming "invisible"—which the patient was obviously producing by food manipulation.

There was a general feeling among the team members that the earlier shifts would focus on household and grounding, and the later shifts on moving toward a mutual discipline. From this point of view, basic attendance is not simply "supporting" another person, it also involves turning over to them the means by which they can support themselves.

One month later, I happened to talk with the therapist about the patient. She said that everything had changed. They now met twice a week and hardly ever in the office. They took walks together and had their meetings outside, usually sitting by a creek that runs through town. The aftermath of the presentation was not that she needed to create a team, but that the whole idea of a team and basic attendance had somehow liberated the therapy. She and the patient had become much more free with each other and they were both less depressed about their relationship. The patient was planning to do some volunteer work with children and the therapist had offered to help her do that.

The varieties of basic attendance and the different possibilities for teamlike treatment make it possible for any of us to wonder how we might apply them to our own experience. How might we think of helping John Perceval if we visited him in the hospital at the time he was trying to gain his release? What use might we make of time spent with John Custance if we dined with him at the same hotel from which he was making his forays into East Berlin? Would we have anything to offer to Donald Crowhurst, if by some strange coincidence we ran into him in a tavern on the coast of Brazil where he had made his clandestine stop? Or to Henri Michaux as a young child, before he decided to enter the world, when he sat in his room all day and refused to talk or eat?

But the most important question of all is how we might apply what we know to someone in our own family who may be developing or recovering from a psychotic ordeal.

CHAPTER 7

Creating a Therapeutic Home

CHAPTER

ON YOUR DOORSTEP

The full effects of psychiatric "deinstitutionalization," which began thirty years ago, have only recently become obvious. Chronically ill patients were discharged from the state hospital facilities to be "maintained" on long-term antipsychotic medications. They were supposed to be cared for and to have their medications regulated by local community mental health centers. This event virtually flooded the mental health centers, which never received the proper funding to look after the returning veterans of chronic hospitalization. No mental health center had adequate resources to meet this challenge. As the number of returnees grew, their care deteriorated into often little more than monthly manipulation of their medications. It is now well known that many of these patients gravitated toward a life on the streets and meld with the 3 million homeless people in America today.

But they did not simply go from the hospitals and mental health centers into the streets. Most of them first tried to return home, to their parental families. This event might have been expected. If you talk to people who are now in hospitals you will hear a constant refrain: They just want to go "home." Sometimes it doesn't seem to matter to them what those homes were like or what terrible conditions they might have lived under at home. And at times they are not concerned that they may not be wanted, or that they have already tried to live at home and failed, and have had to return to a hospital. Recently, I spoke with a young woman, who had been living for a year on the chronic ward of a large state hospital, in regard to her possible discharge. Her family had split up; her mother lived with another man in a situation of extreme domestic violence, and her father was an alcoholic on the verge of being homeless. They never contacted her in the hospital and only visited her once when the social worker insisted on it. But the patient only wanted to leave the hospital and live with one of her parents.

I consulted with a young boy who has lived for the past ten years in detention centers and adolescent hospital wards, who continually dreams of returning to live with his parents, in spite of the fact that both of them have died. The boy knows very well that he is involved in something of a delusion, but he says he cannot help wishing for his family home. A middle-aged woman who is actually doing very well at a halfway house episodically has fits of longing to return home to live with her highly disturbed and abusive mother. Does she really think she is capable of caring for her mother, who actually doesn't want her? Isn't her urgent need to go home a painful reflection of a delusional tie to her mother? No, she says, she simply belongs at home. There is something timeless and natural about this desire to return to live with one's family.

Clearly, the idea of returning home to recover is a powerful drama in the minds of many people suffering from psychosis. Probably it is more dominant for those in hospitals who are struck by the contrast between life as an inmate as compared to their imagined freedom of home life. In this sense, going home is an archetypal idea for anyone who feels imprisoned for whatever reason. But for those who are in the throes of psychotic confusion, the idea of going home to recover has more intelligence and sanity to it than merely deliverance from painful circumstances.

By the time John Perceval was hospitalized at the Brisslington sanatorium, he had not lived at home for many years, and he was actually furious at his family for incarcerating him. Yet even in the midst of confusion, with everyone around him assuming triple and quadruple identities, he fixed his sights on "home":

> My earnest desire, my intense inward prayer to the Deity whom I imagined conversing in me, was, 'Oh! take me home, Oh! take me to Ealing [the family home]. I shall never know what I am to do here; all is so new, so strange, so perplexing. If I were one fortnight, one week, three days in the library at Ealing, left to myself, I should know how I was to act—what I was to do.' My brothers, my sisters, and my mother were always in my thoughts; my constant longing was to be with them. Nearly all I did that was extravagant, nearly all the voluntary suffering I brought on myself was with a view to my finding myself miraculously amongst them, or them about me.[1]

About 70 percent of those who have been in intensive care for major mental illness attempt to return home. They stay with their families for short or long periods of time. Currently, more than one-third of all long-term mentally ill adults are living with their families. One California survey found more than 50 percent living with relatives. When patients do return to live with their families, the results have usually been chaotic and sometimes even tragic. Families are dreadfully unprepared for the type of household that is required. Little information about the problems to be faced has been passed on to them, mostly because professionals in mental health have themselves not known how to prepare families.

Recently, a written collection of family experiences that describe the difficulties of such home life has been gathered in a book called *A Family Affair*.[2] This book of firsthand experiences of parents has been endorsed by the family organization called the National Alliance for the Mentally Ill, as representative of what life is like when trying to keep a chronic mentally ill family member at home. The book concludes that the psychiatric profession has been both uninformed and untrained to deal with the problems of the family. One family reports that their son "has been in and out of hospitals for . . . five years at least six times. Each time it has been advised by doctors that he [should] not come home, but no one comes up with any place for him to live, so he comes home."[3] Another family says:

> Our son has been abused, neglected, and released from the hospital when he was not able to care for himself. He had to find a place to stay for himself. Invariably he was evicted since he is up at night and sleeps during the day. After several such experiences, we retrieved him and took him home, against the advice from the 'experts' who tell us that we should never have taken him in, even if it's 20 below zero and he is starving. These humanitarians tell my husband and myself that our son will never get better until we let him fall in the gutter.[4]

One response by the psychiatric profession has been that such families need ongoing "family therapy," although it is generally agreed that such therapy is expensive and hard to find. A survey of psychiatrists finds that 85 percent of them are disinterested in working with the chronic mentally ill and their parents. While all the families feel very lonely in their singular struggle to create a therapeutic household and welcome the opportunity to share their problems, they find that professional psychological therapy is simply not "practical" enough to meet the needs of the family. More and more they turn to self-help support groups where much of the emphasis is on survival.

The families live in dread that patients will suddenly stop taking antipsychotic medications, as most will do at some point when living at home or on their own. The families feel powerless and overcome with responsibility when the patients leave home. They feel unable to integrate the patient into family life. They are usually unable to get the patient to care for his own personal hygiene, clean his room, help around the house, have meals with the family, be less self-absorbed and more considerate of others. They are frustrated by the patient's tendency to sleep during the day and be awake all night. They worry about the patient's gravitation toward the subculture of homeless patients, the use of street drugs and alcohol, and the lack of genuine motivation for health.

In many situations where the patient is living at home, the quality of life for the whole family deteriorates to the point that it endangers the health of everyone living there. It is not unusual to find home situations that are continually on the verge of domestic violence. Family members often live with the inescapable feelings of guilt from wishing the patient were disabled enough to be rehospitalized or would die. They are torn between their love for the patient—usually for who the patient has been or could become—and their desire to be rid of the patient and live an ordinary life. The book *Is There No Place on Earth for Me?* chronicles the life of one such family and exposes the many instances where a patient and family are subtly or overtly torturing each other.[5]

The families hope, wait, and lobby for mental health agencies to provide needed resources: for day-care treatment facilities; for programs to monitor medication usage; for the development of new, more effective medications; for programs that can bring patients "out of the house," to be among people and not simply rely on families; for reeducation of patients; for job training and placement; for more and better-trained psychiatrists who are not discouraged by chronic mental illness; for changes in state and government funding; for better insurance coverage. Ultimately, they await the creation of more shelter and treatment opportunities where the patient can live away from home but where the family understanding, energy, and caring for the patient can still be of service.

It was inevitable that many psychiatric authorities would begin to question the value of deinstitutionalization and come to advocate for a return to prolonged and custodial hospitalization.[6] The general discouragement one finds among the psychiatric profession about the care and treatment of major mental illness is reflected in the alarming rate at which new psychiatric hospitals are being built. For example:

> Denver finds itself in the midst of a psychiatric hospital building boom. At a time when the only other boom in town is in the practice of bankruptcy law, we are jarred with the prospect of doubling or more likely tripling the number of psychiatric beds in the metropolitan area. Not only are large national hospital chains vying with each other for prime building locations, but existing general hospitals are adding psychiatric beds in an attempt to deal with declining census figures . . . [which] are often more profitable than general medical beds.[7]

At the same time, there is an increasing reliance on electroshock treatment. Lithium, once thought to be the wonder drug for treating manic-depressive psychosis, is now felt to be less effective than previously believed and inferior to the use of bilateral electroconvulsive therapy as a "mood-stabilizing treatment."[8]

It is now commonly stated by families that they have been financially exhausted by the cost of repeated private psychiatric hospitalization of a relative, and that when their funds and insurance run out the patient is either discharged home or to a state facility. Except for the hospitalization of adolescents (which has become a psychiatric growth-industry), insurance coverage for long-term patients—because of its overuse—has become difficult to come by.

More than they realize, both patients and families are faced with funding and insurance situations that are very similar to those taking place in regard to homelessness in general, where a complicated bureaucracy of rules and regulations is based on the principle of "deterrence."[9] In this case, all the infamous obstacles to receiving financial subsidy, disability benefits, and other aid have been wittingly or unwittingly designed to discourage their usage and thereby deter the cause of illness or homelessness, as if they were needless indulgences. It may be suspected that what underlies this principle is a thinly disguised desire to "punish" those who are ill. It is a resurgence of an ever-recycling attitude discovered by John Perceval: a belief that people in psychosis must be "humiliated" for treatment to be effective.

What is even more problematic for the families is that most patients are living with aging parents who are becoming increasingly incapable of caring for their children. At least three studies show that 85 percent of family caregivers are parents in their late fifties or sixties.[10] Sometimes, aging parents see their home life with the patient as their unique personal burden, their "cross to bear." Here are examples of their concerns:

> The unsolvable problem of what is to become of our son upon our deaths or disability plagues my husband and me ceaselessly. State facilities as they now exist are unacceptable. Residential care is nonexistent, or cost prohibitive, or both. He cannot make it alone, and we fear his falling into the hands of uncaring, unscrupulous persons. We are currently in the process of revising our will to a trust fund which will specify that his needs be met after we die, but we can't come up with how to furnish him with *people who will love him* and care for him. That is our dilemma.[11]

> We worry about what will become of him when we are dead—the only future we can see for him is living out his life in a mental institution if he is lucky enough to be admitted to one, or in a

prison. Society has really done us a disservice by emphasizing
'main-streaming.' It means that experts have removed themselves from responsibility, and have left the agony to people who
are totally untrained and unprepared to handle the problems of
the mentally unstable person.[12]

What is happening is that *other* members of the family (usually
brothers and sisters, even aunts and uncles) are the ones who
inherit the care of the patient. Many of these relatives, years
beforehand, become aware of the responsibility that will fall
upon them, but others will find—when they least likely expect
it—the patient on their doorstep. They will have to make decisions about care: What is best for the patient, for the family,
what method of treatment works, and what is affordable. They
will often end up living with the patient and find that their lives
are beset by all the same problems that made their parent's lives
so difficult. They too, are beginning to form self-help affinity
groups to deal with the specific problems of brothers and sisters
who try to create therapeutic households.[13]
    This new generation of family caregivers—in spite of their
determination not to make the same "mistakes" they feel their
parents made—also lives with the uneasy feeling that they are
providing inadequate care at home and that they are not receiving proper guidance in actual home-care practicalities. This next
generation is becoming more interested in the possibilities of
creative alternative care.

HOUSEHOLDS IN CRISIS

It is most likely that—if not now, then sometime in the future—
anyone's own household may need to become a therapeutic
home. As well as caring for relatives in extreme mental states,
there are also aging parents, disabled spouses, children who
become ill, and friends who may need a safe haven. All of these
will require some changes in the nature of one's household. The
strength of the household will undoubtedly be tested and all the
relationships within it may be strained. But if this hospitality and
generosity can be offered properly, it benefits the lives of anyone who lives near and around it.
    I have noticed that when capable mothers and mothers-in-law
come to help out at the house when their new grandchild is

born, they just naturally dedicate themselves to environmental concerns. They cook, clean, relax, and uplift the environment. They are not intrusive, and they give the new parents time alone together. They answer the phone, help change the infant, and arrange flowers. They might do the shopping and help host friends and neighbors. Sometimes they even arrange their own rest to fit the baby's sleeping schedule. This is the spirit of basic attendance and it is the atmosphere for creating a therapeutic household.

If your household is in the crisis of trying to care for someone recovering from psychosis, there are things that can be done to bring your home to its fullest therapeutic potential.

In the Windhorse project, and in many other therapeutic homes that I have observed, the key to providing an environment of recovery is the *housemates.* They live with the patient and they experience, more than anyone on a treatment team, the fullest range of emotions that can be evoked by caring for someone recovering from psychosis. There is no problem or conflict that family members living with patients have that is not also glimpsed by housemates, to a much lesser extent, of course. But the housemates have an intimate understanding of a family's dilemma by living under similar conditions and having similar feelings toward the patient. There tends to be an ease of "exchange" between parents and housemates. It is often the case in Windhorse households that when relatives of the patient visit the household for extended periods, they feel their closest bond to the housemates.

Here is an example of a particularly demanding experience that is known to any family member living with a patient and to all the housemates I have known. *The patient is missing.* He went out for a walk and did not come back. Or, there was an argument in the house and he left and is gone all night. Or, he goes out to meet friends who drink alcohol and do drugs and is away for several days. Whoever is living with the patient at this time experiences a degree of anxiety, which can sometimes be frantic. You are unable to locate him and you cannot help but wonder if he is causing harm—to himself or other people. You may know from past experience that he has been suicidal, or aggressive, or completely out of touch with his surroundings. In any case, he is out there suffering. Even by his very absence he is causing you anxiety. Does he mean to do this? Is he punishing you, manipulating you? Or is he so incognizant or inconsiderate that he is unaware of your feelings, unable to exchange? You are beset by thoughts of self-doubt of whether you are doing the right thing. Should you call the police, his therapist, his friend, or just wait it out? You and another relative or housemate have to make decisions. There may be an atmosphere of blame—someone, or an inadequate environment, has been blamed for the patient's dangerous disappearance. The doubt continues: Are you capable of doing a therapeutic home? Might this work even be harming your own growth and development because of the continual focus on the patient, his welfare, safety, and at times survival? Is all this time and energy worth it? What is recovery anyway, does it exist? When he runs away like this, how "real" can islands of clarity be?

If such a crisis repeatedly happens in a household, you will naturally wonder if there might not even be something morally wrong with devoting so much energy and concern to only *one* person. But what it really means is that you are doubting your own experience of the patient's islands of clarity: the reality of his sanity, the availability of his awareness, the moments of mutual warmth and opening to each other.

In a Windhorse-style therapeutic home, the team responds to a crisis of the patient being "missing" by continuing its shift work, *even in the patient's absence.* The team continues to attend to the entire household, particularly to the housemates who need to take time off from worrying and having to sit a vigil at home. And the team members can prevent a home in crisis from falling into the disarray that happens so commonly during a household crisis. It is surprising to see how quickly a treatment environment can deteriorate during a crisis. On their shifts, the team members will maintain the kitchen and see that meals are available. They allow the housemates to leave and may even attend to them by doing their chores or just talking with them. In general, when the patient is missing, the home should not be left empty; it should be maintained in such a way that the patient feels welcome to come back into it. An emergency team meeting might be called and, if need be, the home will become a temporary command center.

All of these possibilities also apply to the household where a patient lives only with his family. The slogan during a crisis to *"Shift the Household"* can be met by friends, other family, or perhaps people from one's support group. In general, families that live alone with a patient have a tendency to become isolated. They are embarrassed by their life-style and, in their own absorption of worrying about the patient, they close themselves off from friends. Just the opposite is needed. In the same spirit of generosity in which they opened their home to the patient, they could also be kind to themselves by inviting outside help. In order for a therapeutic home to work, it is clear that some kind of direct help is needed, not only during a crisis, but in an ongoing way.

A *team leader* is the key to this help: someone who can translate the principles of basic attendance into the particular home situation; who might gather and train volunteer help if the family cannot afford a team; initiate and lead the essential meetings, at least establish a basic household meeting; help the patient work with a schedule of activities; advise on a household budget; be a liaison with the psychiatrist or mental health agency; do the necessary research and inform the family about the patient's particular medications and their side effects. Perhaps this is a way in which the formal mental health system might come in, by providing team leaders to work with families in these situations.

Another obvious reason why a team leader (or a person or persons who fulfill team-leader functions) is needed is that there is usually a long-standing enmeshment between the family and the patient. There is nothing like a crisis in the household to expose this more. Anger, guilt, shame, fear, hopelessness, and depression are parents' common feelings when they are alone in their struggle to create a therapeutic household. They feel confused about when to be compliant and when to "draw the line." They continually talk of "setting boundaries" and the real meaning of "tough love." They go through phases of being attracted to, and trying out for weeks at a time, one treatment philosophy or another. This week it is behavior modification or reliance on medications, next week it is some kind of family therapy. They alternate between treating the patient as a "disease" and as a real person who needs help with daily living.

In the Windhorse style of treatment it is said: *"The Household Is for Everyone."* It is a slogan that could well be applied to any family living alone with a patient. It means that the household is meant for the well-being of everyone who lives in it, and not just the patient. This is especially noticeable in Windhorse households that have children living in them, where household and team meetings also include discussions of the children's health, schoolwork, friends, allowance, and house chores. "Everyone" also means the other team members, including their families. For example, a crisis in the life of one of the team members may have high priority at a team meeting where the patient has equal opportunity to express his concern and offers to help. The lives of the housemates themselves need to receive continuous attention. Just like the family members alone with a patient, the housemates and the environment need to be enriched by the team's interest—in their relationships with friends, their jobs, education, and their need for retreats and vacations. The key point is that a treatment household (or any other household) should be an uplifted environment and a healthy place in which to live and work.

In spite of all the family enmeshments, which center around hopes and fears for the patient, *this attitude of complete environmental awareness needs to permeate the culture of a therapeutic home.* The family who does this work alone is not merely accommodating a "border" in their home or making temporary adjustments and sacrifices in their lives to shelter an ill person. *Their home is no longer an ordinary home.* For it to be successful it must recognize and acknowledge itself as a therapeutic home. And a therapeutic home is very inclusive: it is meant for the protection and welfare of the entire family. If this principle is compromised, not only is there increased suffering for the patient, but the valuable opportunity for the patient to continually expand his awareness is lost. In this sense, *environmental awareness is not only the tool to create sanity in the household, it is also the fundamental healing discipline that the patient needs.*

In the family treatment home, as well as in an extended family situation of a Windhorse household, there are many opportunities for arousing and sharpening environmental awareness. When a family first takes in someone recovering from psychosis, they are primarily concerned with his essential needs. But gradually, they realize that some kind of agreement needs to be reached that what they are doing together is a "treatment household," that is not a hospital or just a home for several people. They need a contract of "no harm," agreeing that they will not harm themselves nor each other. Thus, seemingly private events and habits affect everyone, like constant cigarette smoking and caffeine usage, alcohol and drug use, day-night reversals, or any other activity of self-abuse; no matter who is doing it, it affects the health of those around them.

It needs to be recognized that much of a patient's actions of self-abuse or transgressions against others may stem from a painful "boredom." In a recent study, when patients recovering from psychosis in the community were interviewed about their lives, "their principal complaint was of boredom—rated by them as much more problematic than psychotic symptoms," and the high prevalence of their using stimulants and mind-altering drugs and sleeping excessively is a consequence of what they feel to be empty or uninteresting lives.[14] This boredom is magnified by antipsychotic medications, even when they are taken in just slightly more than the minimal dosage. And when the medications are used for long-term "maintenance" or "prophylaxis," not only is the boredom magnified, but added to it are fits of anxiety and an underlying restlessness. When many patients say they "must" reduce their medications, they are attempting to deal with the accumulative effects of boredom that leave them feeling lethargic, lazy, and uninspired.

This kind of boredom can only be addressed by a shift of allegiance toward sanity within the entire household. Everyone in the household needs to cultivate their own relationship to sanity. They can have a full life beyond the household and the patient. Too often, families use their time-consuming interest for the patient's welfare as an excuse to forsake their own development. This will only breed resentment—on both sides. The family members, too, need to take the opportunity of a creating a therapeutic home to improve their own lives by renewed concern for diet, behavior, and working with their minds (as described in chapter 5). It may also be useful for them to be familiar with the skills of basic attendance (as described in chapter 6). The goal here is not to make family members into therapists—in fact, that is a position they should abandon—but simply good housemates. The purpose is not to create a special hospital-home so much as it is to create the foundation of an enlightened social structure:

> The nowness of your family situation is that foundation. From it, you can expand. By regarding your home as sacred, you can enter into domestic situations with awareness and delight, rather than feeling that you are subjecting yourself to chaos. It may seem that washing dishes and cooking dinner are completely mundane activities, but if you apply awareness in any situation, then you are training your whole being so that you will be able to open yourself further, rather than narrowing your existence . . . Shambhala vision is based on living on this earth, the real earth, the earth that grows crops, the earth that nurtures your existence.[15]

The importance of bringing awareness to household discipline is legendary within the Zen Buddhist tradition. Among the profound philosophical and psychological works by the great Zen patriarch Dogen Zenji are descriptions of how to care for a kitchen—how to organize a kitchen, how to clean the ladles, where to hang the ladles.[16]

When a family goes on a camping trip, even when one of them is struggling with his mind, many of the issues that trouble them in the household may suddenly dissolve. They must all relate individually and communally to the elements of earth, water, fire, wind, and space. All of those aspects of their intelligence can be articulated. Such direct confrontation with the elements naturally activates mindfulness. The continually changing weather, the simplified living, and the time to be all together are in sharp contrast to their home life. For a short time then, they develop a collaborative effort to establish a campsite. Everyone has a natural part to play in tending the fire, gathering wood, cooking, hauling water for clean up, and helping each other. There is a glimpse of a natural hierarchy where everyone does what he is needed to do. When they return home, most families experience a deeper level of family bonding, even if it lasts for only a few days.

The activities of creating and tending a homesite on earth are unique in their ability to shift one's allegiance to sanity. These are critical activities in the recovery from psychosis because they provide the opportunity for work, relaxation, friendship, and art. All of these become the means for synchronizing mind and body, for "joining heaven and earth," or, as John Perceval called it in his personal slogan for recovery, keeping "one's head to one's heart." From this point of view, household is a microcosm of human action, which can become a healing circle, or the original meaning of "hospital."

By using one's own basic sanity and intelligence, one's home can be the right place for recovery. If the home environment is good, it is the best place in which to recover from an illness, as it is said to be the best place in which to be born and to die. At any such time, a home takes on the immediacy of a therapeutic household. It is the basic element of recovery, the element of earth.

I have heard that in rural areas of Japan, many patients who had been cared for at home are returning to the large custodial mental hospitals. When elderly parents cannot continue their care of their chronically ill children, by custom they turn toward their healthy children to assume this burden. But most young people are moving away to the big cities in search of greater opportunities. So, the patients return to the hospitals.

This same scenario is probably occurring in many rural areas. Even in urban areas, family members are unavailable to care for patients because they find the task so difficult and because there is so little help available. In part, they lack the confidence to create a therapeutic home and even the knowledge that it can be done at all.

Because of this, I sometimes lead workshops with both professionals and nonprofessionals in mental health about how to transform an ordinary household into a therapeutic home. The main exercise here occurs in small groups where each member presents his own home, or a relative's home, for discussion of how to make it into a treatment household. It is to be set up for someone who needs care now, or who will in the future. By using the principles of care described in the previous chapters—perceiving moments of recovery, cultivating environmental awareness, gathering a team to do basic attendance—one tries to design a home situation that will meet the whole family's needs.

One such discussion involved an elderly grandmother who is losing her memory and orientation but is fiercely independent and refuses to move from her home. She is becoming increasingly withdrawn and alone, and has bouts of paranoia that she will suddenly be evicted from her house if she leaves it to go shopping, or when she sleeps. In this case, the grandson who presented her became the team leader. His sister and a college friend of hers became people who might do shifts. The team was augmented by an elderly friend of the grandmother and one of her friends from church. We in the group imagined what her household could be like and how such a supporting team might relax her predicament.

Another discussion attempted to create a household for someone's autistic child, and it turned out to be similar to the household created by a family described in a book called *Son Rise,* where an autistic child was successfully worked with in a treatment household.[17] Another discussion might be about a delinquent adolescent, one who has no choice but to return home to live.

The idea in this exercise is to take a chance, try something, and become more aware of the potential possibilities. One might begin by thinking: "If my _____ became ill with psychosis (or any other calamity) and I had the opportunity to do something creative with home care (rather than using an institution), what would I do?"

A PLAN FOR A HOSPITAL

What should be done for the treatment of the vast majority of indigent people suffering from psychosis, those who *should not* be in a hospital but who *cannot* live at home or alone? This is the question I was confronted with in 1988. It was similar to the question of clinical care that arose when Karen was coming out of the hospital and I had to create an alternative home treatment environment for her. But in this case, it meant creating a therapeutic household for a group of people and at the lowest possible cost. It was naturally of great interest to me to see what could be done with Windhorse treatment in the public sector.

The Naropa Institute, represented by myself, approached Ms. Phoebe Norton (the executive director of the Mental Health Center of Boulder County), with an offer. The institute wished to go further in its fourteen-year collaboration with the center. Each year most of the students from the psychotherapy department of the institute do their one-year of clinical internship training at the center. Now, after some years of providing Windhorse-style alternative care for people recovering from major mental illness, we had much energy and enthusiasm to extend further into social action. Our idea was to train more socially committed therapists. Ms. Norton quickly identified an area of need within the Boulder community: people who no longer need emergency psychiatric care but who would be (and have been) damaged by prolonged and expensive hospitalization. This includes all those who are known as "revolving door" patients—who are in and out of hospitals and are the dilemma of every community mental health center.

One possible solution was to jointly establish an alternative treatment center, which later became known as Friendship House. It was born from an unusual, if not unique, collaboration of public and private institutions.

Ms. Norton was familiar with the Windhorse style of treatment, having been on the board of directors of Maitri Psychological Services (as I was on the board of the Boulder County mental health center), and she suggested that we establish a group treatment home following the same principles of home care and team treatment that we had already developed. We had become proficient at setting up treatment homes for individual patients, but how would we do it for a group of patients? How would we extend the treatment design? How would we fund it at no cost to the center or the institute? How would we staff it with only volunteer labor?

We gathered a team of people, a task force, to work with these questions. We decided to create a combined treatment and teaching facility: five teams of therapists working with five patients within one large household, which would also be a training opportunity for our interns. The administrative and planning team met once a month, and in less than one year Friendship House was opened. Mr. Jeffrey Fortuna (who had been the senior team leader of the Windhorse project) was chosen as the program director of Friendship House for its first year of operation. I became the treatment consultant and supervisor of psychotherapy. Five patients and two housemates now live at the House and work with a staff of thirty team therapists.

The United Nations had declared 1988 as the "Year of Shelter," to recognize and acknowledge a global concern for the growing number of homeless people in the world. This event seemed to magnetize a variety of organizations to our project. At first we bought an old, four-story brick house with federal funds made available to the mental health center from the Stewart-McKinney Act, which provides funds for shelter resources. The University of Colorado School of Environmental Design (working with the American Association of Architects as part of their nation wide program "Search for Shelter") donated its effort to draw up renovation plans. The renovations were completed by volunteer labor, material, and funds from the HAVEN-Habitat for Humanity Foundation, which had already been involved with creating shelter opportunities for the homeless. This was its first venture devoted to the welfare of the chronic mentally ill. The Swanee Hunt Foundation provided start-up funding for the training of staff. All expenses of Friendship House (salaries for eight key staff members, food budget, utilities, maintenance, and so on) were to be covered by monies allocated from federal Medicaid insurance and Colorado Foster Care to the patients who lived at the house. The Naropa Institute provided the unpaid student interns who were to basically attend the entire residence. A number of other volunteers (from other departments at the institute, alumni from the psychology training program, and graduate students from other schools) gradually joined the House community. Thus, Friendship House was created by a surprising consortium of people.

This team became the "steering committee" for the House. The obstacles were so numerous (e.g., sudden changes in state funding procedures, zoning difficulties, neighborhood resistance, construction permits, insurance restrictions) that I was never confident from one meeting to the next if the House would really happen.

After an extensive search, we selected and hired five team leaders and two housemates. Now, all that remained was to choose the five patients who would live there. The program director and I jointly interviewed about a dozen people who we selected from a long list of available patients. All of them were homeless in the sense that for the past ten to twenty years they had lived with no home outside of repeatedly returning to residential and inpatient facilities. We met with them at the local acute and chronic treatment facilities in which they were then hospitalized. Some were confined at the hospital they were in, and others could come and go, but each of them was an "involuntary" patient, having been committed to treatment by the courts. One of them had to come out of the seclusion room to meet with us.

These were some of the most poignant interviews I had ever had. We were offering the patients a quality of care that is largely unprecedented for people in their condition. We tried not to seduce them to the idea of the House because we were apprehensive about raising their expectations and then disappointing them if they were not accepted. And, of course, we did not know if the House would really work! It was very difficult to explain the plan and the treatment design of the House to these prospective patients (we wished we had brought a diagram with us). Over the years, all the patients had developed a distrust for institutional treatment of any kind, and some of them could not really hear what we were saying, or thought it was a dream or a joke. One woman, bearing the scars of years of autism, oscillated moment to moment about her interest in the House, while walking back and forth through the door. But just two words were sufficient for all of them to connect to the idea of the House: a "team" of people to help you do what is needed, and a long-term "home" environment in which to live.

How ill a patient was, or the duration of illness, or the diagnosis were not important issues. What most interested me in these interviews was each patient's potential for a shift of allegiance to sanity, because ultimately, that was the opportunity we offered at Friendship House. We looked for gaps in their otherwise solid thought processes. We were inquisitive about their experiences of islands of clarity. We looked for signs of their potential body-mind disciplines. It was astonishing for us to watch one man delicately and meticulously roll a cigarette in the midst of being mindless and morbidly distracted in everything else he did. We talked with the patients about what they needed to work on in their lives and what their problems were in the hospital. We tried to contact their natural warmth for other people and we imagined ourselves as team members working with them. One woman, who was excitedly swinging her feet throughout the interview, would have sudden surges of expansion and was unable to stay on a topic from one moment to the next. She found it remarkable that we could completely follow along and laugh hilariously with her, yet still return to the original point of conversation. She said, "You guys are great to hang out with. But how do you do that? Do they teach you that at the House?" In our interactions with each patient we tried to manifest the quality of care they might experience at the House. Every patient we interviewed felt that the medications they were being given (which were considerable, and in patchwork combinations) made them feel unhealthy and somehow undermined their intelligence. We told each patient that we had been deeply concerned about this for many years and that our long-term goal at the House was to reduce and withdraw patients from medications. All the patients thought that this was a valuable dream. In the end, we had profound moments of intimacy with everyone we interviewed.

During the month between selecting the five patients and moving into the House we began to do basic attendance shifts with the patients at the places where they were hospitalized. The team leaders and interns of their respective teams visited them and introduced themselves. At the same time, we began a program of staff training, which consisted of transmitting to the housemates, team leaders, and interns what we had learned in the Windhorse project.

On the appointed day, all five of the selected patients moved into the House. Immediately, difficulties arose because four of the five aggressively refused to take their medications. But there was also a general confusion about kitchen use, smoking areas, rules, and so on, and everyone was fearful that we had made a big mistake of taking on more than we could handle. The housemates were frustrated and frightened. At 9:00 that night, I asked to have our first emergency community meeting, bringing together the patients, housemates, and team leaders. We met on the top floor of the House, in a large open space with a skylight at its apex. We all sat on the floor on cushions since there was no furniture for that room. At this point, all our agency support was irrelevant: We were on our own, a group of strangers, and maybe a "ship of fools." The atmosphere was one of restless irritation and fearfulness.

I led the meeting, as I was already considered something of an "elder" to the patients and staff. I felt it was imperative that we all got down to the bottom line of what we wanted for ourselves, and that we once again taste the inspiration for being together. I welcomed everyone to this just-born community. I said that our being together was based on a mutual trust that something worthwhile would come from working together. I reminded everyone that we were attempting to form a community from scratch. Our community started there, with all our ideas, discomforts, and fears, all of which were part of our community and the ground on which we would build. It was not just any community in search of a community spirit; it was meant to be a "healing community" that could benefit all our lives.

I reminded everyone that we were not in an ordinary hospital, and in any case we were trying to do something different. I said, "We do not have it all together in regard to rules and policies because we plan on doing that work as a community, with *everyone* being able to say what they want and need. No one can do this for us, we must simply work through every obstacle together. That is the only way our experimental community will work." I reminded the patients of what each had said during the interviews: that most of all they wanted to reduce or be off their medications because they felt their health was in jeopardy. I said that we would *all* study the medications and their effects. This was not just a matter for pharmaceutical "experts," not one of whom had had any real personal experience with the drugs. Any genuine understanding of the medications, and how not to be dependent on them, required putting together all of our own experiences with them. All of us were hoping that we could set up our community so that gradual reductions of medications could take place. I promised them that this would be a high priority at the House. I asked everyone to please be patient with each other. It was difficult for all of us, like setting up a campsite in the middle of a storm.

In the next few days the structure of the treatment community became fully operational. The treatment design consists of five Windhorse-style teams, one for each of the five patients living in the House. One difference at Friendship House is that these are five *interlocking teams* (see diagram on page 305). Each team has a team leader who supervises the team's activities of basic attendance, but who is also the principal, or individual, psycho-therapist for a patient on *another* team. Each intern or volunteer serves on two different teams. Each of the two housemates is a member of every team. All of the essential meetings (whole-community meetings, team meetings, household meetings, team-leader meetings, supervision meetings) are held at the House. As was the case in the Windhorse project, all decisions are reached by consensus except in an emergency.

Each patient has at least one three-hour basic attendance shift a day. The original plan was for each patient to also be in individual psychotherapy three times a week, but because we were working with a very limited budget it was cut to twice a week. Even as I was concerned about whether twice a week would be sufficient, I also wondered once again whether individ-ual psychotherapy was needed at all. It took me about six months of supervising the team leaders in their individual psy-chotherapy work to feel confident that we had made the right decision in including this mode of therapy in the treatment design. It became clear to me that it is a question of "bonding." All our patients had experienced only tenuous (if any) bonding in their interpersonal relations for many years previously. Now, at the House, there was bonding at the community level, the household level, the team level, and at the basic attendance shift level. Individual psychotherapy is still another dimension of bonding. I am long familiar with the quality of intimacy that can develop between a therapist and a patient whose mind is in great turmoil. I know that such a therapist develops intense feelings for the patient, dreams about the patient, is occasionally overly dedicated, feels solely responsible for the patient, and may even feel unhealthy when the patient fails to thrive. Whatever the

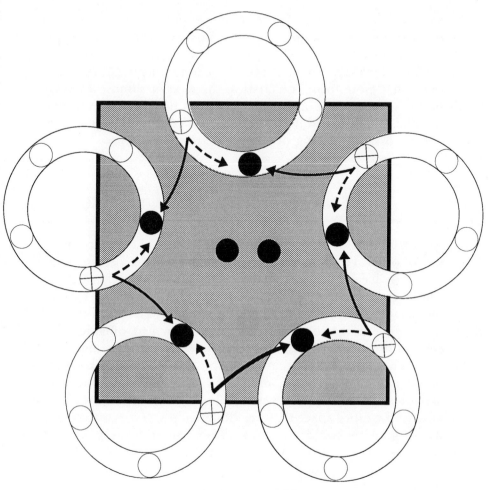

PLAN FOR A HOSPITAL

so-called countertransference to the patient might be, I wanted there to be someone in the community who cared *that* deeply about the welfare of each patient.

One way to view the history of this community might be to see that it has gone from one crisis to the next on almost a weekly basis. Another view of the community is that almost every patient has experienced, to one degree or another, a shift of allegiance to sanity during our first year together.

HEALING COMMUNITY: THE BINDING FACTORS

After a lifetime of being involved in one kind of healing community or other, I am amazed at the tremendous range of meanings and styles it can exhibit. My father was a family physician and the whole ground floor of our house was his office. My earliest memories include playing with his patients and their children in his large waiting room and in the garden just outside. Our refrigerator usually contained food given to us by his patients, sometimes the payment of poor people. My mother worked with him to maintain the office, and as I got older I would sometimes assist him in simple procedures. There was even one room in back of the office space that was designated a "recovery room," where patients could recuperate from minor surgery, or just rest. Eventually, this room became my bedroom, except when it was urgently needed. The whole situation was a sort of family hospital.

During my education, and up to the present time, like many people I have lived or worked in a large array of environments that attempted to be "community"; that is, communities that were more than just assemblages of people trying to survive and get along. Whether it was on the wards of Bellevue Hospital or in luxurious psychiatric treatment centers, each worked on the basis of a model, or a subconscious ideology about what true community might be. Each community—whether it was an educational, therapeutic, or contemplative one—seemed to have an implicit notion that the sum is greater than the parts; that the total effect is larger than just the combination of people, like the power that exists in a great library. Each community had a binding factor that was a dedication to some kind of self-knowledge, and each incorporated a form of practice to bring that about. But of most relevance here is my involvement with those communities that self-consciously constitute themselves as "heal-ing," or "therapeutic," communities. From my own upbringing, I had come to see therapeutic community along the lines of a "family hospital."

The notion of "therapeutic community" as a specialized form of healing community began in England and Scotland after the Second World War. It was the best effort of the time to address the challenge of the "asylum mentality" that was crippling the existing hospitals. For the next twenty years there was a plethora of treatment centers that called themselves "therapeutic com-munities." Everyone began to believe that they were a "thera-peutic community" if they only had a large community meeting. The founder of the therapeutic community movement, Dr. Max-well Jones, regrets this corruption of the movement. The deteri-oration of its values and practices he attributes solely to a perni-cious tendency toward the abuse of therapeutic power.[18] When I had the opportunity to study with Jones, I consulted with him about the Windhorse project community. He felt that every-thing was in order, except that he was appalled that we had not yet instituted a periodic total-community meeting; one that fol-lowed the principles of shared and alternating leadership, as well as other principles of the decorum needed for a community to function as an "open system."[19] He agreed that we could begin slowly but more community meetings had to be instituted.

When we began Friendship House, we built a weekly total-community meeting into the treatment design. Six months later, we were able to add a second community meeting. But it takes more than meetings, structures, and schedules to create a heal-ing community. That is only the *outer* aspect of community. At the *inner* level there needs to be powerful community binding factors.

The *spiritual binding factor* is the most important. This has been known for millennia in many cultures. The Christian church itself literally means community. In India, the varieties of the Hindu ashram were designed to be models for communal living. The Buddhist monastic tradition gives precise instructions, founded in spiritual practice, for the healthy functioning of com-munity. Anyone who visits the ruins of the great Pueblo commu-nity of the mysterious Anasazi Indians at Chaco Canyon Na-tional Monument, New Mexico, comes to realize that an extraordinary community of twelve thousand people once flourished there. All roads of the Anasazi empire lead to Chaco. At its most majestic settlement, called Pueblo Bonito, over six hundred rooms have been identified, where people practiced an idea of community in relative peacefulness for four hundred years. What did they know, and what did they transmit about community to their modern Pueblo children, the Zuni, Hopi, and Pueblo Indians? Huge, underground ceremonial meeting places (called kivas), some of them capable of holding hundreds of people, are the central feature of each settlement in the canyon. Whatever the secret Anasazi practice of community was (still closely guarded by the Hopi Indians), it undoubtedly took place in the kiva. From the number and different sizes of kivas found at Chaco, it is probable that these people held more community meetings than any other people on earth. Community was inseparable from the spiritual life of the people.

There appears to be a universal longing for genuine community. It is everywhere one looks. Even young children dream of being part of an ideal or utopian peaceful community. When we interviewed the patients who came to Friendship House, without realizing it we tapped into this longing when we described to them our concept of "home." In the terms of the environmental principle of "joining heaven and earth" (chapter 5), "home" for these people was the heaven principle. This yearning has been pointed to by a host of ancient philosophers and modern psychologists. For the philosopher Friedrich Hegel, the "authentification" of spiritual consciousness can *only* take place and be witnessed within community. Now many say that it is a fundamental human longing that is largely ignored in our modern culture, and that its breakdown has contributed to the current ecological calamity.

At Friendship House, spirituality does not mean cavorting with spirits. All of our patients have had enough of that. There is hardly any chronic mentally ill patient who is not involved (or has not been in the past) with spirit-presences who guide them, praise them, attack them. (While taking a walk with her individual therapist, one patient girlishly asked, "Do you have any spirits?" The therapist said that he was unaware of any contact with spirit-presences. She was surprised at this, as she herself had a wonderful contact with what sounded like a childhood "imaginary companion," and she offered to help him to learn how to make contact. She felt he was missing something.) As a community we have become accommodating to every variety of spirituality. But the spirituality we address at the House is not disembodied, ethereal, metaphysical, or unearthly. The spirituality of a community attempting to live productively and creatively together is very earthy. It has to do with sharing the earth together, and working the earth together. I have described this previously as the domestic disciplines of maintaining a household and of basic attendance. Although these were discussed (chapter 6) in terms of body-mind synchronization, mindfulness, and resting the mind, their ultimate effect is on taming the process of ego. And this is what is needed for our patients, because it is ego, speed, and manic consciousness that is at the root of their disability, and throughout the course of their recovery will be their great vulnerability.

In the Buddhist tradition, dissolving egocentricity is the basis of anything that can be called "spiritual." Although it is a highly personal journey of development, it can be cultivated and protected at the level of community. This is the place where therapeutic community and spirituality meet. The materialism of ego—its territoriality, possessiveness, need for confirmation, attachment to self, protection of self, and eventual aggrandizement of self—is the greatest threat to both the patient's recovery and a harmonious community. Relaxing one's personal territory and being able to open up to the experience of others is a fruition of true community. Thus, a spirituality that recognizes and relates to a world of experience beyond the confines of ego is the bottom-line individual and collective discipline of genuine community. With a gradual shedding of the restricting blinders of ego comes greater appreciation of the sensory world and the possibility of recognizing sacredness and dignity in ordinary life. This, I have found, is *the* most powerful medicine for recovery from psychosis, and a major inspiration to shift one's allegiance to sanity.

In the Windhorse project and at Friendship House, we find that three other binding factors are needed to facilitate a community spiritual journey: *work, practice, and study.* These are the same principles we use at the Naropa Institute, when twice each year we establish a space awareness practice community in the mountains (from ten days to three months). This community is involved with the five-color "room" practice of maitri space awareness (chapter 5). As well as offering the opportunity to explore one's relationship to space and stimulate environmental awareness, these communal living situations are designed to be model therapeutic communities. From these experiences, we have concluded that the binding factors of work, practice, and study are necessary for the health of every therapeutic community.

Work involves all the domestic disciplines needed to maintain any form of shelter. (In the middle of a supervision group at the House, two of the team leaders had to suddenly leave in order to deal with an overflowing toilet bowl.) The maintenance of the shelter itself is everyone's business. All staff and patients alike are required to be involved with domestic disciplines.

Practice is the means for working with one's own mind and emotions in a way that gives rise to the experience of acceptance and kindness of one's inner world (called *maitri*). It naturally arises out of the practice of mindfulness-awareness meditation. As the experience of maitri develops in the practice of many community members, it begins to pervade the entire community. This is a most important antidote to the tendency toward "asylum mentality." As mentioned previously, it is not necessary (or advisable for some patients) that they do this practice, but it is essential that a critical mass of staff members *do* have some means to cultivate maitri. All the disciplines of basic attendance are also meant to radiate the experience of maitri.

In a sense, basic attendance itself is a spiritual practice, to soften the process of professional solidification into "healers" and "sick people." The original working name for the community was Maitri House, but some of our funding sources felt that this name might indicate religious proselytizing. Finally, we all agreed that the name Friendship House would fully capture the maitri principle of "loving kindness," and at the same time highlight the creative tension between formal therapy and genuine patient-therapist friendship, on which all Windhorse community is based.

As the community meeting is the sine qua non of anything called a therapeutic community, learning to hold one's mind reasonably steady during a community meeting is still another form of practice. Being at these meetings can be uncomfortable, especially when one's mind and body are filled with distraction and restlessness. Learning to be at ease in the meetings (including household meetings, team meetings, etc.) gradually allows one to experience the joyfulness that is possible within community. Nevertheless, every therapeutic community is familiar with the difficulties of getting patients and staff to attend these meetings. At Friendship House we do everything we can to encourage people to attend the community meeting. We continuously invite people to come, before and during the meeting. We will not "drag" them to it, pay them for attending, or punish them for not attending, as is the prescription in many other communities. If patients do not come along to the meetings, then there is something wrong with the meetings. Some examples of what may obstruct people from attending the meetings are: they are simply not interesting enough; not inclusive enough of the patients; too linear, too tied to an agenda; too serious, not playful enough; not personal enough, or when they are, they tend to call the patients to account. All of these lead patients to feel that what they have to contribute to meetings is not of great value, and that their presence may even be a burden.

So, at Friendship House, we continue to invite people to attend the meetings as a place where everyone can be heard, where the center and fringe of the community can freely communicate, where there is no attempt to change or coerce anyone, and where the obstructions to community can be uncovered. In the end, what brings a patient to a community meeting is his inquisitiveness and curiosity. Recently, at the House, there had been a year-end turnover of the interns and volunteers. This transition, of losing old and making new relationships, for good reason, is usually the plague of any community that is also a teaching facility. But at our first community meeting, meant to be a greeting for the new team members, all the patients came, and were more present and wakeful than ever. They wanted to see the new faces and personalities; they had become curious and were magnetized by a sense of community passion.

And, when everyone is present at the community meeting—whether it be a meeting of a family alone, of a team, or a community of teams—sometimes there is a sudden recognition of everyone's interdependence, of a commitment to each other's health, and a reaffirmation of the basic goodness that exists in all of us. This alone is what ultimately brings people to participate in therapeutic community.

Study refers to some kind of intellectual or insightful activity, as happens in clinical supervision groups. But the study of the nature of therapeutic community is the most intriguing. Daily, we are learning more about the nature and means of community. It doesn't stop: Community is always a "work in progress"—evolving, running into obstacles, devolving.

How to introduce more awareness discipline into the House is one of our continuing studies. One day, some of the interns brought a small bell into the community meeting with the idea than when it rang, everyone would stop talking and keep several seconds of silence. This was modeled after a Vietnamese Zen community practice, which the interns had just learned at a workshop. We tried it for a couple of meetings and it did have the effect of stopping the community mind and producing a gap in the middle of a feisty discussion. But no one liked the little bell, it made us apprehensive.

As promised, the staff and patients studied the effects of medication together. No other subject could arouse the patients' interest more than this! Their major contact with health of any kind was a desire for wellness by being free of medications. More than anything else, the medication issues sparked their intelligence and inquisitiveness. At the same time, no other issue can drive such a wedge into a community—splitting patients from staff—like the enforced taking of medication. One evening, I gave a presentation to the community about the effects of medications, as I understood them to be. Beforehand, all the staff and patients had read the section from *Dr. Caligari* about the reduction of medications. The discussion turned out to be more frightening than I had expected, and for the next two weeks almost all the patients periodically refused to take their medications. We formed a task force to design a medication reduction for each particular patient at the House, including a schedule of what needed to be accomplished in order to begin a gradual withdrawal.

It was clear to us that when the patients stopped taking medications on their own, and without support, it was usually with the intention of wanting to "feel better." Released from the tranquilization, they felt they could be "more of themselves." Yet, when our patients tried such private reductions, they always seemed to lose control of their minds just as they began to feel better. For some people, the energy and speed arising from withdrawal is more than they are accustomed to handling. Eventually, everyone became convinced that a scheduled withdrawal, under the right conditions and with team support, was the only sensible way to reduce medications. As of this time, three of the patients have experimented with very slight withdrawals, and the conflict about medications no longer preoccupies the community.

Historically, "therapeutic community" was meant to be an ideal democratic process, and it left little room for the final binding factor: *natural hierarchy.* No community can survive without the presence of teachers or elders who can transmit the wisdom of the community and train others to become teachers.

In this way the practices of the community can stay alive and have a continuity beyond the teachers. Just as the presence of a knowledgeable team leader catalyzes an individual therapeutic home, such leadership responsibility is crucial in larger treatment communities. The continuity of Windhorse-style treatment, and of projects like Friendship House, are completely dependent on skillful team leadership. *It is my opinion that in the whole field of mental health there is no higher priority than the training of new team leaders.*

It is impossible to convey the amount of staff dedication that has gone into the founding of the Friendship House community. Obviously, the housemates bear the heaviest burden. "In turn, the housemates may begin to wonder if they are therapists, friends, or, perhaps, even patients themselves! Not only are their personal domestic lives fully exposed to the patients and other team members, but their professional lives are also open to view and completely supervised."[20] Aside from their day-to-day stress, they must protect—sometimes alone and against everyone's forgetfulness—the important transmission that the House is a home, not a hospital. It is a home to the housemates as much as it is to the patients, and when community members enter the House they need to remember that it is not a hospital, or a school, or a clubhouse, but that they are a guest in someone's home.

THE BRILLIANCE OF RECOVERY

At this time, all the popular and professional literature express hopelessness about recovery from psychosis. It is seen simply as a terminal illness, although several studies indicate that, about twenty years after being released from state hospitals, 20 to 50 percent of patients have settled down in their lives (usually on long-term medications) and do not require custodial care.[21] This is not exactly inspiring news. However, the evidence from the Windhorse project and Friendship House suggests that recovery is much more immediately available than is generally believed.

There were numerous difficulties during the first year of life at Friendship House. Most noteworthy were several incidents of extreme anger and flashes of violence toward the staff. Police officers had been summoned, and twice a patient had to be removed from the community and hospitalized for a brief stay. Several of the patients had reversed sleep patterns and, to the dismay of the house staff, enjoyed a surreptitious nightlife, nights often filled with nightmarish, terrifying struggles in the realms of hell. The house staff often experienced a conflict between living as ordinary, eye-level roommates with the patients and authoritatively setting behavior limits. A summary of the first six months reports:

> The politics of communication remains a charged issue. On the other hand, a vital learning environment and a safe, stable household are slowly taking root. The training of socially committed therapists with a speciality in comprehensive care of the severely disturbed is being carried out with increasing precision. The patients are settling into their new community home with a renewed sense of personal dignity and appreciation of human relatedness. They are beginning to treat each other with more consideration, exercising long-neglected compassionate impulses. The patients are simply waking up to their current life circumstances. At the same time, they may experience fleeting glimpses of the possibility for recovering a meaningful life.[22]

How can one evaluate the "success rate" at Friendship House? For people who have lived largely in psychiatric institutions against their will for at least fifteen years, how does one talk about "cure"? Certainly, there have been achievements. Although one of the patients had to return to a hospital after two months, all five of the patients who entered the House were under legal certification to treatment; by now, at the end of one year, all have become voluntary patients. All were under legal order to take medication; now none are required to take them. No patient had lasted more than six months in any other treatment setting; after one year, no one wants to leave. While currently the continually inflating cost at most treatment facilities ranges from about $300 a day (in the public sector) to more than $1000 (in some private hospitals, and often for the most mediocre care), the cost for each patient at Friendship House is about $86 a day. Meanwhile, five expensive inpatient beds have been vacated by the patients who moved to Friendship House and are now available for other acutely ill patients. Construction is about to begin at the House to add two more bedrooms, a large meeting room, and an outside deck. Also, the mental health center is interested in beginning another treatment home of the same design.

On entering the House during the day, one is likely to find a child playing in the living room or watching television while waiting for his parent who is at a team meeting. Generally, the atmosphere is light and spacious. Now there are many more cookouts and picnics than there are emergency meetings.

My own observations over the year about our patients' journeys of recovery are more difficult to describe and will not help those who depend on statistics to document mental health. The general health of all the patients has improved (although everyone smokes too much). Since coming to the House each patient dresses better, smiles more easily, is more interested in their lives, and is much more judicious about the use of alcohol and drugs. They have more friends, and they have learned something about community. They have come a long way from the early days of resenting each other, to being more considerate, kinder people. Their senses of humor seem to be restored and more easily accessible. Usually, there is a wakeful glint in their eyes and it makes you want to smile at them.

In terms of how the patients handle their minds, one observation is striking: They seem to be less "caught up" in their minds. They are better able to dissolve escalations of ideas and emotions. When they *are* too much involved in a "thought-world," they often come out of it quickly, as if suddenly freed from a fixed delusion. Not one of them seems to take their thought-worlds as seriously as they did before.

How many people have witnessed someone in the gradual and painstaking recovery from psychosis? It seems to be quite rare. Most modern treatment facilities are not the environments in which to make such observations. We have become sanguine and prejudiced about the possibility of recovery at all. But if one does have the privilege of knowing someone as he extricates himself from psychosis and shifts his allegiance to sanity, it is like watching a flower bloom. It touches you deeply. Like any parent who is comforting a child as he awakens from a terrible nightmare, you feel a sense of tenderness and even mystery. You see, and then you remember in your own life, the power of mind to encase one in a delusional conviction of reality. You feel your own fragility.

But in the night, when you are alone with the awakening child, it is also peaceful and joyful: He has returned.

He may cling to you, but he is wiser; he wonders if he has only entered another dream. His hesitation is palpable. Only your presence makes the situation bearable. It makes you want to do everything you can to protect his wakefulness. When it is done, when the nightmare has been broken through, you may look again at the human condition, and feel a renewed appreciation for the power of recovery, which is intrinsic to all of us.

Epilogue

The intention of this book is to inspire our culture to more compassionate care for the mentally ill. To one degree or another this applies to all of us, for madness is everyone's concern: If you have a mind, it can go mad; as long as there is egocentricity, there is always the possibility for egomania. Moreover, anyone can lose their mind if they do not care for it properly; if one does not know how to protect the mind, there remains a possibility for severe mental imbalance. Dangerous repercussions can follow from cultivating any habitual distractibility or absences of mind—concentration becomes scattered and, in a moment, one can become caught between the jaws of the "thought-world."

Glimpsing the interior of these extreme mental states opens the way for understanding and empathic response:

John Perceval demonstrated that whatever else insanity is, it involves a deliberate interference with the delicate balance of mental forces. Genuine recovery is just as willful, requiring great courage, effort, and the release of compassionate impulses. For him, patient advocacy was the true fulfillment of recovery.

John Custance indulged and explored the biological founda-

tions of his fascination, even craze, with attaining psychospiritual power. He drove himself to the heights and depths
of madness by trying to harness the energy of extreme mental
speed.

Donald Crowhurst exposed a seemingly ceaseless urge toward
self-transformation, to become someone other than who he
was, where no height of largeness or greatness was ever final
enough—a kind of psychospiritual malignancy.

Henri Michaux discovered the essential "wound" of madness
that unleashes the energies of the undermind to create alternative realities, super-realities, and cosmic realities. He unveiled the terrible psychic energetics of psychosis.

Uncovering the existence of spontaneous, innate flashes of sanity can become the building blocks of recovery. Upon these can
be built a whole structure of treatment and a fresh approach to
intensive care of the mind and body in psychosis.

Learning the necessary skills of this approach, especially the
methods of *basic attendance,* allows human intimacy to become
the catalyst for recovery. The secret of such intimacy can be
learned and practiced; it is called the discipline of "exchange."

Empowered in this way to take mental health into our own
hands, we need no longer rely simply on "experts" to banish
madness. By understanding the importance of environment, an
ordinary home can become a natural place for healing. This can
have great consequences for everyone involved in such a project: One's inherent human goodness can be appreciated and
nurtured.

This presentation of mental breakdown and recovery points
to a general rule of mind: Some kind of mental discipline of
being present, of nowness, or of mindfulness is necessary to
maintain the health of the mind. This is not a matter of psychology or spirituality—protecting the mind is like protecting one's
eyes. It is precious, and ultimately it is one's own natural responsibility. Even in the midst of psychotic exaltation or disaster one
can learn to hold one's seat and maintain one's dignity. This,
along with gentle human companionship, is the key to recovery.

Notes

Introduction

1. From a task force of the American Psychiatric Association, reported in *Psychiatric Times*, Oct. 1987.
2. This same claim has been made continuously, beginning in 1810. See Andrew Scull, *Museums of Madness: The Social Organization of Insanity in Nineteenth-Century England* (New York: St. Martin's Press, 1979).
3. American Psychiatric Association study on electroshock therapy, Boulder, Colorado, *Daily Camera*, 22 Dec. 1989.
4. Ivan Illich, *Medical Nemesis: The Expropriation of Health* (New York: Pantheon Books, 1976).
5. Thomas Bittker, "The Industrialization of American Psychiatry," *American Journal of Psychiatry* 142 (1985): 2.
6. Manfred Bleuler, letter to the author, October 1984. By permission of Dr. Bleuler.

Chapter 1: Perceval's Courage

1. John Perceval, *Perceval's Narrative: A Patient's Account of His Psychosis,* ed. Gregory Bateson (Palo Alto: Stanford University Press, 1961).
2. Ibid., 6.
3. Ibid., 12.
4. William James, *Varieties of Religious Experience* (New York: Random House, 1902).
5. Søren Kierkegaard, *Philosophical Fragments* (Princeton: Princeton University Press, 1952), 13.

6. Perceval, *Perceval's Narrative*, 19.
7. Ibid., 22.
8. Ibid., 29.
9. Ibid., 43.
10. Michel Foucault, *Madness and Civilization: A History of Insanity in the Age of Reason* (New York: Pantheon Books, 1965); Andrew Scull, *Museums of Madness: The Social Organization of Insanity in Nineteenth-Century England* (New York: St. Martin's Press, 1979); Andrew Scull, ed., *Madhouses, Mad-Doctors, and Madmen* (Philadelphia: University of Pennsylvania Press, 1981); William Parry-Jones, *The Trade in Lunacy* (London: Routledge and Kegan Paul, 1972); and others.
11. John Perceval, *A Narrative*, Vol. II (London: Effingham Wilson, 1840), 23.
12. Ida Macalpine and Richard Hunter, *George the Third and the Mad-Business* (New York: Pantheon Books, 1969).
13. Perceval, *Perceval's Narrative*, 70.
14. Chögyam Trungpa, *Glimpses of Abhidharma* (Boston: Shambhala Publications, 1975).
15. Perceval, *Perceval's Narrative*, 44.
16. D. P. Walker, *Unclean Spirits: Possession and Exorcism in France and England in the Late Sixteenth and Early Seventeenth Centuries* (Philadelphia: University of Pennsylvania Press, 1981).
17. Perceval, *Perceval's Narrative*, 46.
18. Ibid., 285.
19. See Chögyam Trungpa, "The Six Realms" in *Cutting Through Spiritual Materialism* (Boston: Shambhala Publications, 1973).
20. Perceval, *Perceval's Narrative*, 54.
21. Ibid., 151.
22. Ibid.
23. Ibid., 63.
24. Ibid., 103.
25. Ibid., 294.
26. Ibid.
27. Ibid., 295.
28. Ibid., 305.
29. Ibid., 329.
30. Ibid., 321.
31. Ibid., 243.
32. Perceval, *A Narrative*, Vol. II, 114.
33. Bruno Bettelheim, *Surviving, and Other Essays* (New York: Alfred A. Knopf, 1979).
34. Perceval, *Perceval's Narrative*, 220.
35. Nick Hervey, "Advocacy or Folly: The Alleged Lunatics' Friend Society, 1845–63," *Medical History* 30 (1986): 245.
36. From the annual report of the Oskar Diethelm Historical Library, New Soul Hospital.
37. Hervey, "Advocacy or Folly," 245.
38. John Perceval to Sir James Graham, *Collected Letters* (London: Effingham Wilson, 1846), 115.
39. John Perceval, ed., *Poems from Bethlehem Hospital* (London: Effingham Wilson, 1851).

40. John Perceval, "The Case of Dr. Peithman," *Journal of Contemplative Psychotherapy* 3 (1985).
41. See, for example, one of the latest studies, "Inside Looking Out," in *Southern Exposure,* Fall 1989.
42. From "In Conversation with Maxwell Jones," *The Bulletin of the Royal College of Psychiatrists* 8, no. 9 (1984).
43. Foucault, *Madness and Civilization.*
44. Perceval, *Perceval's Narrative,* 74.
45. Ibid., 47.
46. Ibid., 99.
47. "A Letter to the Right Hon. W. E. Gladstone, M.P., on the separation of the Irish Church from the State, and in favour of a dissolution of the Union between England and Ireland" (London: Effingham Wilson, 1868).

Chapter 2: Mania and the Risk of Power

1. Daniel Schreber, *Memoirs of My Nervous Illness,* ed. Ida Macalpine and Richard Hunter (London: Dawson and Sons, Ltd., 1955).
2. John Custance, *Wisdom, Madness and Folly* (New York: Pellegrini and Cudahy, 1952), 187.
3. Mark Sedler, "Falret's Discovery: The Origin of the Concept of Bipolar Affective Illness," *American Journal of Psychiatry* 140 (1983): 9.
4. John Custance, *Adventure into the Unconscious* (London: Christopher Johnson, 1954), 1.
5. Ibid., 15.
6. Carl Jung, "Forward to Wisdom, Madness and Folly," in *Collected Works of Carl Jung,* vol. 18 (London: Bollingen Foundation, 1976), 349.
7. Custance, *Adventure into the Unconscious,* 9.
8. Ibid., 45.
9. Ibid., 28.
10. Ibid., 81.
11. Ibid., 70.
12. Ibid., 85.
13. Ibid., 88.
14. Ibid., 185.
15. Custance, *Wisdom, Madness and Folly,* 187.
16. Custance, *Adventure into the Unconscious,* 57.
17. Ibid.
18. Ibid., 32.
19. Ibid., 56.
20. Ibid., 32.
21. Ibid., 52.
22. Ibid., 54.
23. Ibid., 16.
24. Ibid., 36.
25. Ibid., 34.
26. Ibid., 53.
27. Ibid., 55.
28. Ibid., 47.
29. Custance, *Wisdom, Madness and Folly,* 18.

30. Custance, *Adventure into the Unconscious,* 20.

31. Ibid., 16.

32. Custance, *Wisdom, Madness and Folly,* 20.

33. William James, *On Exceptional Mental States: The 1986 Lowell Lectures,* reconstructed by Eugene Taylor (New York: Charles Scribner and Sons, 1982).

34. Custance, *Adventure into the Unconscious,* 58.

35. Ibid., 16.

36. Ibid., 59.

37. Custance, *Wisdom, Madness and Folly,* 46.

38. Custance, *Adventure into the Unconscious,* 113.

39. Thomas De Quincey, *Confessions of an English Opium Eater* (New York: Penguin Books, 1971).

40. Custance, *Adventure into the Unconscious,* 4.

41. Edward Podvoll, "Psychosis and the Mystic Path," *The Psychoanalytic Review* 66 (1979–80).

42. Edward Podvoll, "The Experience of Dreaming and the Practice of Awareness," *Naropa Institute Journal of Psychology* 3 (1985).

43. William Wordsworth, *Prelude,* in Custance, *Adventure into the Unconscious,* 3.

44. Custance, *Adventure into the Unconscious,* 2.

45. Clifford Beers, *A Mind That Found Itself* (Pittsburgh: University of Pittsburgh Press, 1981); Anton Boison, *The Exploration of the Inner World* (Philadelphia: University of Pennsylvania Press, 1936).

46. Custance, *Adventure into the Unconscious,* 129.

47. Jung, "Forward to Wisdom, Madness and Folly."

48. Custance, *Adventure into the Unconscious,* 148.

49. Ibid., 187.

50. Ibid., 117.

51. Chögyam Trungpa, *Shambhala: The Sacred Path of the Warrior* (Boston: Shambhala Publications, 1984).

52. Custance, *Adventure into the Unconscious,* 203.

53. Ibid., 207.

Chapter 3: The Epic of Megalomania

1. Michel Foucault, ed., *A Case of Parricide in the Nineteenth Century,* chapter entitled "I, Pierre Riviere . . ." (New York: Random House, 1975).

2. The description of events relating to the life and strange adventure of Donald Crowhurst comes from the excellent work of N. Tomalin and R. Hall, *The Strange Last Voyage of Donald Crowhurst* (New York: Stein & Day, 1970). All quotations are from their work unless otherwise specified.

3. This event was reported only in a survey article, G. Bennet, "Psychological Breakdown at Sea: Hazards of Singlehanded Ocean Sailing," in *British Journal of Medical Psychology* 47 (1974).

4. Tomalin and Hall, *Strange Last Voyage,* 237.

5. Chögyam Trungpa, *Cutting Through Spiritual Materialism* (Berkeley: Shambala Press, 1973).

6. See Sigmund Freud, *The Interpretation of Dreams* (New York: Basic Books,

1955). See especially examples of the dream dramas that are woven around interrupting outside stimuli.

7. Tomalin and Hall, *Strange Last Voyage*, 265.

Chapter 4: Major Ordeals of Psychotic Mind

1. Described in Karl Jaspers, *General Psychopathology* (Manchester: Manchester University Press, 1962).
2. Henri Michaux, *Miserable Miracle* (San Francisco: City Lights, 1956), 89.
3. Antonin Artaud, *The Peyote Dance* (New York: Farrar, Straus and Giroux, 1976).
4. Henri Michaux, *Ecuador*, trans. Robin Magblum (Seattle: University of Washington Press, 1970).
5. R. Gordon Wasson, *Maria Sabina and Her Mazatec Mushroom Velada* (New York: Harcourt Brace Jovanovich, 1974).
6. Henri Michaux, *Major Ordeals of the Mind and Countless Minor Ones* (New York: Harcourt Brace Jovanovich, 1974), 13.
7. Michaux, *Miserable Miracle*, 7.
8. Henri Michaux, *Light Through Darkness* (New York: The Orion Press, 1963), 1.
9. Henri Michaux, *Infinite Turbulence* (London: Calder and Boyars, 1975), 61.
10. Michaux, *Major Ordeals*, 4.
11. Michaux, *Infinite Turbulence*, 121.
12. Michaux, *Light Through Darkness*, 162.
13. Ibid., 166.
14. Michaux, *Major Ordeals*, 16.
15. Michaux, *Miserable Miracle*, 66.
16. Michaux, *Major Ordeals*, 37.
17. Michaux, *Miserable Miracle*, 63.
18. Michaux, *Light Through Darkness*, 6.
19. Michaux, *Miserable Miracle*, 87.
20. Michaux, *Major Ordeals*, 51.
21. Ibid., 52.
22. Ibid., 60.
23. Ibid., 92.
24. Ibid., 93.
25. Ibid., 96.
26. Ibid., 9.
27. Ibid., 10.
28. Ibid., 20.
29. Michaux, *Infinite Turbulence*, 139.
30. Michaux, *Light Through Darkness*, 3.
31. Michaux, *Miserable Miracle*, 83.
32. Michaux, *Light Through Darkness*, 131.
33. Michaux, *Major Ordeals*, 13.
34. Ibid., 23.
35. Ibid.

36. Michaux, *Light Through Darkness*, 175.
37. Hsüan-tsang, *The Doctrine of Mere-Consciousness*, trans. Wei Tat (Hong Kong: 1973).
38. Hervey de Saint-Denys, *Dreams and How to Guide Them* (London: Duckworth, 1982).
39. Michaux, *Miserable Miracle*, 72.
40. Ibid., 67.
41. Michaux, *Light Through Darkness*, 135.
42. Michaux, *Infinite Turbulence*, 148.
43. Henri Michaux, *Selected Writings*, trans. Richard Ellman (New York: New Directions, 1968), xvi.
44. Michaux, *Light Through Darkness*, 156.
45. Ibid., 157.
46. Michaux, *Major Ordeals*, 4.
47. Michaux, *Infinite Turbulence*, 173.
48. Sally Clay, "Stigma," *Journal of Contemplative Psychotherapy* 4 (1987).
49. Oliver Sacks, *Awakenings* (New York: E. P. Dutton, 1983), 306.
50. Michaux, *Miserable Miracle*, 37.
51. Jeremy Hayward, *Perceiving Ordinary Magic* (Boston: Shambhala Publications, 1985).
52. Michaux, *Miserable Miracle*, 10.
53. Michaux, *Major Ordeals*, 117.
54. Ibid.
55. Michaux, *Light Through Darkness*, 158.
56. Henri Michaux, *Vers la completude* (Paris: Editions G.L.M., 1967).
57. Terry Clifford, *Tibetan Buddhist Medicine and Psychiatry* (York Beach, Maine: Samuel Weiser, 1984).
58. Michaux, *Major Ordeals*, 120.
59. Ibid., 42.
60. Ibid., 10.
61. Technically, this has been stated to be so by the neuropsychologist Dr. Karl Pribram. After some skepticism, the noted neuroanatomist Dr. Walle Nauta agreed that it was probably correct.
62. Two remarkable examples of this are A. R. Luria, *The Man with a Shattered World* (Chicago: Henry Regnery, 1968); and Helen Wulf, *Aphasia, My Life Alone* (Detroit: Wayne State University Press, 1973).
63. Anesthetics: Chloralose, Ketamine.
64. Richard D'Ambrosio, *No Language But a Cry* (New York: Doubleday, 1970).
65. Bruno Bettelheim, *The Empty Fortress* (New York: The Free Press, 1967).
66. August Strindberg, *Inferno/From an Occult Diary* (New York: Penguin Books, 1979), 92.
67. Gérard de Nerval, *Selected Writings* (Ann Arbor: University of Michigan Press, 1970), 115.
68. Later in his work with mescaline, Michaux gave a remarkable account of the inseparable functioning of both systems. He described the personal reality of hallucinogens working through a subtle nervous system, one which recapitulates the physiology of the Buddhist and Hindu yoga tantras (see Michaux, *Major Ordeals*, "The Four Worlds").

69. Michaux, *Miserable Miracle,* 88.
70. Sacks, *Awakenings,* 306.
71. Ibid., 211.
72. Ibid., 93.
73. Ibid., 50.
74. Ibid., 314.
75. Ibid., 103.
76. Ibid., 224.
77. Ibid., 53.
78. Ibid., 56.
79. Ibid., 223.
80. Ibid., 220.
81. The "recruiting response," as it is known in classical neurophysiology, is an interesting example. When you "drive" (via electric pulsing) the great ascending system that leads to the cerebral cortex, the cortex responds with a gathering of electrical waves, becoming "recruited" into synchrony, and producing larger and larger wave forms. This response can only occur when the pulsing is applied within a narrow frequency band. It is also greatly facilitated by barbiturate anesthesia.
82. Michaux, *Light Through Darkness,* 138.
83. Sacks, *Awakenings,* 153.
84. Ibid., 222.
85. Michaux, *Light Through Darkness,* 178.
86. Ibid., 180.
87. Henri Michaux, *By Surprise* (Madras: Hanuman Books, 1987). From the Introduction by Allen Ginsberg.
88. L. A. Velinsky, *Henri Michaux* (New York: Vantage Press, 1977), 8.
89. Ibid., 5.
90. Ibid.
91. Ibid., 6.
92. Ibid., 4.
93. Michaux, *Selected Writings,* 193.
94. Michaux, *Infinite Turbulence,* 38.
95. Niko Tinbergen and Elisabeth Tinbergen, *"Autistic" Children: New Hope for a Cure* (London: George Allen and Unwin, 1983).
96. Erik Stromgren, *European Journal of Psychiatry* 1, no. 2 (1987): 45–52.
97. Tinbergen, *"Autistic" Children,* 66.
98. Ibid., 67.
99. Ibid., 119.
100. Ibid., 67.
101. Henri Michaux, *Les Commencements* (Montpellier: Fata Morgana, 1983), 43.
102. The psychoanalyst Donald Winnicott has suggested that a remnant of autism might even be discovered in the phenomenon of "momentary withdrawal."
103. Michaux, *Major Ordeals,* 21.
104. Michaux, *Light Through Darkness,* 45.
105. Henri Michaux, *A Barbarian in Asia* (New York: New Directions, 1949), 57.
106. Velinsky, *Henri Michaux,* 106.

107. Michaux, *Barbarian in Asia,* vi.
108. Michaux, *Miserable Miracle,* 89.
109. Ibid., 43.
110. Michaux, *Infinite Turbulence,* 65.
111. Ibid., 163.
112. Michaux, *By Surprise,* xvi.
113. Jay Stevens, *Storming Heaven* (New York: Harper & Row, 1987).
114. See, for example, "Barrett *vs.* United States," *New York Law Journal,* May 1987.
115. R. Gordon Wasson, *The Wondrous Mushroom: Mycolatry in Mesoamerica* (New York: McGraw-Hill, 1980).
116. Alvaro Estrada, *Maria Sabina: Her Life and Chants* (Santa Barbara: Ross-Erikson, 1981).
117. Ibid.
118. Michaux, *By Surprise,* 108.

Chapter 5: Discovering Islands of Clarity

1. Konrad Lorenz, "The Nature of Instinct," in *Instinctive Behavior,* ed. Claire Schiller (New York: International Universities Press, 1957).
2. Black Elk, *The Sacred Pipe,* recorded and edited by Joseph Epes Brown (New York: Penguin Books, 1971).
3. William Le Parry-Jones, "The Model of the Geel Lunatic Colony and Its Influence on the Nineteenth-Century Asylum System in Britain," in *Madhouses, Mad-Doctors, and Madmen,* ed. Andrew Scull (Philadelphia: University of Pennsylvania Press, 1981).
4. Ibid.
5. Ibid.
6. Eugeen Roosens, *Mental Patients in Town Life: Geel, Europe's First Therapeutic Community* (Beverly Hills: Sage Publications, 1979).
7. Ida Macalpine and Richard Hunter, *Three Hundred Years of Psychiatry* (London and New York: Oxford University Press, 1963).
8. Under the auspices of what was called Dana Home Care for the Elderly.
9. Chögyam Trungpa, *Shambhala: The Sacred Path of the Warrior* (Boston: Shambhala Publications, 1984).
10. *I Ching,* trans. Richard Wilhelm (Princeton: Princeton University Press, 1967), 143: "The [hexagram] Family shows the laws operative within the household that, transferred to outside life, keep the state and the world in order. The influence that goes out from within the family is represented by the symbol of the wind created by fire."
11. David Richman, *Dr. Caligari's Psychiatric Drugs* (Berkeley: private printing, 1984).
12. Terry Clifford, *Tibetan Medicine and Psychiatry: The Diamond Healing* (York Beach, Maine: Samuel Weiser, 1984).
13. Thomas De Quincey, *Confessions of an English Opium Eater* (New York: Penguin Books, 1971).
14. Richman, *Dr. Caligari's Psychiatric Drugs,* 57.
15. Medication reduction task force of Friendship House.
16. E. Thelmar, *The Maniac* (New York: The American Psychical Institute, 1937), 13.

17. Ibid., 44.
18. Ibid., 110.
19. Ibid., 253.
20. Ibid., 254.
21. From The Ramayan, *The Sri Ramacharitamanasa* (Delhi: Motillal Bernarsidass, 1989).
22. Designed in 1970 with the collaboration of the Tibetan Buddhist teacher Chögyam Trungpa, Rinpoche, and the Japanese Zen teacher Suzuki Roshi. Students in the Naropa Institute Psychotherapy program spend three months doing this practice in the context of a model therapeutic community in a rural setting. See also *Journal of Contemplative Psychotherapy* 7 (1990).
23. Chögyam Trungpa, "Creating an Environment of Sanity," *Journal of Contemplative Psychotherapy* 2 (1983).
24. William James, *Psychology: Brief Course* (New York: Dover, 1961), 424.
25. It is called the Abhidharma. In later stages of the development of this psychology, it is called Yogacara and Madhyamika.
26. For a rare instance in the psychiatric literature that suggests how a person in psychosis may exert control over his mind, see Alan Breier and John Strauss, "Self-control in Psychotic Disorders," *Archives of General Psychiatry* 40 (1983).
27. See Ken Wilber, Jack Engler, and Dan Brown, *Transformations of Consciousness* (Boston: Shambhala Publications, 1986); Ilan Kutz, J. Bonysenko, and H. Benson, "Meditation and Psychotherapy," *American Journal of Psychiatry* 142 (1985): 1; and Gerald May, *Will and Spirit: A Contemplative Psychology* (San Francisco: Harper & Row, 1983).
28. Karl Jaspers, *General Psychopathology* (Manchester: University of Manchester Press, 1962), 425.
29. Rachel Corday, "The Experience of Psychosis," *Journal of Contemplative Psychotherapy* 6 (1989).
30. Ibid.
31. Thich Nhat Hanh, *The Sutra on the Full Awareness of Breathing* (Berkeley: Parallax Press, 1988).

Chapter 6: Learning Basic Attendance

1. Notable practitioners of this tradition of psychotherapy are Dr. Frieda Fromm-Reichaman and Dr. Harry Stack Sullivan. My personal teachers have been Dr. Harold Searles and Dr. Otto Will.
2. Feeling the illness of a sufferer is a basic principle of most indigenous healing disciplines. See Mercea Eliade, *Shamanism* (Princeton: 1964).
3. Jamgon Kongtrul, *The Great Path of Awakening: An Easily Accessible Introduction for Ordinary People,* trans. Ken McLeod (Boston: Shambhala Publications, 1987).
4. Santideva, *A Guide to the Bodhisattva Way of Life* (Dharamsala: Library of Tibetan Works and Archives, 1979).
5. Karl Jaspers, *General Psychopathology* (Manchester: Manchester University Press, 1962), 425.
6. Chögyam Trungpa, "Creating an Environment of Sanity," *The Naropa Institute Journal of Psychology,* 2 (1983).

7. Edward Podvoll, "The History of Sanity in Contemplative Psychotherapy," *The Naropa Institute Journal of Psychology,* 2 (1983).
8. Manfred Bleuler, "Some Results of Research in Schizophrenia," *Behavioral Science,* 15 (1970).
9. Bonnie Rabin and Robert Walker, "A Contemplative Approach to Clinical Supervision," *Journal of Contemplative Psychotherapy,* 4 (1987).

Chapter 7: Creating a Therapeutic Home

1. John Perceval, *Perceval's Narrative: A Patient's Account of His Psychosis,* ed. Gregory Bateson (Palo Alto: Stanford University Press, 1961).
2. The Group for the Advancement of Psychiatry, *A Family Affair: Helping Families Cope with Mental Illness.* (New York: Brunner/Maze, 1986).
3. Ibid., 57.
4. Ibid.
5. Susan Sheehan, *Is There No Place On Earth For Me?* (New York: Vintage Books, 1983).
6. L. Bachrach and H. Lamb, "What Have We Learned from Deinstitutionalization?" *Psychiatric Annals* 19 (January 1989): 1.
7. G. Mizner, "The Psychiatric Hospital Boom," *Colorado Psychiatric Society Newsletter,* June 1988.
8. G. Sachs and J. Rosenbaum, "Options Needed to Treat Bipolar Affective Disorder," *Psychiatric Times,* August 1989.
9. Jonathan Kozol, *Rachael and Her Children: Homeless Families in America* (New York: Fawcett Columbine, 1988).
10. "Housing Shortage for the Mentally Ill in Colorado," publication of the Colorado Alliance for the Mentally Ill, December 1987.
11. The Group for the Advancement of Psychiatry, *A Family Affair,* 44.
12. Ibid., 47.
13. M. Moorman, "A Sister's Need," *New York Times Magazine,* September 1988.
14. Richard Warner, *Recovery from Schizophrenia* (Boston: Routledge and Kegan Paul, 1985).
15. Chögyam Trungpa, *Shambhala: The Sacred Path of the Warrior* (Boston: Shambhala Publications, 1984).
16. From the Tenzo Kyokun, cited in Charlotte Joko Beck, *Everyday Zen* (San Francisco: Harper & Row, 1989).
17. Barry Kaufman, *Son Rise* (New York: Warner Books, 1976).
18. Maxwell Jones, "In conversation with Maxwell Jones," *The Bulletin of the Royal College of Psychiatrists* 8 (1984).
19. Maxwell Jones, *The Process of Change: From a Closed to an Open System in a Mental Hospital* (Boston: Routledge and Kegan Paul, 1982).
20. Jeffrey Fortuna, "Therapeutic Households," *Journal of Contemplative Psychotherapy* 4 (1987).
21. Courtney Harding, G. W. Brooks, T. Ashikaga, and J. Strauss, "The Vermont Longitudinal Study," vols. I and II, *American Journal of Psychiatry* 144, no. 6 (1987).
22. Jeffrey Fortuna, "The Friendship House," *Journal of Contemplative Psychotherapy* 6 (1989).

Select Bibliography

BEERS, CLIFFORD. *A Mind That Found Itself.* Pittsburgh: University of Pittsburgh Press, 1981.

BETTLEHEIM, BRUNO. *The Empty Fortress.* New York: The Free Press, 1967.

BLEULER, EUGENE. *Dementia Praecox.* Translated by J. Zinkin. New York: International Universities Press, 1950.

BLEULER, MANFRED. *The Schizophrenic Disorders: Long-Term Patient and Family Studies.* New Haven: Yale University Press, 1978.

BOISEN, ANTON. *The Exploration of the Inner World.* Philadelphia: University of Pennsylvania Press, 1936.

BYNUM, W. F., R. PORTER, and M. SHEPHERD. *The Anatomy of Madness: Essays in the History of Psychiatry.* Vols. I and II. London: Tavistock Publications, 1985.

CLIFFORD, TERRY. *Tibetan Buddhist Medicine and Psychiatry.* York Beach, Maine: Samuel Weiser, 1984.

CUSTANCE, JOHN. *Adventure into the Unconscious.* London: Christopher Johnson, 1954.

CUSTANCE, JOHN. *Wisdom, Madness and Folly.* New York: Pellegrini and Cudahy, 1952.

D'AMBROSIO, RICHARD. *No Language But a Cry.* New York: Doubleday, 1970.

DE QUINCY, THOMAS. *Confessions of an English Opium Eater.* New York: Penguin Books, 1971.

ELIADE, MERCAE. *Shamanism.* Bollingen Series LXXVI. Princeton: Princeton University Press, 1964.

ESTRADA, ALVARO. *Maria Sabina: Her Life and Chants.* Santa Barbara, Calif.: Ross-Erikson, 1981.

FOUCAULT, MICHEL. *Madness and Civilization: A History of Insanity in the Age of Reason.* New York: Pantheon Books, 1965.

FOUCAULT, MICHEL. *Mental Illness and Psychology.* New York: Harper & Row, 1976.

FREMANTLE, FRANCESCA, and CHÖGYAM TRUNGPA. *The Tibetan Book of the Dead.* Translation and commentary by Shambhala Publications. Boston: Shambhala Publications, 1975.

GROUP FOR THE ADVANCEMENT OF PSYCHIATRY. *A Family Affair: Helping Families Cope with Mental Illness.* New York: Brunner/Mazel, 1986.

HANH, THICH NHAT. *The Sutra on the Full Awareness of Breathing.* Berkeley: Parallax Press, 1988.

ILLICH, IVAN. *Medical Nemesis, The Expropriation of Health.* New York: Pantheon Books, 1976.

JAMES, WILLIAM. *On Exceptional Mental States: The 1896 Lowell Lectures.* Reconstructed by Eugene Taylor. New York: Charles Scribner and Sons, 1982.

JAMES, WILLIAM. *Varieties of Religious Experience.* New York: Random House, 1902.

JAMGON, KONGTUL. *The Great Path of Awakening: An Easily Accessible Introduction for Ordinary People.* Translated by Ken McLeod. Boston: Shambhala Publications, 1987.

JASPERS, KARL. *General Psychopathology.* Manchester: Manchester University Press, 1962.

JONES, MAXWELL. *The Process of Change: From a Closed to an Open System in a Mental Hospital.* Boston: Routledge and Kegan Paul, 1982.

KAPLAN, BERT, ed. *The Inner World of Mental Illness.* New York: Harper & Row, 1964.

LURIA, A. R. *The Man with a Shattered World.* Chicago: Henry Regnery, 1968.

MICHAUX, HENRI. *Infinite Turbulence.* 1957. Reprint. London: Calder and Boyars, 1975.

MICHAUX, HENRI. *Light Through Darkness.* 1961. Reprint. New York: The Orion Press, 1963.

MICHAUX, HENRI. *Major Ordeals of the Mind and Countless Minor Ones.* 1966. Reprint. New York: Harcourt Brace Jovanovich, 1974.

MICHAUX, HENRI. *Miserable Miracle.* 1956. Reprint. San Francisco: City Lights, 1963.

PARRY-JONES, WILLIAM. *The Trade in Lunacy: A Study of Private Madhouses in England in the 18th and 19th Century.* London: Routledge and Kegan Paul, 1972.

PERCEVAL, JOHN. *Perceval's Narrative: A Patient's Account of His Psychosis.*

Edited by Gregory Bateson. Palo Alto, Calif.: Stanford University Press, 1961.

PETERSON, DALE. *A Mad People's History of Madness.* Pittsburgh: University of Pittsburgh Press, 1982.

SACKS, OLIVER. *Awakenings.* New York: E. P. Dutton, 1983.

SAINT-DENYS, HERVEY DE. *Dreams and How to Guide Them.* 1867. Reprint. London: Duckworth, 1982.

SANTIDEVA. *A Guide to the Bodhisattva Way of Life.* Dharmsala, India: Library of Tibetan Works and Archives, 1979.

SCHREBER, DANIEL. *Memoirs of My Nervous Illness.* Edited by I. Macalpine and R. Hunter. London: Dawson and Sons, Ltd. 1955.

SCULL, ANDREW. *Museums of Madness: The Social Organization of Insanity in Nineteenth-Century England.* New York: St. Martin's Press, 1979.

SEARLES, HAROLD. *Collected Papers on Schizophrenia and Related Subjects.* New York: International Universities Press, 1965.

SHEEHAN, SUSAN. *Is There No Place On Earth For Me?* New York: Vintage Books, 1983.

STRINDBERG, AUGUST. *Inferno/From an Occult Diary.* New York: Penguin Books, 1979.

THELMAR, E. *The Maniac.* New York: The American Psychical Institute, 1937.

TINBERGEN, NIKO, and ELISABETH TINBERGEN. *"Autistic" Children: New Hope for a Cure.* London: George Allen and Unwin, 1983.

TOMALIN, N., and R. HALL. *The Strange Last Voyage of Donald Crowhurst.* Briarcliff Manor, N.Y.: Stein and Day, 1979.

TRUNGPA, CHÖGYAM. *Cutting Through Spiritual Materialism.* Boston: Shambhala Publications, 1973.

TRUNGPA, CHÖGYAM. *Glimpses of Abidharma.* Boston: Shambhala Publications, 1975.

TRUNGPA, CHÖGYAM. *The Myth of Freedom.* Boston: Shambhala Publications, 1976.

TRUNGPA, CHÖGYAM. *Shambhala: The Sacred Path of the Warrior.* Boulder, Col. and London: Shambhala Publications, 1984.

Index

Father, dead, 125
Fear, 36
  psychosis and, 132–33
Five-color room, 239, 309
"Flicker fusion," 82
Food. *See also* Diet
  psychosis production by, 176
Fortuna, Jeffrey, 300
Foster care, homelike, 214–15
Foucault, Michel, 63, 66
Fox, Edward, 22
Fox, George, 215
Fragmentation, call to, 202
Freud, Sigmund, 241
Friendship, discovery of, in basic
    attendance, 277–79
Friendship House, 299
  establishment of, 307
  success rate, 314
Functional psychosis, 172
Furor therapeuticus, 3

Genetic markers, autism and, 192–93
Gentleness, 245
Gide, André, 130
Ginsberg, Allen, 190
God(s)
  formless, 112
  movement beyond, Crowhurst's
      experience of, 106, 107
  power of, 113
  proclamation of being, 83
  realm of, 36
Grandeur, delusion of, 75, 91–92
Grasp reflexes, 187
"Great opening," 198
Greed, realm of, 35
Gross nervous system, 177
Groundlessness, experience of, 126
Group discussion, in basic attendance,
    260–62
Group treatment home, establishment of,
    299–306
Guidance, speaking with, 29

Hallucinations
  command, 13
  Custance's, 79
  in megalomania, 114
  uninterrupted, 31
Hallucinogens, 176, 201–3. *See also* LSD;
    Mescaline; Peyote; Psilocybin
  body rhythmic effects of, 185
  experimentation with, 129–31, 133,
      150, 178
  organic, 178
  use of, 201–3
  weak, 178
Healing center, 213–15
Healing circle, 224

Healing communities, 222, 306–13
  meetings of, 310–11
Healing diet, 213
Healing environments, 211–16
Health. *See also* Mental health
  Perceval's allegiance toward, 47–48
Heaven, joining of earth with, 308
  healing through, 212–13
Hegel, Friedrich, 308
Hell, realm of, 36
Heroin, 202
Hidden opposite, reaction to, 95
Hierarchy, natural, in therapeutic
    community, 312–13
Home. *See also* Household; Therapeutic
    home
  concept of, 308
  return to, 285–87
Homelike treatment, 4
Honesty, autism through, 196
Hope, 35
Hospital(s)
  alternative, 213–16, 299–306
  litigations against, 61
  recovery in, 216–23
Hospitalization
  costs of, 290
  custodial, 289
Household. *See also* Home
  in crisis, 291–98
  therapeutic, 265
  transformation into therapeutic home,
      298
Household meetings, in basic attendance,
    262
Housemates, 292
  in basic attendance, 256
Human contact, avoidance of, by autistic
    child, 195
Humiliation, 290
  of asylum patients, 65
Hyperexcitability, 210
Hyper-lucidity, 149

Ideas, 188
  repetition of, 156
Identification
  in megalomania, 113
  psychotic practices of, 126
  successive series of, in megalomania,
      116–17
Identity
  personal, 145–46
  productive, 260
Idiopathic psychosis, 172
Illusion(s), 42, 44
  visual, 78
Images
  perception of, 155
  repetitions of, 156